The Fast Forward MBA in Financial Planning

THE FAST FORWARD MBA SERIES

The Fast Forward MBA Series provides time-pressed business professionals and students with concise, one-stop information to help them solve business problems and make smart, informed business decisions. All of the volumes, written by industry leaders, contain "tough ideas made easy." The published books in this series are:

The Fast Forward MBA in Investing
   (0-471-24661-1)
   by John Waggoner

The Fast Forward MBA in Hiring
   (0-471-24212-8)
   by Max Messmer

The Fast Forward MBA in Business
   (0-471-14660-9)
   by Virginia O'Brien

The Fast Forward MBA in Finance
   (0-471-10930-4)
   by John Tracy

The Fast Forward MBA Pocket Reference
   (0-471-14595-5)
   by Paul A. Argenti

The Fast Forward MBA in Marketing
   (0-471-16616-2)
   by Dallas Murphy

The Fast Forward MBA in Financial Planning

ED MCCARTHY

John Wiley & Sons, Inc.

New York • Chichester • Weinheim • Brisbane • Singapore • Toronto

To my wife, Diane,
who really does have the patience of a saint.

Copyright © 1999 by Ed McCarthy. All rights reserved.

Published by John Wiley & Sons, Inc.
Published simultaneously in Canada.

This publication is designed to provide accurate and authoritative
information in regard to the subject matter covered. It is sold
with the understanding that the publisher is not engaged in
rendering professional services. If professional advice or other
expert assistance is required, the services of a competent
professional person should be sought.

Library of Congress Cataloging-in-Publication Data:
McCarthy, Ed (Edward), 1955–
    The fast forward MBA in financial planning / by Ed McCarthy.
      p.   cm.
    Includes index.
    ISBN 0-471-23829-5 (pbk. : alk. paper)
    1. Finance, Personal. 2. Investment analysis. I. Title.
HG179.M37418   1998
332.024—dc21   98-13504

Printed in the United States of America.

10 9 8 7 6 5 4 3 2 1

ED McCARTHY

Ed McCarthy has published numerous articles on finance and business topics for professional audiences and the general public. These articles have appeared in *CFP Today, Financial Consultant, Financial Planning, Journal of Financial Planning, Modern Maturity, Pension Management, Personal Financial Planning, Providence Business News, Real Estate Finance, Rhode Island Monthly,* and the *Loose Change* and *Retirement Planning Advisor* newsletters. From 1991 through 1995, he wrote a technology review column for *CFP Today* magazine, and he currently writes a monthly technology column for *Ticker* magazine. His first book, *The Financial Advisor's Analytical Toolbox: Using Technology to Optimize Client Solutions,* was published by McGraw-Hill in early 1997. As an instructor, McCarthy has taught courses and seminars for the University of Rhode Island, Bryant College, Community College of Rhode Island, Holland America Cruise Lines, and other companies. He also served as a committee member and vice president on the national Board of Directors of the Institute of Certified Financial Planners.

McCarthy earned his Bachelor of Arts at the University of Rhode Island, and a Master in International Business (MIB) degree from the University of South Carolina. He has completed advanced professional education courses in estate planning and individual income taxation, and he is currently finishing his Ph.D. in Finance at the University of Connecticut. He also worked as a stockbroker with several major brokerage firms in the early 1980s, and he holds the Certified Financial Planner (CFP) license.

McCarthy has spoken before many organizations on finance topics and has been listed in *Who's Who in Industry and Finance.* He has been quoted in local and national publications, including the *Wall Street Journal, Investor's Business Daily, US News & World Report, USA Today, The Christian Science News Monitor, Boston Globe,* and the *Providence Journal-Bulletin.*

He has been a frequent guest on local (Providence, Rhode Island) television, including WJAR-TV's *Newswatch 10 at Sunrise* and *These Are the Days,* WLNE-TV, and he has made instructional videos for the financial services industry.

This book will help you learn and implement the techniques of successful personal financial planning. It is written for those readers who want practical advice on managing their finances and reaching their financial goals. The material fills a need that results from a gap in the American education system. While attending school, you learn a great deal, much of which is designed to provide you with the skills required to pursue a career. In all those years of formal education, however, generally you receive no instruction on handling finances. You learn the skills needed to make a living, but not how to manage your personal finances effectively after you begin working.

The results of this knowledge gap are evident. In 1996, despite a strong economy and relatively low levels of unemployment, over *1 million* Americans filed for personal bankruptcy. Among those who have not reached the crisis stage yet, there are other signs of financial strain. National consumer debt is approaching the *$1.2 trillion* mark, and total debt has reached an average 17 percent of disposable income, a level not seen since 1989. Roughly 6 million people, or 3½ percent of credit card users, are skipping payments, which is the highest level since the 1981 recession. Obviously, many people are having difficulty managing their finances effectively.

The philosophy behind this book is straightforward: You are responsible for your personal financial success or failure. It is up to you to acquire the information and skills needed to manage your finances effectively. The days of relying on a benevolent lifetime employer and the government to take care of your financial needs are gone. Today's uncertain economic environment calls for increased self-reliance, and you will find the tools you need to achieve financial independence in this book.

Fortunately, the goal of financial independence is within your grasp. You won't reach it overnight—realistically, it will take years of planning and persistent effort. You will not achieve it by simply reading this book, either—you must translate the book's concepts and suggestions into actions. Specifically, to achieve financial success, you must do the following:

● Evaluate your current financial condition.
● Develop specific financial goals and plans to reach those goals.
● Integrate your goals with your financial activities.
● Implement the plan and track your progress.

If you think these steps resemble Business Planning 101, you're right. Many of the principles of successful personal financial planning correspond directly to those found in business planning. You will find that some of the topics in this book, such as developing financial statements to track financial progress, creating a spending plan, and evaluating financial risk exposures, are very similar to their business plan equivalents.

In fact, we can carry the analogy one step further: You are a financial enterprise. Your goal is to apply the same disciplined, rational approach to managing your personal finances that you would apply to managing a business. Businesses have short- and long-term goals, and they develop plans to reach those goals. As you read this book, you will develop short- and long-term goals and the plans to reach them. Businesses allocate resources, evaluate financial risks, and attempt to create equity for their owners. Similarly, you must allocate your resources, evaluate risks and protect yourself against them, and create the wealth needed to ensure your financial security. Of course, there are differences between a company's financial affairs and yours. Businesses don't have to put their children through college, they don't get divorced (at least not in a marital sense), and they don't worry about retirement. The process of planning, implementing, and reviewing is still common to both companies and individuals, though.

You can approach the book in several ways. If you have enough time, read the chapters sequentially. The material follows a building-block approach, with the first few parts serving as a foundation for the remaining sections. If you need immediate advice on a specific topic, you can start with that chapter and return to the other material as your schedule permits. Whichever method you choose, as you read the material I strongly suggest that you personalize the examples and re-create them for your own goals and with your own figures. Personal financial planning is not a spectator sport: You must go through the process to make it work. Re-create the worksheets and work the calculations with your own personal data as you encounter them in the book. If you don't want to develop your own forms and worksheets, and you have a PC, buy one of the personal financial management software programs readily available today. A program can help you get organized and started on the right track. If you don't have access to a PC, or you just don't have time to do your own planning, read the book and hire a competent financial planner. You will have to pay for the advice and services you receive, but after reading this book you will be better prepared to work with an advisor. No matter which approach you take, get started and stick with it! The information you need is in these pages, but it's up to you to make something of it.

ED MCCARTHY

Warwick, Rhode Island
July 1998

ACKNOWLEDGMENTS

Several people helped made this book possible, and I am grateful to them. Debra Englander, my editor at John Wiley & Sons, Inc., provided the original concept and motivation for the book. In addition, the following individuals generously supplied software and research materials:

Tisha Findeison, The Vanguard Group

Ed Giltenan and Steve Norwitz, T. Rowe Price Associates, Inc.

Tenna Merchent, Golden Rule

Mark Miltner, Standard & Poor's

Tracy Sherman, UNUM

Shannon Stubo and Rod Cherkas, Intuit, Inc.

Tom Taggart, Charles Schwab & Co.

CONTENTS

PART 4
RETIREMENT AND
ESTATE PLANNING

PART 5
OTHER ISSUES

The Fundamentals

CHAPTER 1

Personal Financial Statements

PERSONAL BALANCE SHEET

Looking back over the past 12 months, how would you rate your financial progress? You might have difficulty answering that question with confidence unless you keep an up-to-date *personal balance sheet*. This document lists your *assets* (what you own), *liabilities* (what you owe), and *owner's equity* (assets minus liabilities).

KEY CONCEPT — Tracking Your Net Worth

Developing and maintaining your personal balance sheet is not just an exercise. The information in the balance sheet is useful for the following purposes:

- Evaluating your financial condition.
- Retirement planning.
- Estate planning.

Developing Your Balance Sheet

The balance sheet is a snapshot that shows the value of your assets and liabilities *at a specific point in time.* By listing your assets' and liabilities' values on that date, you create a benchmark that you can use as a future standard. This chapter includes a sample balance sheet to illustrate the document's typical layout.

Balance Sheet Item: Assets

Assets are the items you own: financial accounts, personal property, real estate, and so on. As you list your assets, remember the following:

- *Use realistic values.* It is easy to get a market value for some items. If you own 100 shares of IBM stock and the stock's price today is $125 per share, your shares are worth $12,500. Other assets are more difficult to value, however. If you own a home, you probably have a rough idea of its value, but you can't know its exact market value unless you sell it. This problem of inexact valuations is even more pronounced for assets that lack a formal market, such as privately held businesses and collectibles like artwork. If you own such assets, the best tactic is to value them conservatively.

- *Avoid unnecessary complexity.* It is tempting to provide great detail on your personal balance sheet, but a detailed balance sheet will require more maintenance in the future, increasing the risk that you will get tired of updating the information. Start by keeping it simple, and make it more complex only as needed. It is better to have a simple balance sheet that you update regularly than a complicated model that you ignore.

Balance Sheet Item: Liabilities

Liabilities are debts or amounts that you owe. These include the following:

- *Short-term liabilities* that you will pay off within the next 12 months.
- *Long-term debts* that require longer than 12 months to repay (e.g., mortgages and car loan balances).

As you list your debts, use the current outstanding balance. If you don't have that information for an account, contact the creditor.

Balance Sheet Item: Net Worth

After you have listed the values of your assets and liabilities, you can calculate your net worth. The formula is simple:

Net worth = assets – liabilities

Your goal is to increase your net worth to achieve a desired degree of financial security.

Typical Categories: Basic Balance Sheet

Assets

Monetary assets. Cash, checking accounts, savings accounts.

Other assets. Personal property.

Liabilities

Short-term. Utility bills, credit card payments, loan payments.

Long-term. Loan balances.

Typical Categories: More Complex Balance Sheet

Assets

Monetary assets. Cash, checking and money market accounts, tax refund.

Investments. Stocks, bonds, mutual funds, retirement plan balances, life insurance cash values, real estate investments.

Personal assets. Furnishings, clothing, autos, home.

Liabilities

Short-term. Utilities, credit card payments.

Long-term. Auto loans, mortgages.

Occasionally the distinction between short- and long-term liabilities is unclear. Use this rule of thumb to avoid confusion: If you will pay off the debt in the next 12 months, list the balance as a short-term debt. But if the payoff date is more than 12 months away, list the balance as long-term debt. *Be consistent.* Otherwise it becomes difficult to compare statements over time.

After you develop your balance sheet, revise it once each year. If you organize your financial records each spring to file your tax return, that is an ideal time, because you have many of your documents easily available.

Sample Balance Sheet

Figure 1.1 shows a personal balance sheet for a fictional couple to assist you in constructing your own. Add or omit details to make the format fit your own situation.

CASH FLOW STATEMENT

"Where did the money go?" If you have ever asked yourself this question, you are not alone. The average person can recall most of his or her major expenditures each month: mortgage payment, car loan payment, insurance premiums, and so on. But once they move beyond the large, recurring expenses, most people cannot account for a good part of their spending.

Developing a reasonably accurate *cash flow statement* can solve the problem of disappearing income. This document lists your *sources* of cash (income, interest, etc.) and its *uses* (living expenses, loan repayments, and so on). If you don't track your cash flow, it is very difficult to redirect the flow of funds to achieve your financial goals. The cash flow statement is the first step in gaining control over your spending.

FIGURE 1.1 SAMPLE BALANCE SHEET.

Date: January 1, 1997

Assets	Wife	Husband	Joint	Total
Financial assets				
Cash			$ 200	$ 200
Checking			3,000	3,000
Money market accts.			7,000	7,000
Savings	$ 4,000	$ 2,000		6,000
Certificates of deposit	6,000			6,000
Payments receivable	10,000			10,000
Total financial assets	$ 20,000	$ 2,000	$ 10,200	$ 32,200
Personal assets				
Clothing	$ 6,000	$ 6,000		$ 12,000
Furnishings			$ 15,000	15,000
Autos	8,000	12,000		20,000
Home			150,000	150,000
Other		1,100		1,100
Total personal assets	$ 14,000	$19,100	$165,000	$198,100
Investments				
Stocks				
Bonds				
Mutual funds			$ 25,000	$ 25,000
Retirement plans	$ 60,000	$30,000		90,000
Life insurance cash values				
Business interests	50,000			50,000
Real estate				
Total investments	$110,000	$30,000	$ 25,000	$165,000
Total assets	$144,000	$51,000	$200,200	$395,200

Liabilities	Wife	Husband	Joint	Total
Short-term				
Utilities			$ 500	$ 500
Credit cards			2,000	2,000
Other				
Total short-term debt			$ 2,500	$ 2,500
Long-term				
Auto loans	$ 3,000			$ 3,000
Student loans				
Home mortgage			$ 76,000	76,000
Other	15,000			15,000
Total long-term debt	$ 18,000		$ 76,000	$ 94,000
Total liabilities	$ 18,000		$ 78,500	$ 96,500

Net Worth	Wife	Husband	Joint	Total
Total assets	$144,000	$51,000	$200,200	$395,200
Less total liabilities	−18,000		78,500	96,500
Net worth	$126,000	$51,000	$121,700	$298,700

Trade-Offs

Unless you have unlimited income, you must make decisions that involve financial trade-offs. For example, you can buy a new television set or invest the same amount of money in a mutual fund. If you don't know where your money goes, you cannot measure the impact of these decisions on your finances. Tracking your cash flow will show how you currently spend your money, and that knowledge will allow you to redirect your spending if necessary.

 **Developing Your Cash Flow Statement**

Your personal balance sheet lists values for a *single point* in time—December 31, 1998, for example. Your cash flow statement will show activity over a *period* of time, such as one year. A cash flow statement has two sections: *sources of income* and *expenses.* Sources include any activity that produces cash for you to spend. The expenses section lists your expenditures (mortgage or rent payments, utilities, food, and so on). It is helpful to divide expenses into two categories: *fixed* and *variable.* Fixed expenses are payroll deductions such as income taxes and those bills that you must pay regularly—rent and loan repayments, for instance. Variable expenses are under your control. Dining out and vacations are two examples of variable costs.

 Developing an accurate record of your cash flow can be a challenge. To make the process less intimidating, start with a short time period. It is much easier to track your cash flow for one month than to estimate it for the next year.

Cash Flow Statement Section: Income

The income section of the statement includes *all* sources of cash. Typical categories include wages, pensions, investment income, cash gifts received from others, and loans. Do not confuse sources of cash income with taxable income: While much of your cash income is taxable, other sources of cash are not taxable income. For example, if you take out a $10,000 loan to buy a car, that is a source of cash, but it is *not* taxable income.

Cash Flow Statement Section: Payroll Deduction Expenses

Payroll deductions probably are one of your largest expenses during your working years. Some of these expenses are relatively fixed—taxes and health insurance contributions, for example. Other payroll deductions are more flexible—retirement plan contributions, charitable contributions, and so on.

Cash Flow Statement Section: Fixed Expenses

Fixed expenses are usually contractual. Mortgage payments and loan payments are two examples. Once you sign the loan agreement, you make regular repayments. Other expenses are not contractual, but are often unavoidable. Utility bills and property taxes are common categories.

Cash Flow Statement Section: Variable Expenses

You have the greatest control over these expenses, although some of them require a minimum expenditure. You need food, but you decide on the type, amount, and dining location. Clothing is another requirement, but you decide how much you will spend, based on taste, climate, and so on.

Typical Categories: Income

Source

Employment.   Wages, salary (including self-employment income), bonuses.

Retirement.   Social Security, pension, retirement plan distributions.

Savings and investments.   Interest, dividends, capital gains (from sale of assets), rental property income.

Other: Loans received, insurance benefits, unemployment benefits, alimony and child support, sale of assets, gifts received from others.

Typical Categories: Payroll Deductions

Income taxes.   Federal, state, and local.

Social Security.

Retirement plans.   401(k), 403(b) plans.

Benefits.   Medical insurance premiums.

Other.   Union dues, U.S. savings bonds, parking fees, charitable contributions.

Typical Categories: Fixed Expenses

Rent and mortgage.   Including fixed-payment home equity loans.

Utilities.   Heat, electric, telephone.

Insurance.   Homeowner's or renter's, auto, life, disability.

Property taxes.   Real estate, personal property (auto).

Loans.   Auto, student, personal.

Savings and investment plans.

Typical Categories: Variable Expenses

Charitable contributions.

Clothing.

Education.

Entertainment/travel/vacation.

Food.

Gifts.

Sample Cash Flow Statement

Figure 1.2 illustrates an annual cash flow statement using these typical categories for a fictional couple to assist you in constructing your own. Add or omit details to fit your situation as needed.

 Keep your cash flow records as simple as possible. Excessively detailed records require more maintenance, increasing the risk that you will get tired of updating the information. It is better to have a simple statement that you update regularly than a complicated tracking system that you ignore.

 Sources of Information
The information you need to accurately track your cash flow will come from several sources, including the following:

Paycheck stubs.   Income and payroll deductions.

Checking account register.   Expenses paid by check or automatic deduction from checking account.

Credit card purchases register and statements. Details of purchases that you are paying for with this statement.

Bank and investment account statements.   Deposits and withdrawals.

Cash transactions register.

 The Credit Card Register
One drawback to using monthly credit card statements as a source document is the lack of information they provide about each purchase. This lack of detail can lead to gaps in your cash flow tracking if you cannot remember the details of a credit card purchase.

FIGURE 1.2 SAMPLE ANNUAL CASH FLOW STATEMENT.

Period: 1/1/97–12/31/97

Sources of Cash	Wife	Husband	Joint	Total
Wages/salary	$42,000	$35,000		$77,000
Interest	400	100	$ 400	900
Mutual fund distributions			1,200	1,200
Total sources	$42,400	$35,100	$ 1,600	$79,100

Expenses	Wife	Husband	Joint	Total
Payroll deductions				
Federal income tax	$ 8,000	$ 6,000		$14,000
Social Security tax	3,150	2,625		5,775
State income tax	2,000	1,500		3,500
Medical insurance premium		2,400		2,400
401(k) plans	4,000	3,500		7,500
Total payroll deductions	$17,150	$16,025		$33,175

	Wife	Husband	Joint	Total
Fixed expenses				
Mortgage			$ 7,800	$ 7,800
Loan payments	$ 3,600			3,600
Utilities			5,000	5,000
Insurance			3,000	3,000
Property taxes			3,000	3,000
Investment plans			6,000	6,000
Total fixed expenses	$ 3,600		$24,800	$28,400

	Wife	Husband	Joint	Total
Variable expenses				
Charitable contributions			$ 2,400	$ 2,400
Clothing	$ 1,500	$ 1,500		3,000
Education				
Food			5,000	5,000
Gifts			2,000	2,000
Travel/vacation			3,000	3,000
Total variable expenses	$ 1,500	$ 1,500	$12,400	$15,400

To avoid this problem, keep a credit card transactions register. At the end of each day, record the amount and details of each credit card purchase you made. When you pay the bill, use the register to allocate the payment among your expense categories.

The Cash Transactions Register

 Americans are slowly reducing their dependence on cash in favor of electronic transactions, but most people still use cash for small payments. Even though each cash transaction might be small, the total amount can represent a significant portion of a month's expenses. The simplest way to track cash payments is to maintain a daily cash expenses register. At the end of each day, record the amount and purpose of each cash payment you made. Total the amounts at the end of the month and add the sums to the appropriate category in your cash flow statement.

 If you make frequent cash withdrawals from your bank's automated teller machines (ATMs), it can be very difficult to track the small cash amounts you spend. To increase your cash flow tracking accuracy, limit your ATM withdrawals to one per week and pay by check whenever possible.

Your first cash flow statement is the most difficult to develop. Fortunately, each successive statement will be easier because you can use the knowledge and forms from previous periods. Also, if you have access to a PC spreadsheet or a financial management program, you can automate much of the work.

END POINT

Your balance sheet provides a snapshot of your financial condition on a particular date. By regularly updating the values of your assets and liabilities listed on your balance sheet, you can track your progress toward your financial goals. It is important to use realistic estimates for asset values—if there is some doubt about an asset's value, use a conservative figure. Inflating numbers will not change the asset's true value.

Understanding the sources of your cash income and your expenses is a critical step in taking control of your finances. Financial decisions frequently involve trade-offs: You must allocate a limited income among competing goals. By learning where your money goes each month, you can begin to redirect your expenditures toward your financial priorities.

Analyzing Your Financial Statements

The personal balance sheet and cash flow statement contain important—but limited—data for measuring your financial status. It is the interpretation of those statements' data that determines your financial condition.

KEY CONCEPT — PERSONAL FINANCIAL RATIOS

Your *financial ratios* measure liquidity, use of debt, growth of income, and net worth. By tracking your ratios, you can develop accurate measures of your financial progress.

KEY CONCEPT — LIQUIDITY RATIOS

Liquidity is a measure of the speed at which an asset can be converted into cash without a loss of value. Cash (currency) is the most liquid asset, followed by checking and money market accounts. Investment real estate is an *illiquid* asset: If you tried to sell it quickly, a buyer probably would impose a steep discount on the price. Financial assets, including most publicly traded stocks, bonds, and mutual funds, are also liquid, although changes in the assets' market values impose a risk that you might be forced to sell at a loss.

Most households require a minimum amount of liquidity in the form of *monetary assets* to pay bills and to handle routine expenses. The basic categories of monetary assets are cash, checking and money market accounts, and savings accounts. If you use a less restrictive definition of liquid assets, such as "assets that can be converted quickly to cash," you can expand the list to include certificates of deposit (CDs) and most publicly traded stocks, bonds, and mutual funds.

Basic Liquidity Ratio

Basic liquidity ratio = liquid monetary assets ÷ average monthly expenses

- *Purpose:* To determine target holdings of liquid monetary assets.
- *Data sources:* Liquid monetary assets: balance sheet; average monthly expenses: cash flow statement.

This ratio uses a restrictive definition of liquid assets: cash, checking, money market, and savings accounts. Each of these assets is readily available without penalty. Average monthly expenses include both fixed and variable expenditures, calculated by dividing annual expenses by 12 to get a monthly average. Figure 2.1 demonstrates the sources of data for the ratio's calculation using the illustrations from Chapter 1.

Calculation:

Basic liquidity ratio: $16,200 / ($43,800 ÷ 12) = 4.4 months

Interpretation: This couple has sufficient liquid assets to pay roughly 4½ months' expenses. Depending on income stability and predictability of expenses, two months is the recommended minimum, so the amount they are keeping in liquid assets is acceptable.

FIGURE 2.1 ASSETS AND EXPENSES.

	Wife	Husband	Joint	Total
Liquid assets				
Cash			$ 200	$ 200
Checking			3,000	3,000
Money market accts.			7,000	7,000
Savings	$4,000	$2,000		6,000
Total liquid assets	$4,000	$2,000	$10,200	$16,200

	Wife	Husband	Joint	Total
Annual expenses				
Fixed	$3,600		$24,800	$28,400
Variable	1,500	$1,500	12,400	15,400
Total annual expenses	$5,100	$1,500	$37,200	$43,800

If your income is steady, your job is secure, and your expenses are predictable, you will not need as much in liquid assets as someone whose income fluctuates or whose job is in jeopardy. Lines of credit can also meet unexpected cash needs, but those generally are an expensive source of funds.

If you keep less than two months' expenses in liquid assets, you increase your risk of a cash crunch. A chronic shortage of funds can lead to an increased reliance on short-term credit, and the interest charges on that credit further increase your expenses. Avoid this cycle by keeping enough funds available to pay your expenses and debts as they come due.

Expanded Liquidity Ratio

Expanded liquidity ratio = liquid assets
÷ average monthly expenses

- *Purpose:* To determine target holdings of liquid assets.
- *Data sources:* Liquid assets: balance sheet; average monthly expenses: cash flow statement.

This ratio uses a less restrictive definition of liquid assets. It includes those assets used in the basic liquidity ratio (cash, checking, money market, and savings accounts), plus other financial assets that can be converted to cash easily with minimum delay and risk of loss. These additional assets include savings bonds, certificates of deposit, and low-volatility mutual funds such as short-maturity bond funds. The data for monthly expenses is the same as the basic liquidity ratio. Figure 2.2 demonstrates the sources of data for the ratio's calculation using the illustrations from Chapter 1.

Calculation:

Expanded liquidity ratio: $22,200 / ($43,800 ÷ 12) = 6.1 months

FIGURE 2.2 LIQUIDITY RATIO.

	Wife	Husband	Joint	Total
Financial assets				
Cash			$ 200	$ 200
Checking			3,000	3,000
Money market accts.			7,000	7,000
Savings	$ 4,000	$2,000		6,000
Certificates of deposit	6,000			6,000
Total financial assets	$10,000	$2,000	$10,200	$22,200

Interpretation: This couple has sufficient liquid assets to pay roughly six months' expenses.

If your income and expenses are stable, use the expanded liquidity ratio to set lower and upper targets for the amount of liquid assets you keep. While keeping insufficient liquid funds can lead to a cash crunch, holding excessive amounts of liquid assets incurs an opportunity cost (e.g., forgone interest earnings from less-liquid accounts).

Don't include in your calculations amounts that you plan to spend. If you have $40,000 in relatively liquid accounts, but plan to spend $25,000 next month on a new car, use the remaining balance ($15,000) to calculate your ratios.

DEBT RATIOS
Debt-to-Asset Ratio

Debt-to-asset ratio = total debt ÷ total assets

- *Purpose:* To determine percentage of financial leverage used.
- *Data source:* Balance sheet.

A common long-term financial goal is to become debt-free, especially as retirement approaches. The debt-to-asset ratio is useful for tracking progress in debt reduction. Figure 2.3 demonstrates the sources of data for the ratio's calculation using the illustrative balance sheet from Chapter 1.

Calculation:

Debt-to-asset ratio: $96,500 ÷ $395,200 = .24

Interpretation: This couple owes roughly 25 cents for every dollar in assets. Their goal should be to reduce this ratio as they approach retirement.

Debt-to-Gross-Income Ratio

Debt-to-gross-income ratio = annual debt repayments ÷ annual gross income

FIGURE 2.3 DEBT RATIOS.

	Wife	Husband	Joint	Total
Total assets	$144,000	$51,000	$200,200	$395,200
Total liabilities	18,000		78,500	96,500

- *Purpose:* To determine ability to make debt repayments.
- *Data source:* Cash flow statement.

Figure 2.4 demonstrates the ratio's calculation using the illustrative cash flow statement from Chapter 1.

Calculation:

Debt-to-gross-income ratio: $11,400 ÷ $79,100 = .14

Interpretation: A ratio below .30 indicates an adequate income for existing debt repayments. At .14, this couple's ratio shows that their debts are moderate compared to their income and they could assume more debt if necessary.

Debt Service Ratio

Debt service ratio = annual debt repayments
÷ annual take-home pay

- *Purpose:* To determine ability to make debt repayments.
- *Data source:* Cash flow statement.

Figure 2.5 demonstrates the ratio's calculation using the illustrative cash flow statement from Chapter 1. Take-home pay is defined as gross income minus payroll deductions.

FIGURE 2.4 DEBT-TO-INCOME RATIOS.

	Wife	Husband	Joint	Total
Total income	$42,400	$35,100	$1,600	$79,100
Debt repayments				
Mortgage			$7,800	$ 7,800
Loan payments	$ 3,600			3,600
Total debt payments	$ 3,600		$7,800	$11,400

FIGURE 2.5 DEBT SERVICE RATIO.

	Wife	Husband	Joint	Total
Gross income	$42,400	$35,100	$1,600	$79,100
Payroll deductions	17,150	16,025		33,175
Take-home pay	$25,250	$19,075	$1,600	$45,925
Fixed Expenses				
Mortgage			$7,800	$ 7,800
Loan payments	$ 3,600			3,600
Total debt payments	$ 3,600		$7,800	$11,400

Calculation:

Debt service ratio: $11,400 ÷ $45,925 = .25

Interpretation: A ratio below .40 indicates an adequate income for existing debt repayments. At .25, this couple's ratio shows that their debts are moderate in comparison to their income and they could assume more debt if necessary.

If your debt service ratio is high, do not overlook the impact of voluntary savings plan deductions (such as 401(k) plans) on the calculation. When you save money in these plans, you increase your debt service ratio because your take-home pay decreases, although the overall impact on your finances is positive.

KEY CONCEPT — SAVINGS RATE RATIOS

Using income for current consumption or to acquire personal assets does not create the wealth needed for financial security. This wealth is created by deferring consumption and diverting income into long-term investments. The savings rate ratios measure the amounts being saved and invested.

Investment-Assets-to-Net-Worth Ratio

Investment-assets-to-net-worth ratio
= investment assets ÷ net worth

- *Purpose:* To track increase of income- or wealth-producing assets.
- *Data source:* Balance sheet.

Figure 2.6 demonstrates the ratio's calculation using the balance sheet from Chapter 1.

FIGURE 2.6 SAVINGS RATIOS.

	Wife	Husband	Joint	Total
Investments				
Stocks				
Bonds				
Mutual funds			$ 25,000	$ 25,000
Retirement plans	$ 60,000	$30,000		90,000
Life insurance cash values				
Business interests	50,000			50,000
Real estate				
Total investments	$110,000	$30,000	$ 25,000	$165,000
Net worth	$168,000	$51,000	$121,700	$298,700

Calculation:

Investment-assets-to-net-worth ratio: $165,000 ÷ $298,700 = .55

Interpretation: A common financial goal is to achieve financial independence. Reaching this goal requires accumulation of sufficient income-producing investments. This ratio should increase over time, especially as retirement approaches.

Be conservative when valuing assets like investment-quality collectibles or a business. Overoptimistic valuations can lead to a false sense of financial progress.

Do not include amounts that you plan to spend. For example, if you have earmarked funds (held in your name) for a child's education, do not include those funds in your investment-assets-to-net-worth ratio.

Savings-to-Income Ratio

Savings-to-income ratio = amount saved
÷ annual income

- *Purpose:* To determine percentage of income saved each year.
- *Data source:* Cash flow statement.

Figure 2.7 demonstrates the ratio's calculation using the balance sheet from Chapter 1.

Calculation:

Amount saved ÷ annual income: $13,500 ÷ $79,100 = .17

Interpretation: This couple is saving 17 percent of their income, which is very good. This ratio should increase over time after major financial obligations such as a mortgage or childrens' educations are paid.

Do not overlook the money that employers add to your savings and retirement plans. For example, many companies provide a matching contribution to an

FIGURE 2.7 SAVINGS-TO-INCOME RATIO.

	Wife	Husband	Joint	Total
Total income	$42,400	$35,100	$1,600	$79,100
Investments				
401(k) plans	$ 4,000	$ 3,500		$ 7,500
Investment plans			6,000	6,000
Total investments	$ 4,000	$ 3,500	6,000	$13,500

employee's 401(k) plan. Once you have ownership of those contributions (i.e., you are fully vested) you can count them as part of your annual savings.

Do not rely on simple formulas based on age ("Save 10 percent in your thirties, 15 percent in your fifties," etc.) to determine if you are saving enough. As you'll read in Chapters 18 and 19, the amount of savings required to reach financial goals varies significantly between persons.

REAL GROWTH RATIOS

Although the average annual inflation rate in the 1990s has been relatively low, small annual increases in the cost of living have a compounded effect. If inflation averages 3 percent per year for 10 years, an item that costs $100 today will cost roughly $134 in 10 years. If your income and net worth do not at least keep up with inflation, your ability to accumulate wealth will be impaired. The real, or inflation-adjusted, growth ratios for income and net worth measure your financial progress after inflation.

Growth of Income Ratio

Growth of income ratio = [(income this year – income last year) ÷ income last year] – inflation rate

- *Purpose:* To determine if income kept pace with inflation.
- *Data source:* Current year's and prior year's cash flow statements; annual Consumer Price Index (CPI) as reported by the Bureau of Labor Statistics.
  Calculation:
  [(79,100 – 75,000) ÷ 75,000] – .03 = .025
  Interpretation: The fictional couple has current-year income of $79,100 and a prior-year income of $75,000 (assumed), with an assumed 3 percent inflation rate over the current year. The result indicates a growth in real income of roughly 2.5 percent.

Growth of Net Worth Ratio

Growth of net worth ratio = [(net worth this year – net worth last year) ÷ net worth last year] – inflation rate

- *Purpose:* To determine if net worth kept pace with inflation.
- *Data source:* Current year's and prior year's balance sheets; inflation rate (CPI).

Calculation:

[(298,700 − 275,000) ÷ 275,000] − .03 = .056

Interpretation: The fictional couple has current net worth of $298,700 and a prior-year net worth of $275,000 (assumed), with an assumed 3 percent inflation rate over the current year. The result indicates a growth in real net worth of approximately 5.6 percent.

END POINT

Think of your financial ratios as a report from your annual financial health checkup. By calculating the ratios over time, you can spot problem areas (e.g., too little savings, too much debt) and evaluate your progress toward reaching your financial goals.

CHAPTER

3

Setting and Reaching Financial Goals

This chapter examines strategies and techniques for developing successful financial plans. Although a plan cannot guarantee the desired results, it does increase the likelihood of a satisfactory outcome.

THE PLANNING PROCESS

Most people rarely achieve financial goals by accident—winning the lottery is a rare event. Instead, these goals require detailed planning, implementation, and monitoring, as shown in Figure 3.1.

Using vague statements such as, "I want to be financially independent," will not produce the desired results. The general goal of financial independence must be clarified: What is a reasonable date for reaching this goal? How much money will this goal require? Where will you find the needed funds?

Although it isn't always easy to develop initial plans for reaching financial goals, monitoring and revising your plans after they are in place takes much less time if you do so. Also, as with any other skill, planning becomes easier with practice.

Identifying Personal Values

For some people, the acquisition and display of wealth is its own reward. This mentality was reflected in the popular 1980s slogan, "Whoever dies with the most toys wins." For others, wealth is a means to an end, not an end in itself. These individuals value

FIGURE 3.1 THE PLANNING PROCESS.

Identify personal values.
↓
Set general goals that match values.
↓
Refine and prioritize goals (target amounts and dates, resources).
↓
Implement steps to reach goals.
↓
Monitor progress; revise plans as needed.

wealth because it allows them to achieve specific results that they find rewarding.

The second view of wealth leads to an obvious question: If wealth allows you to reach your financial goals, *what are your goals?* Your financial goals need to be specific, with targeted dates, amounts, and action plans. While some goals, which are discussed shortly, are common to most individuals, your personal goals must reflect the values that are important to you. It is easy to take the idea of values for granted, especially when terms such as *family values* are used loosely. But identifying your key values is a prerequisite for developing goals, because if your goals do not reflect your values, achieving those goals will not produce much satisfaction. Figure 3.2 lists several values that are widely held in the United States.

Identifying your values will help you set goals that generate personal satisfaction. If you value autonomy, the goal of owning your own business could be appropriate for you. If you value simplicity, the requirements of being in a position of authority might not appeal to you. Although it is possible for you to achieve financial success without identifying key values, you face the risk of losing your motivation, especially if the objectives you are pursuing clash with your unidentified values.

If you do not identify with the values listed in Figure 3.2, or if you cannot narrow your selections from the list, imagine that you have just inherited enough money so that you never have to work again. What would you do differently in your life? The activities you select under this scenario provide a good indication of your values.

Do not identify with a value simply because it is popular at the moment. Fads change, creating a risk that this year's deeply held values will be considered unfashionable next year.

FIGURE 3.2 WIDELY HELD VALUES.

Achievement
Aesthetics
Authority
Adventure
Health
Independence
Integrity
Intimacy
Pleasure
Recognition
Security
Service (to others)
Simplicity
Spiritual growth
Wisdom

Adapted from New England Financial Advisors, Searching for the Perfect Balance *(Boston: The New England, 1986).*

In recent years the value of simplicity has become important for many people. Here are some tips to help you simplify your financial life.

- Charge everything to a single credit card.
- Have one checking account.
- Use a cash management account.
- Pay your bills automatically.
- Use electronic banking.
- Keep your investments at a single brokerage firm or mutual fund company.
- Keep good financial records.

General Financial Goals

CONCEPT   Although financial goals are unique to each individual, there are several common goals that are widely shared. Figure 3.3 lists some of these goals in four categories: organization, risk management, and wealth accumulation. As you review the list, identify the goals that are important to you.

At a minimum, your goals should include the following:
- Organized financial records.
- Adequate health, disability income, life, property, and liability insurance.
- Basic estate plan, including a written will.

FIGURE 3.3 GENERAL FINANCIAL GOALS.

Organization

- Develop a realistic spending plan.
- Create a record-keeping system for important financial documents.
- Create or review wills, trust agreements, powers of attorney.

Risk Management

- Identify risks to family income and current standard of living; develop plan for protecting income.
- Identify risks to assets; develop plan for protecting assets.

Wealth Accumulation

- Accumulate assets for the following:
   Children's college costs.
   Improvement in standard of living.
   Major purchases (auto, home, vacations, etc.).
   Support of other family members.
   Financial independence/retirement.

Estate Planning Goals

- Reduce income and estate taxes to legal minimums.

While these goals do not contribute directly to your net worth, they can reduce the impact of unexpected setbacks.

 **Selecting and Planning for Specific Goals**

After identifying goals, the next step is to develop detailed plans for reaching these goals. These plans should include a *target date* for reaching the goal, *an estimate of the amount needed,* and a *funding plan.* It is convenient to categorize goals by time required to completion: *Short-term goals* generally have a target date of under one year and *long-term goals* of over one year. To estimate the future costs of intermediate- and long-term goals, use the time value of money (TVM) methods from Chapter 4. Here is an example of setting an intermediate-term goal to demonstrate the process.

   Goal: Purchase new automobile in three years (36 months).
   Current cost: $22,000.

Anticipated cost (5 percent annual inflation): approximately $25,500.

Funds available today: $10,000.

Future value of available funds (8 percent annual return): $12,600.

Balance required: $12,900 ($25,500 – $12,600).

Monthly savings to accumulate balance of $12,900 (8 percent annual return): $316.

Do not use overly optimistic assumptions in your planning or you may fall short of your targets. The auto purchase example assumes a 5 percent inflation rate for the car's price and an 8 percent average annual return on the funds saved for the purchase. If the price increases by more than 5 percent or if the savings grow at less than 8 percent, there will be insufficient funds available. It is better to use conservative estimates and to risk overfunding a goal.

Ranking Goals

Because most people have more financial goals than money to fund those goals, it becomes necessary to allocate funds. Assume that you have two long-term (five-year target dates) goals: taking a luxury cruise and paying off the mortgage on your home. Unfortunately, you cannot afford both simultaneously—you must choose between them.

Prioritizing goals and choosing among them is not easy, but having a clearly defined set of values helps immensely in these situations. If you value pleasure and adventure more than the security of having no mortgage, you will save for the cruise. If you value financial peace of mind, you will pay off the mortgage.

Getting Advice

If you require assistance in developing plans to reach your financial goals, you should consider getting professional advice. Because goal setting requires an understanding of your overall finances, look for an advisor with a broad background in personal finance. These individuals usually will hold the Certified Financial Planner (CFP) or Chartered Financial Consultant (ChFC) designations. Several organizations provide referrals to financial planners, including the Institute of Certified Financial Planners (800-282-7526), the International Association for Financial Planning (800-945-4237), and the National Association of Personal Financial Advisors (800-333-6659). Before hiring anyone, ask about an advisor's professional education, experience, how he or she gets paid for working with you, and whether he or she works with clients whose circumstances are similar to yours. To check your potential advisor's regulatory background, call the Financial Adviser Alert service (800-822-0416). For $39, the service will check with several regulatory agencies to learn if the advisor has had any problems with regulators.

THE PSYCHOLOGY OF MONEY MANAGEMENT

People tend to approach their finances primarily from a quantitative perspective: dollars and cents, interest rates, rates of return, and so on. But numbers are only part of the story—it is just as important to understand the person behind the numbers. If you think that a person's money psychology is unimportant, think for a moment about how the people you know handle their finances. Some of these people probably are very frugal and hate spending money—any money! You probably also know a "shopaholic" who is happiest when spending money and uses shopping binges as a mood enhancer.

How do you manage your finances? If you asked another person who knows you well to describe your psychological profile with money, would any of the categories fit you? It is possible that your behavior is a mix of profiles that vary with the situation. For instance, you might spend very little money on personal luxuries for yourself but enjoy giving lavish gifts to friends and relatives. Or you might be uncomfortable with financial success, but still work 70 hours a week to achieve it.

If you have been experiencing increasing stress in your life or relationships, do not overlook money problems as a possible cause. Because many Americans find it difficult to talk about money, finances can be a silent source of problems in life.

 Identifying Influencing Factors

Where did your current attitudes toward money originate? These feelings usually represent a blend of influences from parents, culture, and personal experiences. If your parents practiced sound financial management and taught you those principles, you probably learned good habits from them. In contrast, if your parents were not adept at managing their finances, you may have picked up some of their problems, unless you consciously recognize their mistakes and work to avoid them. Parental influences are not always apparent, though—they can also have a subconscious impact on our behavior.

The culture we grow up in also plays a role in attitude toward money. In her book, *Talking Dollars and Making Sense: A Wealth Building Guide for African-Americans,* financial advisor Brooke Stephens discusses attitudes that are common among African-Americans. These include "The Lord will take care," "Money is evil," "Investing is for white people," "Looking rich is being rich," and "Advancement is betrayal," among others.[1] Stephens argues that African-Americans will not begin to realize their full economic potential until they recognize the debilitating effect of these attitudes and move beyond them.

Other sources of cultural influence extend beyond race. Attitudes toward money gleaned from television shows and other news and entertainment media or founded on religious beliefs can all influence your actions.

Personal experience is a major source of money attitudes. You can see this in the different ways older and younger people approach debt. Older Americans, especially those who experienced the Depression firsthand, tend to avoid debt. They often prefer to pay cash for transactions, and if they use a credit card, they do not carry a balance. Younger people (under age 50 in this example) are much more comfortable with debt. They owe more than their parents' generation and see debt as a useful tool for buying homes and cars, putting children through college, and financing their lifestyles.

Work-related experiences also affect your financial behavior. If you feel confident about your job, you probably become more relaxed with larger debts and fewer liquid assets. When the climate changes, though, as it has for many employees who have been downsized and "reengineered" out of their jobs, your financial attitude becomes much more cautious and conservative.

KEY CONCEPT — The Money Personality

Olivia Mellan is a psychotherapist and business consultant from Washington, D.C., who specializes in the field of money conflict resolution. In her book, *Money Harmony: Resolving Money Conflicts in Your Life and Relationships,* Mellan identifies the following five categories of money personality[2]:

- *Amasser.* Likes accumulating, spending, and investing large amounts of money.
- *Avoider.* Feels anxious about money management; avoids it whenever possible.
- *Hoarder.* Enjoys holding onto money; dislikes spending.
- *Money monk.* Feels guilty about accumulating wealth.

- *Spender.* Derives pleasure from spending; has difficulty saving.

Identifying your money personality is only an intermediate goal. The real purpose of the exercise is to understand how your profile affects your behavior, especially if you are in a long-term relationship. Mellan's book is an excellent guide to understanding and working with your profile.

Here are some tips for avoiding money arguments with your significant other[3]:

- Talk about money openly and matter-of-factly.
- Keep track of your separate debts before and after marriage.
- Settle the issue of joint versus separate accounts.
- Decide which spouse will handle the routine financial chores like paying bills.
- Keep track of your individual and joint accounts and investments.
- Agree on your estate plans, especially if there are children from previous marriages.
- Do not deny your spouse occasional personal luxuries.
- Discuss and agree on big purchases before making them.
- Spend some time planning your financial goals each year.
- Find financial advisors with whom both of you are comfortable.

This chapter presents an introduction to the psychology of money management and its potential impact on personal financial decisions. If finances are causing problems in your life, seek professional advice. Find a financial planner or counselor with experience in advising clients on their relationship with money. Until you recognize the factors influencing your financial behavior, it will be difficult to modify that behavior.

END POINT

Relying on luck to achieve financial fantasies makes it almost impossible to achieve financial success. By developing detailed, realistic plans for specific goals, you increase the likelihood of reaching those goals. The next chapter demonstrates the integration of your goals with a spending plan to allocate the needed funds.

It is easy to underestimate the important role that psychology plays in personal financial management.

Parents' behavior, culture, and individual experiences all influence your relationship with money. Problems can develop when these influences cause destructive behavior or prevent a person (or couple) from reaching their financial goals. In particular, when the individuals in a relationship have different attitudes toward money, conflicts can develop. The first step toward preventing and resolving these conflicts is to recognize the predominant behavior pattern and its impact.

4

The Time Value of Money

The easiest way to understand the concept of money's time value is by example. Imagine that you had a choice between receiving $100 today or $100 one year from now. When would you prefer to receive the money?

Intuition should tell you to take the $100 today. By taking the money now, you can spend it and receive immediate gratification or you could invest it with the goal of making it grow. From another perspective, if you waited a year to take the money, there is a good chance prices will increase and the $100 would buy less than it would today.

KEY CONCEPT — MONEY HAS A TIME VALUE

This example demonstrates a basic financial principle: A dollar that you receive today is generally worth more than a dollar to be received in the future. In other words, *money has a time value*. Depending on the amount of time and the rate of return that you can earn on your money, the difference between a dollar's *present value* and its *future value* can be substantial.

Time value of money (TVM) calculations answer the following types of questions:

- If college costs increase by 7 percent each year, how much will it cost to send my children to the local university in five years?

- My pension plan has offered me a choice between receiving a lump-sum payment or an annual pension when I retire. Which option should I take?

This material requires only a standard calculator. If you plan to work extensively with TVM calculations, you should consider using a PC spreadsheet program or a financial calculator. These tools can handle TVM problems easily and speed up your work considerably.

 **Present Value versus Future Value**

The first step in working with TVM problems is to understand the time dimensions. Trying to estimate a value for some future date is a *future value* problem. Here is an example. Home prices in your area are increasing by 5 percent annually, and you want to estimate your home's value in three years. If you put these dates on a timeline, it would look like this, with time passing as you move along the arrow to the right.

Three-Year Future Value Timeline

Present value   Future value
(known)   (unknown)

|————————————►|

Today   Three years from today

In contrast, *present value* problems bring future amounts back through time. Say you are expecting a $10,000 payment in five years, and you want to know what that $10,000 is worth today. The timeline looks like this:

Five-Year Present Value Timeline

Present value   Future value
(unknown)   (known)

|◄————————————|

Today   Five years from today

 **SINGLE OR MULTIPLE CASH FLOWS**

The second step in working with TVM problems is to decide whether you are working with a *single* cash flow or *multiple* cash flows. A single cash flow problem (present or future value) will involve an amount that occurs once, while multiple cash flows occur more than once. (Multiple cash flow problems are also known as *annuities.*)

Future value problems

Single cash flow: If you deposit $1,000 in an account earning 5 percent, what will the account be worth in five years?

Multiple cash flows: If you deposit $1,000 *each year* for the next five years in an account earning 5 percent, what will the account be worth in five years?

Present value problems

Single cash flow: You will receive a $10,000 payment in five years. What is that $10,000 payment worth today?

Multiple cash flows: You will receive $5,000 *each year* for the next 10 years. What are those payments worth today?

 Timing of Multiple Cash Flows

Some multiple cash flows occur at the beginning of the period—mortgage and rent payments, for instance. Other financial transactions, like loans, can be structured so payment is due at the end of the period. When the cash flow occurs at the beginning of the period, the TVM problem is called an *annuity due,* while cash flows at the period's end are *ordinary annuities.* The formulas and tables in the following sections calculate ordinary annuity values, but it is simple to convert their results into annuities due.

 If you are unsure about a problem's structure (present or future value, single or multiple cash flows, multiple cash flow timing), sketch a timeline. Placing the cash flows and dates on paper will help you visualize the problem so you can approach it properly.

There are several tools for solving TVM problems: formulas, tables, financial calculators, and spreadsheets. Your choice of a solution method will depend on access to a tool and the convenience of using it.

 TVM FORMULAS

The TVM formulas require you to provide the interest rate you plan to use and the number of periods involved in the problem. The formulas use the notation *i* for the interest rate you will use and *n* for the number of periods. You will need a calculator to work through the examples in this section.

Formula 1: Future value, single cash flow

$$\text{Future value} = \text{amount} \times (1 + i)^n$$

Example: Your local college costs $7,000 per year today. If costs increase 6 percent each year, how much will your son's first year cost when he starts school in five years?

Calculation:

$$i = .06, n = 5 \qquad \$7{,}000 \times (1 + .06)^5 = \$9{,}368$$

Formula 2: Future value, multiple (equal) cash flows (ordinary annuity)

Future value (ordinary annuity) =

$$\text{amount} \times \frac{(1 + i)^n - 1}{i}$$

Example: You invest \$2,000 into an Individual Retirement Account (IRA) at the *end* of each year for the next 15 years. If the account grows by an average of 10 percent each year, how much will you have in the account after 15 years?

Calculation:

$$i = .10, n = 15$$

$$\$2{,}000 \times \frac{(1 + .10)^{15} - 1}{.10} = \$63{,}545$$

Conversion to annuity due

Multiply the result of your ordinary annuity calculation by $(1 + i)$.

Example: You invest \$2,000 into an IRA at the *beginning* of each year for the next 15 years. If the account grows by an average 10 percent each year, how much will you have in the account after 15 years?

Calculation:

$$\text{Previous result} \times (1 + i),$$

$$\text{or } \$63{,}545 \times 1.10 = \$69{,}899$$

Formula 3: Present value, single cash flow

$$\text{Present value} = \frac{\text{amount}}{(1 + i)^n}$$

Example: In the earlier example, you estimated that the first-year cost for your son's college education would be \$9,368. If you can earn 12 percent on your investments, how much should you invest today to have that amount (\$9,368) available in five years?

Calculation:

$$i = .12, n = 5 \qquad \frac{\$9{,}368}{(1 + .12)^5} = \$5{,}316$$

Formula 4: Present value, multiple (equal) cash flows (ordinary annuity)

$$\text{Present value (ordinary annuity)} =$$

$$\frac{\text{amount}}{i} - \frac{\text{amount}}{i \times (1 + i)^n}$$

Example: You are injured in an auto accident and the insurance company offers you a settlement. You can receive $50,000 today or $7,500 annual payments at the *end* of each year for the next 10 years. If you can earn 6 percent on your money, which offer should you take?

Calculation:

$$i = .06, \ n = 10 \qquad \frac{\$7,500}{.06} - \frac{\$7,500}{.06 \times (1.06)^{10}}$$

$$= \$55,201$$

You should take the annual payments because their present value ($55,201) is greater than the lump-sum payment ($50,000).

Conversion to annuity due

Multiply the result of your ordinary annuity calculation by $(1 + i)$.

Example: You are injured in an auto accident and the insurance company offers you a settlement. You can receive $50,000 today or $7,500 annual payments at the *beginning* of each year for the next 10 years. If you can earn 6 percent on your money, which offer should you take?

Calculation:

$$\text{Previous result} \times (1 + i), \text{ or } \$55,201 \times 1.06$$
$$= \$58,513.$$

 TVM TABLES

CONCEPT   An alternative to the formula method is to use TVM tables, which list each formula's results for a range of periods and interest rates. Figures 4.1 and 4.2 list part of the TVM table for Formula 1 (future value, single cash flow).

Follow these steps to use the tables. (Complete versions of Figures 4.1 through 4.5 may be found in the appendix.)

1. Determine the number of periods and the interest rate in the problem.

FIGURE 4.1 FUTURE VALUE (PARTIAL), SINGLE CASH FLOW.

Period	1%	2%	3%	4%
1	1.010	1.020	1.030	1.040
2	1.020	1.040	1.061	1.082
3	1.030	1.061	1.093	1.125
4	1.041	1.082	1.126	1.170
5	1.051	1.104	1.159	1.217

2. Determine if you are dealing with a single cash flow or multiple flows.

3. Go to the corresponding table and cross-reference the period and interest rate.

4. Use the cross-referenced factor in the TVM formula.

The previous problems are repeated here to demonstrate the method.

Future Value, Single Cash Flow

Example: Your local college costs $7,000 per year today. If costs increase 6 percent each year, how much will your son's first year cost when he starts school in five years?

Solution technique: In Figure 4.2, move across the interest rate row until you reach the 6 percent column. Go down the column until you are across from the Period equals 5 row and you will find the factor, 1.338.

Use that factor in the following formula:

Future value = amount × future value factor

That results in $7,000 × 1.338 = $9,366, which is very close to the previous result of $9,368. (There is

FIGURE 4.2 FUTURE VALUE, SINGLE CASH FLOW.

Period	1%	2%	5%	6%
1	1.010	1.020	1.050	1.060
2	1.020	1.040	1.103	1.124
3	1.030	1.061	1.158	1.191
4	1.041	1.082	1.216	1.262
5	1.051	1.104	1.276	1.338
6	1.062	1.126	1.340	1.419
7	1.072	1.149	1.407	1.504

some rounding because Figure 4.2 uses only three decimal points.)

Future Value, Multiple (Equal) Cash Flows (Ordinary Annuity)

Example: You invest $2,000 into an IRA each year for the next 15 years. If the account grows by an average 10 percent each year, how much will you have in the account after 15 years?

Solution technique: In Figure 4.3, move across the interest rate row until you reach the 10 percent column. Go down the column until you are across from the Period equals 15 row and you will find the factor, 31.772. (Several rows and columns are omitted from Figure 4.3 to save space.)

Use that factor in the following formula:

Future value = amount × future value factor

That results in $2,000 × 31.772 = $63,544, versus the previous result of $63,545.

Conversion to annuity due
Multiply the result of your ordinary annuity calculation by $(1 + i)$.

Present Value, Single Cash Flow

Example: You estimated that the first-year cost for your son's college education would be $9,368. If you can earn 12 percent on your investments, how much should you invest today to have that amount ($9,368) available in five years?

Solution technique: In Figure 4.4, move across the interest rate row until you reach the 10 percent column. Go down the column until you are across from the Period equals 5 row and you will find the factor, 0.567.

FIGURE 4.3 FUTURE VALUE, MULTIPLE CASH FLOWS AT END OF PERIOD.

Period	1%	2%	9%	10%
1	1.000	1.000	1.000	1.000
2	2.010	2.020	2.090	2.100
3	3.030	3.060	3.278	3.310
14	14.947	15.974	26.019	27.975
15	16.097	17.293	29.361	31.772

FIGURE 4.4 PRESENT VALUE, SINGLE CASH FLOW.

Period	11%	12%
1	0.901	0.893
2	0.812	0.797
3	0.731	0.712
4	0.659	0.636
5	0.593	0.567

Use that factor in the following formula:

Present value = amount × present value factor, or
$$\$9{,}368 \times 0.567 = \$5{,}312$$

Present Value, Multiple (Equal) Cash Flows (Ordinary Annuity)

Example: You are injured in an auto accident and the insurance company offers you a settlement. You can receive $50,000 today or $7,500 annual payments for the next 10 years. If you can earn 6 percent on your money, which offer should you take?

Solution technique: In Figure 4.5, move across the interest rate row until you reach the 6 percent column. Go down the column until you are across from the Period equals 10 row and you will find the factor, 7.360.

Use that factor in the following formula:

Present value = amount × present value factor,
or $7,500 × 7.360 = $55,200

Conversion to annuity due
Multiply the result of your ordinary annuity calculation by $(1 + i)$.

FIGURE 4.5 PRESENT VALUE, MULTIPLE CASH FLOWS.

Period	1%	2%	6%
1	0.990	0.980	0.943
2	1.970	1.942	1.833
3	2.941	2.884	2.673
9	8.566	8.162	6.802
10	9.471	8.983	7.360

FIGURE 4.6 PERIOD CONVERSION TABLE.

To Go from Annual To	Divide *i* By	Multiply *n* By
Semiannual	2	2
Quarterly	4	4
Monthly	12	12

Calculating Payments

Figure 4.5 also can be used to calculate annual payments using the following formula:

Payment = amount borrowed ÷ present value factor (from Figure 4.5)

Example: You borrow $5,000 at 10 percent interest. Loan payments are due at the end of each of the next five years. How much must you repay each year?

Solution technique: Go to Figure 4.5 and find the factor for 10 percent, five periods (3.791). Using the preceding formula, $5,000 ÷ 3.791 = $1,319.

TVM Formulas and Tables with Other Periods

The TVM formulas and tables assume that interest rates are annual and that periods are in years, but some TVM problems, like monthly loan payments, require different time periods. Use Figure 4.6 to adjust the formulas' and tables' annual interest rates and periods.

END POINT

The TVM calculations offer a versatile set of tools for dealing with a wide range of common financial calculations that involve time. Although the calculations may seem complex, you can master them with a basic calculator and the tables in the appendix. Later chapters will use TVM tools extensively.

Developing a Spending Plan

The reality of limited resources forces choices: You must decide whether to spend your money on current consumption or save it for the future. In addition, you must allocate your current spending to meet a variety of needs. If you fail to make conscious spending and savings decisions, you are unlikely to achieve any lasting financial success, regardless of your income.

This chapter introduces the *spending plan,* a technique for taking control of your cash flow. By integrating your financial goals with projections of your income and expenses, you redirect your resources toward your highest-priority goals. This integration increases the probability that you will achieve those goals, and it also reduces the wasteful impulse spending that can sidetrack your efforts.

KEY CONCEPT — LINKING GOALS AND FUNDS

Chapter 3 illustrated goal-setting techniques that require target dates and specific amounts. Setting a realistic, specific goal does not guarantee its achievement, though: *You must find and allocate the resources required to implement the plan.* The spending plan will help you identify the resources—it is the link between your cash flow, resources, and goals.

Developing a spending plan forces you to deal with *real dollars,* not abstract amounts. Once you master the mechanics of planning, it is relatively easy to set a financial goal: "I need to save $300 each month and earn a 6 percent annual return for the next two years so I can reach my goal." This plan is stated clearly, with a specific amount and target date. *But where will you find the $300 each month?* Because most people lack unlimited resources, finding funds for goals usually requires modifications in spending patterns and asset allocations. The personal spending plan integrates the financing required for goals with projected cash flow. Chapter 1 developed a balance sheet and cash flow statement for a fictional couple; Figure 5.1 lists the couple's financial goals.

These two goals will require roughly $1,000 per month, or $12,000 per year. The couple's next task is to find the funds for these goals. They start by examining their current spending patterns. Figures 5.2 and 5.3 reproduce part of the couple's cash flow statement from Chapter 1.

 If the changes in spending patterns will affect other family members, involve them in the process as much as possible. Ideally, spouses should make decisions together so that they can compromise when necessary to avoid later conflicts. If your children are old enough to understand your family finances, involve them, too—

FIGURE 5.1 FINANCIAL GOALS.

Goal	Amount Needed	Dates
Pay off home mortgage in 10 years instead of 15.	$500 per month	Monthly for next five years
Buy new car (for cash) in three years.	Projected future cost: $20,000 (including trade-in); monthly savings: approx. $500	Monthly for next three years

FIGURE 5.2 FIXED EXPENSES (FROM CHAPTER 1).

Fixed Expenses	Wife	Husband	Joint	Total
Mortgage			$ 7,800	$ 7,800
Loan payments	$3,600			3,600
Utilities			5,000	5,000
Insurance			3,000	3,000
Property taxes			3,000	3,000
Investment plans			6,000	6,000
Total fixed expenses	$3,600		$24,800	$28,400

FIGURE 5.3 VARIABLE EXPENSES (FROM CHAPTER 1).

Variable Expenses	Wife	Husband	Joint	Total
Charitable contributions			$ 2,400	$ 2,400
Clothing	$1,500	$1,500		3,000
Education				
Food			5,000	5,000
Gifts			2,000	2,000
Travel/vacation			3,000	3,000
Total variable expenses	$1,500	$1,500	$12,400	$15,400

a spending plan is an excellent tool for teaching them about personal finance.

As they examine their fixed expenses, the couple recognizes several opportunities for redirecting their cash flow:

- *Refinance mortgage.* Rates have dropped since they took out their current loan, and refinancing at current rates will reduce their monthly payment by $100. Annual cash flow generated: $1,200.

- *Loan payments.* The wife's auto loan of $3,000 (monthly payment, $300) will be paid off in 10 months. The loan's interest rate is considerably higher than the interest being paid on the couple's savings account, so they withdraw $3,000 from savings to pay off the loan. Annual cash flow generated: $3,600.

- *Insurance.* By increasing their policies' deductibles, the couple can reduce their premiums. Annual cash flow generated: $500.

- *Investment plans.* The couple has been investing $500 each month ($6,000 per year) into mutual funds. They had not established a purpose for the fund account, and they are willing to use future contributions to reach their two goals, if necessary. They will review other sources of cash before deciding whether to use this money.

After reviewing their variable expenses in Figure 5.3, the couple decides the following:

- *Charitable contributions.* Both individuals place a high value on giving to their selected recipients, so they make no changes here. This is an example of personal values influencing a financial decision.

- *Gifts.* They agree to cut back slightly on gifts. Annual cash flow generated: $500.
- *Travel/vacation.* They agree to reduce their spending here by 50 percent. Annual cash flow generated: $1,500.
- *Other variable-expense categories.* Left unchanged.

In summary, the couple has identified the sources of cash (see Figure 5.4) to fund their goals.

The annual target for the couple's goals is $12,000, and they have identified $7,300 in available funds. Because they still are roughly $5,000 short, they decide to allocate their monthly $500 mutual fund investment toward these goals, which will give them a comfortable margin in saving for their goals.

In this example, some of the required cash flow came from reducing discretionary expenditures such as gifts and travel. While spending reductions are often required to free funds, it is not always necessary to reduce the level of activity. For instance, if the couple could buy the same gifts when those items go on sale, they could give as much as they had in the past while reducing their spending. They could use this same smart-shopper approach to their vacations, searching for off-peak-season hotel bargains, airfare deals, and so on. Since $1 of reduced expenses equals $1.25 (or more) of pretax income, it is worth the effort to cut expenses whenever possible.

In this example, the couple decided to take money from savings to reduce their debts. In general, moving funds from low-yielding savings to reduce higher-rate debt is a sound strategy. Be careful that you do not leave yourself strapped for liquid assets, however. If a cash shortage forces you to borrow again, you might be faced with a higher rate than you were paying on the debt that you eliminated.

FIGURE 5.4 SUMMARY OF SAVINGS.

Source	Annual Amount
Mortgage	$1,200
Loan payments	3,600
Insurance	500
Gifts	500
Travel	1,500
Total	$7,300

THE SPENDING PLAN

Having identified sources of funds, the couple can set up their projected annual spending plan, shown in Figure 5.5, assuming that their income remains unchanged.

As you develop and revise your spending plan, leave some flexibility for unexpected expenses. This is particularly important if your income fluctuates, as it can for the self-employed or those working on commission. In the preceding example, the couple deliberately overfunded the amount the needed for their goals. If they should incur an unexpected expense during the year, such as a home or auto repair, they can divert some of the funds from their goals without suffering a major setback.

MONITORING THE SPENDING PLAN

After identifying the changes you wish to make on an annual basis, the next step is to design a system for monitoring your finances each month. Checking your progress monthly does not require an excessive amount of time, but it is frequent enough to spot problems before it is too late to correct them. Figure 5.6 continues the sample couple's spending plan by first

FIGURE 5.5 REVISED ANNUAL SPENDING PLAN.

Expense	Previous Amount	Revised Amount	Change
Mortgage	$7,800	$6,600	−$ 1,200
Loan payments	3,600	0	− 3,600
Utilities	5,000	5,000	0
Insurance	3,000	2,500	− 500
Property taxes	3,000	3,000	0
Investment plans	6,000	0*	− 6,000
Charitable contributions	2,400	2,400	0
Clothing	3,000	3,000	0
Education	0	0	0
Food	5,000	5,000	0
Gifts	2,000	1,500	− 500
Travel/vacation	3,000	1,500	− 1,500
Total change			−$13,300

*They continue to invest the $500 each month but earmark it for their goals.

FIGURE 5.6 MONTHLY PROJECTIONS.

Month: January	Pro- jected	Actual	Monthly Variance	Year- to-Date Variance
Income				
Wages/salary	$6,417			
Interest	0			
Mutual fund distributions	0			
Total sources	$6,492			
Payroll deductions				
Federal income tax	$1,167			
Social Security tax	481			
State income tax	292			
Medical insurance premium	200			
401(k) plans	625			
Total deductions	$2,765			
Fixed expenses				
Mortgage	$ 550			
Loan payments	0			
Utilities	417			
Insurance	208			
Property taxes	0			
Investment plans	0			
Saving for goal 1	500			
Saving for goal 2	500			
Total fixed expenses	$2,425			
Variable expenses				
Charitable contributions	$ 0			
Clothing	0			
Education				
Food	417			
Gifts	0			
Travel/vacation	0			
Total variable expenses	$ 417			

transferring their annual projections onto a monthly worksheet, with January as the illustrative month. The "Monthly variance" column will hold the difference between the "Projected" and "Actual" columns, and the "Year-to-date variance" column will hold the cumulative total of each month's variances. Figure 5.7 summarizes the results.

The assumptions used are as follows:

- Interest paid quarterly (March, June, September, December).
- Mutual fund distribution paid annually in December.

FIGURE 5.7 CASH FLOW SUMMARY FOR JANUARY.

Month: January	Pro- jected	Actual	Monthly Variance	Year- to-Date Variance
Income	$6,492			
Payroll deductions	2,765			
Fixed expenses	2,425			
Variable expenses	417			
Net cash flow	+$ 885			

- Property taxes paid quarterly (March, June, September, December).
- Charitable contributions, clothing, gifts, travel/vacation: no expenditures planned for January.

 Treat the amounts needed for your goals as fixed expenses. This technique reinforces the goals' importance and reduces the likelihood that you will cut funding if you encounter a shortage of cash in any period.

 Some fixed expenses, like property taxes, do not occur monthly; instead, you must pay them quarterly or at some other regular interval. If you do not account for these expenses they can disrupt your spending plan. The easiest way to handle them is to mark them on your calendar at the beginning of the year so you will remember to include them in your monthly projections.

 If you show a projected cash flow surplus for a month, don't make the mistake of spending it. You will need the surplus for those months when you incur nonmonthly or unpredictable expenses. Keep any surplus in a liquid account so you can access it quickly when needed. If you consistently generate surpluses, revise your projections and apply the surplus toward your goals.

 ## DEALING WITH INSUFFICIENT FUNDS

The couple in this chapter's examples found the funds their goals required without making drastic changes in their lifestyle. However, you may lack sufficient funds to achieve all of your goals, in spite of major changes in your spending patterns and asset allocations. In that case, the short-term solution is to rank your goals in order of importance. You should then begin funding your most important goal. In the longer term, you should search for additional sources of income. This income could come from a salary or wage increase, from working overtime, or from starting a part-time business.

END POINT

It is unlikely that you will reach your financial goals by accident. You must link the goal-setting process described in Chapter 3 with a realistic spending plan to provide the funds needed to reach your goals. If you lack sufficient funds to achieve all of your goals, you must rank the goals to decide which ones you will pursue first. You should also consider ways to increase your income to provide the additional funds for your remaining goals.

6

Cash Management

Effective cash management requires a trade-off between the need for liquid assets and the opportunity cost of holding those assets. Holding insufficient liquid assets makes it difficult to pay bills on time and meet unexpected expenses. Because liquid assets such as checking and savings accounts pay low yields, however, holding excess balances means the loss of the potentially higher income available with other investments.

This chapter discusses the tools and techniques of effective cash management so you can meet your liquidity requirements while minimizing the attendant opportunity costs. These tools include traditional bank products, asset management accounts, short-term investments, and electronic banking. If you have not read Chapter 2, you should review it before reading this chapter, so you can estimate your liquidity needs.

BANKS' LIQUID ACCOUNTS

Banks offer a variety of liquid accounts, including the following:

- Checking accounts.
- NOW (negotiable order of withdrawal) accounts.
- Savings and money market deposit accounts.
- Money market mutual funds (through investment subsidiaries).

Bank products have several attractive features, including safety (for FDIC-insured accounts) and convenient access to funds and services at bank branches and ATMs. In recent years, though, many banks have started charging a wider variety of fees and have increased their minimum required account balances. These increasing fees and higher balances can add up. A 1997 study by the U.S. Public Interest Research Group (PIRG) found that the average annual cost to maintain a regular checking account was more than $218 for large banks and $190 for small banks. The average minimum balance required to avoid those fees was $462 at big banks and $554 at small banks.[1]

The first step in selecting the bank account that best fits your needs is to evaluate how you use bank services. Here are some areas to review:

- Your account balances during a typical month (actual and average minimum).
- The number of checks you write each month.
- ATM use (frequency and type of transactions).
- Need to visit local branches for transactions.
- Use of other bank services: debit cards, electronic funds transactions (including direct deposits and payments).

After evaluating your requirements, the next step is to find the institution that can meet those needs at the lowest cost. Ideally, you want a bank with convenient locations, accounts with no minimum balances, no fees, and competitive interest rates on balances. Since it may be impossible to find this ideal combination of features, you should identify the best compromise by ranking the accounts' features in order of their importance to you. The goal of comparing institutions is to find the bank accounts that offer the products and services you need while minimizing your costs. Features to review include the following:

- Minimum required balances.
- Convenience: branches, ATMs.
- Fees: monthly, ATM.
- Number of checks allowed each month without additional fees.
- Interest paid on account balances.
- Other features: overdraft protection; preferential rates on savings accounts, loans, and charge cards.

Do not overlook credit unions, small banks, and on-line banks, which frequently have lower required account minimums, charge lower fees, and pay higher interest rates than large banks. The U.S. PIRG study found that the average cost for a checking account at a credit union was $108, roughly half the cost of having an account at a bank.[2]

MONEY MARKET MUTUAL FUNDS

Money market mutual funds (MMFs) are offered by investment firms. Originally developed as short-term holding accounts for brokerage firms' clients' cash between securities sales, MMFs currently hold roughly $1 trillion of investors' money.[3] The reasons for this popularity include their liquidity (check-writing privileges are standard), their low initial minimums (usually $1,000 to $3,000), and their excellent safety record. There are three basic categories of funds:

- *Standard MMFs.* Invested in short-term corporate and government debt.

- *Government-only MMFs.* Invested in short-term U.S. government and government agency obligations.

- *Tax-exempt MMFs.* Invested in short-term municipal securities; exempt from federal income taxes.

Unlike banks' money market deposit accounts, MMFs are investments, not FDIC-insured accounts. The funds work to maintain a constant price of $1.00 per share, and they pay dividends, not interest, to shareholders. (A fund's price of $1.00 per share is not guaranteed, but MMFs have an outstanding safety record.) The standard MMF will hold short-maturity (less than one year) investments such as U.S. government debt, large bank certificates of deposit, and high-quality corporate debt. You should examine the fund's prospectus for following features before investing[4]:

- *Yield.* Does the fund consistently rank among the highest-yielding? Large MMFs, such as those from Vanguard, Zurich Kemper, and Fidelity frequently have good records of offering competitive yields.

- *Minimum initial investment.* Most fund minimums range from $1,000 to $3,000, although some start at $25,000.

- *Check minimums.* These range from $100 to $500 per check. If you write a large number of checks, look for unlimited check writing.

- *Checks returned.* Helpful for record keeping.

- *Fees.* Avoid funds that impose 12-1 fees on shareholders, since these fees reduce your net yield. Check the "Annual Fund Operating Expenses" in the prospectus for a summary of fund fees.

 Compare tax-exempt MMFs with their taxable counterparts to determine where you will earn the highest *after-tax* yield. To determine a taxable fund's after-tax return, multiply its current yield by 1 minus your federal tax rate. If you are in the 28 percent federal tax bracket, and the fund pays a taxable 5.4

percent yield, that translates to a 3.9 percent after-tax return: $5.4 \times (1 - .28)$.

TERM ACCOUNTS
Banks' Term Accounts

One common feature among the accounts previously described is that the depositor or investor can withdraw his or her funds at any time. In contrast, term accounts require the funds to remain in the account for a specified period of time. With a typical certificate of deposit (CD), for example, the bank will charge a penalty of several months' interest if the depositor withdraws the funds before the account matures. In exchange for this reduced liquidity, banks pay higher rates, with the highest yields being paid on the longest deposit terms, usually five years for CDs. Figure 6.1 lists the national averages for liquid accounts and CDs as of late July, 1997.

Shopping for CDs

You frequently can increase the yield on your CDs by considering out-of-state banks and brokerage firms' offerings. Each issue of *Money, Kiplinger's Personal Finance* magazine, and the *Bank Rate Monitor* lists the nation's highest savings yields, along with bank safety ratings, minimum deposits, and phone numbers. If you prefer to bank with a local institution, try negotiating for a better deposit rate, especially if you have a large balance. Bank branch managers usually can authorize a higher deposit rate if necessary to retain a customer's business.

If you want to try for a higher CD return and can accept some uncertainty, consider an *indexed CD*. The yields on these accounts are tied to a stock market

FIGURE 6.1 COMPARATIVE YIELDS.

Account	National Average Yield
Regular checking accounts	1.35%
Bank money market deposit account	2.64
Taxable money market fund (MMF)	5.14
Tax-exempt MMF	3.13
U.S. government-issue MMF	4.93
Six-month CDs	4.88
One-year CDs	5.17
Five-year CDs	5.68

Sources: Adapted from the September 1997 issue of Money, copyright © 1997 by Time Inc., and from the Wall Street Journal, copyright © 1997 by Dow Jones & Company, Inc. All rights reserved worldwide.

index: If the index performs well, the yield on your CD can increase substantially. The Marine Midland bank's one-year CD that matured in June 1997 paid depositors 12.7 percent, double the return on traditional CD accounts. (The stock market rose 35 percent during that same period, but Marine Midland caps its maximum rate at 15 percent.) If the market drops, you still get your principal back and you have the benefit of FDIC insurance.[5]

If you want to increase the yield on your CDs but don't want to tie up your funds with longer-term deposits, consider staggering the maturities. For instance, you could divide your funds among three-month, six-month, one-year, and two-year maturities. This technique allows you to capture the higher yields available from longer maturities while ensuring that part of your funds will be available fairly soon if needed.

If you keep more than $100,000 in a bank, get advice on structuring your accounts, because the insurance coverage rules are more complex than you might think. Here is an example from the *Your Insured Deposit* booklet[6]:

QUESTION: Are joint accounts owned by the same persons separately insured if different Social Security numbers are used?

ANSWER: No. The use of Social Security numbers does not determine insurance coverage. In addition, insurance coverage is not increased by rearranging the name of the owners or by changing the styles of the names. Furthermore, the use of "or" versus "and" to join the owners' names in a joint account does not affect insurance coverage.

U.S. Savings Bonds

Approximately 55 million Americans (about 20 percent of the population) own over $180 billion of U.S. savings bonds. Not all of these owners are making money on their bonds, though: Of the bonds in circulation, over 7 million of them no longer earn interest because they are past their maturity dates. Savings bonds have several attractive features:

- *Safety.* Backed by U.S. Treasury.
- *Ease of purchase.* Minimum purchase of $25 for a $50 bond.
- *Tax advantages.* Interest is exempt from state and local income taxes; federal income is tax deferred until you redeem the bonds or stop earning interest

after 30 years; lower- and middle-income investors can exclude part or all of Series EE bonds' interest when the bonds are redeemed to pay for postsecondary education.

- *Market-based rates.* Bonds' interest rates track Treasury securities' yields, so your bonds' rates can increase if market rates increase.
- *Liquidity.* You can cash Series EE bonds anytime after six months.[7]

Over the years, bonds have been offered with a variety of guaranteed interest rates, as Figure 6.2 shows.

The yields earned on bonds also depend on the bond's issue date. Bonds issued before May 1995 that are held for at least five years earn the greater of their guaranteed rate or 85 percent of the average of five-year Treasury security yields. EE bonds bought between May 1995 and April 1997 earn short-term market rates during the first five years and long-term market rates from the fifth through seventeenth years. Rates are adjusted every six months, and new rates are announced each May 1 and November 1. Finally, bonds issued on or after May 1, 1997, will earn interest equal to 90 percent of the average yield for five-year Treasuries.

Although they have several valuable features, savings bonds remain unattractive, especially for conservative buyers who plan to hold the bonds for a long time. If you have a short-term goal for the money, such as keeping sufficient cash balances, buy Treasury bills or government debt-only money market mutual funds. If you are planning for a longer-term goal, consider zero-coupon municipal bonds or mutual funds that buy conservative stocks. For retirement savings, you should first save the maximum allowed in any tax-deductible retirement accounts such as 401(k), 403(b), and IRA accounts. Given the wide range of alternatives available today and the lack of a guaranteed minimum rate, savings bonds are no longer the great deal they were on their introduction in 1935.

FIGURE 6.2 SAVINGS BOND GUARANTEED RATES.

Series E/EE issue dated or entering an extension during:	Earn a guaranteed minimum rate of:
11/82–10/86	7.5%
11/86–2/93	6
3/93–4/95	4
5/95–present	No minimum guaranteed rate

Source: Introduction to Savings Bonds, *Bureau of the Public Debt, 1997.*

You can get current values for your savings bonds from several sources. The Department of Public Debt offers printed tables and tracking software. For the printed tables, write to the Bureau of Public Debt, Savings Bonds Operations Office, Parkersburg, VA 26106-1328, and request publication PD 3600. The Bureau also provides free valuation software at its Web site, http://www.ustreas.gov/treasury/bureaus/pubdebt. Several firms also value savings bonds for a fee: The Savings Bond Informer (800-927-1901) and U.S. Savings Bond Consultant (800-717-2663).

DANGER! Plan the timing of any bond redemption carefully so you don't lose accumulated interest. Interest is credited to bonds twice each year, so you should redeem a bond immediately *after* the interest is posted. If your bond's interest is credited in June and December and you redeem it in November, you lose six months' interest. An exception: EE bonds issued between March 1993 and April 1995 have interest credited monthly for the first five years, but semiannually after that.

KEY CONCEPT — SHORT-TERM INVESTMENTS

The key difference between savings accounts and investments is safety of principal. Savings accounts are not subject to swings in market value. Interest rates may vary, but the depositor's original deposit is not at risk. In contrast, the value of an investment fluctuates, although the degree of fluctuation can be moderate. U.S. Treasury bills and notes and short-term bond funds are examples of conservative investments with limited risk. These investments are appropriate for short- to intermediate-term goals where funds will be required within three years. The selection of a three-year horizon is arbitrary—more conservative investors might prefer to use a five-year cutoff.

Treasury Bills and Notes

The federal government sells debt securities to raise the cash needed for its operations. *Treasury bills* are short-term obligations with a term of one year or less, while *Treasury notes* have maturities from one to ten years. Bills and notes are sold by auction. Large investors such as mutual funds and pension plans submit competitive bids for the securities, while individuals usually submit noncompetitive bids. With a noncompetitive bid, the individual investor agrees to accept a rate determined by the auction. The Treasury guarantees that it will accept the noncompetitive bids, relieving the buyer of the uncertainty that his or her bid will be accepted. Figure 6.3 lists the terms of the Treasury's debt sales.

FIGURE 6.3 BUYING TREASURY SECURITIES.

Term	Minimum Investment	Additional Investments	Auction Held
13-week bill	$10,000	$1,000	Weekly
26-week bill	10,000	1,000	Weekly
52-week bill	10,000	1,000	Every four weeks
2-year note	5,000	1,000	Monthly
5-year note	1,000	1,000	Monthly
10-year note	1,000	1,000	February, May, August, November
30-year bond	1,000	1,000	February, August, November

Sources: Buying Treasury Securities *and* General Pattern of Treasury Financing by Security Debt, *The Bureau of the Public Debt, 1997.*

U.S. Treasury securities are considered to be one of the safest investments available, and bills and notes are an ideal investment for funds needed for short-term goals. Although the price of a bill or note can fluctuate, the Treasury guarantees payment of your interest when due and principal at maturity. Treasury securities are also exempt from state income taxes.

You can buy bills and notes through banks and brokerage firms for a fee, but if you plan to invest in these securities regularly, open a *Treasury Direct* account with the Federal Reserve bank that services your part of the country. These accounts offer a convenient way to manage your Treasury securities. You can get details on the Treasury Direct program by requesting the program's free brochure from the Federal Reserve, the Bureau of Public Debt (200 Third Street, Parkersburg, WV 26106), or from the department's Web site at http://www.ustreas.gov/treasury/bureaus/pubdebt.

If you want to capture the higher yields available on longer-term notes but don't want to commit all your funds to the longer maturities, build a bond ladder of staggered maturities. For example, you could split your funds among three- and six-month and one- and two-year notes. That strategy allows you to capture the longer terms' higher yields with the assurance that 50 percent of your investments will be maturing in the next six months.

Short-Term Bond Funds

Short-term bond funds invest in government and corporate debt securities whose maturity date is generally less than three years. These funds usually earn a yield higher than that of money market funds but less than that of long-term bonds. According to Lipper Analytical Services, as of August 28, 1997, the "Short-Term Debt" category of funds had produced a one-year return of 6.78 percent, a three-year average return of 6.38 percent, and a five-year average of 5.27 percent.[8] Short-term funds are less volatile than those with longer-maturity debts, though, producing a risk versus return profile that is more appealing to conservative investors.

Short-term funds are classified by the investments they hold—government or corporate bonds, high- versus low-quality corporate bonds, for example. Another category of funds worth considering are loan-participation or prime rate funds. These funds invest in bank loans made to companies whose credit ratings are below the top (A) rating. The borrowers pay variable rates, so if interest rates move higher, the fund's income also increases. These funds frequently charge fees to investors who withdraw their funds after less than one year, and investors can usually redeem shares only one day each quarter. If you can accept these liquidity constraints, though, loan-participation funds can be a rewarding short-term investment.

DANGER! As you begin to consider alternatives to guaranteed accounts, be sure you fully understand the risks and constraints of any investment before you invest your money. At a minimum, you should understand the scenarios under which you will profit or lose money. For example, if short-term interest rates move up or down 100 basis points (1 percentage point), how will your investment perform? Are there restrictions on selling the investment? If you understand the investment's limitations, you can make a better-informed judgment on its merits.

KEY CONCEPT

ELECTRONIC BANKING

Bank transactions today are largely electronic, although bank customers might not realize that. Even the most old-fashioned bank customers who insist on handling all their transactions in the bank's lobby with a teller are using electronic banking. The teller is merely a human interface to the technology, and the currency and coins the teller handles represent only a fraction of the bank's cash balances. Direct deposit of checks, automatic bill payments, debit cards, and automated teller machines (ATMs) are evidence of electronic banking's growing presence.

On-Line Banking

The growth of on-line networks such as America Online (AOL), CompuServe, and the Internet is making on-line banking more accessible. Industry observers estimate that roughly 600 banks will offer on-line banking by 1998, and about one-third of the nation's largest banks allow computer users direct access.[9] Early concerns about privacy and security have been addressed, and the range of services available through on-line banks continues to expand. For example, the Security First Network Bank (SFNB) now offers checking, credit cards, and savings accounts. There are several types of on-line banking available:

- *World Wide Web access.* Some institutions, such as Wells Fargo and Security First, use the Internet for customer access. This approach requires you to have a Web browser program such as Microsoft's Internet Explorer or Netscape's Navigator.

- *Stand-alone software.* The bank provides proprietary software that you install on your PC and use to dial the bank directly.

- *Network proprietary technology.* Used to link private networks' customers (AOL, etc.) to the bank.

- *BankNOW.* Available from Intuit, makers of Quicken software. Provides AOL members access to a variety of financial service firms.

If you are considering on-line banking, evaluate these features in an account:

- On-line access method (Web, Network, direct).

- Monthly account fee.

- Monthly bill paying fee.

- Additional features (credit and debit cards, savings accounts, local ATM access).

KEY CONCEPT — Debit Cards

Debit cards are becoming a popular solution to the cash-or-check dilemma. Although debit and credit cards look the same and are used similarly, with a debit card the issuing bank does not extend credit to you, so you do not incur new debt. When you use a debit card (or *check card,* as issuers are calling them now), the funds are deducted electronically from your checking account. The debit card's drawback is that you give up the "free ride" on your funds that credit cards provide. Cardholders apparently have learned to live with this shortcoming. In 1996, consumers used debit cards for 1.4 billion transactions totaling $54.5 billion in purchases. Banking experts estimate that almost two-thirds of American households will have debit cards by the year 2000.

Before mid-1997, debit cardholders had less protection than credit cardholders against fraudulent use of their cards. Your liability if your credit card is stolen is a maximum of $50, but the loss limits were much higher with debit cards. If you failed to report a lost debit card within two days of discovering it, you could be liable for up to $500. Should you fail to report the loss within 60 days, your liability was limited only by the amount in your bank account.

In July 1997, MasterCard International announced that it would cap liability for unauthorized use of its U.S.-issued MasterCard debit cards to $50.[10] Several weeks later, VISA USA followed MasterCard's move and announced that it would eliminate the cardholder's liability if the theft were reported within two days of recognizing inappropriate activity in the account. Losses would be capped at a $50 maximum after the two-day period.[11]

These changes in cardholder liability make debit cards a very convenient payment method, and they can also help prevent overspending. If your bank offers debit card, consider using one. It could greatly simplify your cash management practices.

KEY CONCEPT — ASSET MANAGEMENT ACCOUNTS

Asset management accounts, which are offered by brokerage firms, combine an investment account with a money market fund (with checking) and debit cards. The accounts sweep idle cash balances into a money market fund regularly so that your funds are earning interest at all times.

Asset management accounts can simplify investment and cash management significantly. Although they are not designed to replace bank accounts, especially for frequent ATM users, their features have attracted millions of users. Almost 2 million investors use Merrill Lynch's Cash Management account, and Charles Schwab's Schwab One account has over 500,000 users.[12]

The major full-service and discount brokerage firms offer asset management accounts. The key to finding the right account for you is to match an account's features with your requirements. These features include the following:

- Minimum assets to open and maintain account.
- Fees for account maintenance and services.
- Frequency of cash sweeps into money market funds.
- Check writing and ATM privileges.
- Debit cards, direct deposit, and bill payment services.

If you work with a full-service brokerage firm, don't be pressured into signing up for an asset management account if you won't benefit from the account's features. The annual maintenance fees on the full-service accounts can be $100 or more, which is an unnecessary expense if you don't really need the account.

END POINT

Effective cash management requires a trade-off. You need sufficient cash balances to meet your liquidity needs, but keeping excess balances at low yields increases your opportunity cost. Your goal should be to minimize the balances in low-yield or high-cost accounts while maximizing the balances in higher-yield alternatives.

Borrowing and Credit

Used properly, debt can improve the quality of your life by allowing you to obtain and enjoy the use of goods and services while still paying for them. Imagine if you had to pay cash for your home—it would take many years of saving to accumulate the required funds. By borrowing the money, you can live in the house and build equity in it while you pay the mortgage.

Used improperly, debt can ruin your finances and make life miserable. Easily available credit frequently leads to overspending, especially with charge cards, and the resulting repayments can absorb funds from your cash flow that should have been earmarked for achieving financial goals. The growing number of personal bankruptcies in the United States, over 1.1 million cases in 1996, is frequently cited as evidence that many Americans have trouble managing debt properly.[1] This chapter describes the proper uses of debt and offers suggestions for finding the best sources of consumer credit and resolving problems with debt management.

APPROPRIATE USES OF CREDIT

There are times when it is appropriate to use debt:

- Convenience.
- Emergencies.
- To consume earlier than would otherwise be possible.
- To make expensive purchases more obtainable.
- To offset inflationary price increases.

- To obtain an education.
- To consolidate debts.
- To take advantage of free credit.
- To protect against fraud.

These can all be valid reasons for the use of credit, depending on the circumstances at the time of the decision. As a general rule, using credit for purchases and investments that will provide a long-term benefit or increase your long-term wealth is a sound strategy. Borrowing money for long-lived necessities when you lack sufficient funds to pay cash is another valid use of debt.

INAPPROPRIATE USES OF CREDIT

There are times when the use of debt is inappropriate, even if the you lack alternative sources of funds:

- Impulse purchases that would not be made if you did not have available credit.
- Luxury items, such as jewelry or vacations.
- Everyday living purchases that you do not intend to repay in full when the charge card bill arrives.
- High-risk investments that would threaten your financial security if the investment fails to produce the desired results.

The simplest way to avoid debt problems is to monitor the amount of your nonmortgage debt repayments relative to your take-home pay. Garman and Forgue (1994) suggest the limits in Figure 7.1.

If you are approaching the 15 percent limit, avoid taking on additional debt. If possible, reduce your current debt by shifting assets from low-yield savings accounts to high-rate debts, or consider delaying purchases until you can handle more debt.

FIGURE 7.1 DEBT PAYMENT LIMITS.

Percent	For Current Debt	Safe to Add More Debt?
<10	Safe limit	Yes
11–15	Maximum safe limit	No
16–20	Fully extended	No
21–25	Overextended	No
>26	Disastrous	No

Source: Garman, E. Thomas and Raymond E. Forgue, *Personal Finance, Fourth Edition.* Copyright © 1994 by Houghton Mifflin Company. Adapted with permission.

How can you tell if you have taken on too much debt? The National Credit Counseling Services suggests the following tests[2]:

1. Exceeding debt limits and credit limits.
2. Using credit cards in place of cash.
3. Paying only the minimum amount due.
4. Skipping credit payments.
5. Requesting new credit cards and increasing limits.
6. Unable to handle small financial emergencies.
7. Unaware of what you owe versus what you earn.

SOURCES OF LOANS

If you have a satisfactory credit history, steady employment, and modest amounts of debt, you will find a wide selection of lenders willing to loan you money. These sources include commercial banks, credit unions, small loan companies, and any retirement plans you have that allow participant loans. Figure 7.2 lists several of these sources with a brief discussion of each. Figure 7.3 lists the features of different loans.

Review a loan contract carefully for the following clauses before you sign the agreement. If possible, negotiate these clauses out of the loan contract before you sign.

- *Acceleration clause.* Entire debt becomes due if you fail to make a payment.
- *Balloon clause.* Large increase in payment, frequently for final payment, after a period of time.
- *Prepayment penalties.* Extra charge imposed for repaying loan ahead of schedule.

CHOOSING A CREDIT CARD

According to the National Credit Counseling Services, the credit card business in the United States has grown an average 24 percent annually since 1993. In mid-1996, the average American household had four credit cards, with outstanding balances of over $4,800 per household, and the average interest rate on those balances was 17 percent.[3]

To compare credit cards, the first step is to evaluate your usage patterns. If you carry a balance, look for a card with a low interest rate. If you pay your balance in full each month, focus your search on card fees and additional benefits. Do you travel frequently, especially to foreign countries? Some cards offer extensive

FIGURE 7.2 SOURCES OF LOANS.

Source	Discussion
Banks (commercial, savings and loan)	Require good credit rating; favorable rates available for existing customers.
Credit unions	Membership required; rates usually competitive.
Sales finance companies (autos, appliances)	Often have less-restrictive lending policies because loan is secured with purchased merchandise; rates usually high, but promotional rates can be very competitive.
Small loan companies	Less-restrictive lending policies; rates usually high.
Insurance companies (loans from cash value life insurance policies)	Easy to obtain; competitive rates; loan amount based on policy's values; flexible repayment schedule; reduces net death benefit to heirs.
Brokerage firms (margin accounts)	Easy to obtain; rates competitive; loan amount based on securities in account; flexible repayment schedule; risk of forced repayment if market value of securities drops.
Retirement plans	401(k): Easy to obtain; rates competitive; loan terms generally up to five years; payroll deduction repayment; interest paid to employee's account; full repayment due if you leave the employer; risks depletion of retirement funds. IRA: Funds available for 60 days if transferring to new account.

services to travelers. Can you benefit from any of the rebate programs issuers offer? Cards now offer frequent-flier miles and pay rebates on gasoline, cable television bills, and a variety of other items. Assuming the card's other features are competitive, these rebates can offer genuine additional value. Figure 7.4 lists the key features to consider as you evaluate cards.

 There are several information sources that can help you find the best credit card for your needs. These include the GetSmart^{SM} card comparison service (800-719-9595), *Money* magazine's "Your Money Monitor" column, *Kiplinger's Personal Finance* magazine's "Yields & Rates" column, publications from the Bankcard Holders of America (703-389-5445), the Bank Rate Monitor (800-327-7717), and RAM Research (800-344-7714).

FIGURE 7.3 LOAN FEATURES.

Feature	Explanation	Discussion
Secured or unsecured	*Secured:* Lender requires collateral. Example: car loan, mortgage on home. *Unsecured:* No collateral required. Example: personal line of credit (PLC).	Secured loans generally have lower rates than unsecured loans, but if you fail to repay, the lender can claim the collateral.
Fixed or variable rate	*Fixed:* Loan's interest rate is fixed for life of loan. Example: car loan. *Variable:* Rate can change over life of loan. Example: PLC with rate pegged to prime rate.	Borrower knows rate and payments in advance with fixed-rate loans. Variable rate may be lower than fixed rate early in the loan's term, but variable rate can increase.
Installment or revolving	*Installment loans:* Borrower receives full amount of loan at once and makes regular repayments. Example: auto loan. *Revolving credit:* Allows multiple loans up to maximum credit limit. Example: PLC.	Installment loans are useful for single purchases. Revolving credit gives the borrower increased flexibility.
Annual percentage rate (APR)	*APR:* This is the true annual cost of the loan stated as a percentage; includes any extra fees the lender charges.	Use the APR to compare rates between loans.

Avoid the following card features:

- Fees for account application, inactivity, and cancellation.

- Teaser interest rates on outstanding balances that start low but jump to the card's much higher standard rate after a few months unless you can pay off the balance before the teaser rate ends.

- Very short grace periods.

 Benefiting from the Grace Period

The time between your credit card's billing and payment due dates is known as the *grace period*. For example, if your bill is issued on the 5th of each month and payment is due on the 30th, you have a 25-day grace period. During that period, you have interest-free use of the credit card company's funds. (Review

FIGURE 7.4 EVALUATING CREDIT CARDS.

Feature	Explanation	Discussion
Annual fees	Annual fee paid to keep account active.	If you pay off your balance each month, look for no-fee cards.
Grace period	The number of days between the billing and payment due dates.	Look for the longest grace period you can find.
Interest rate	What annual percentage rate (APR) does the card carry? How are interest charges calculated?	If you carry a balance, look for a low APR. Do you pay interest on new purchases from date of purchase or is there a grace period?
Fees and charges	Issuers impose a variety of charges: late fees, cash advance fees, minimum finance charges, late payment fees, inactive account fees.	Look for the lowest fees and most favorable (to you) policies. Fees are increasing, so don't ignore informational mailings from the card issuer.
Additional benefits	These could include travel insurance, shopping discounts, extended warranties, rebates, rental car collision insurance, overseas medical assistance.	Look for the features that will actually benefit you in your current lifestyle.

your cardholder's agreement for details on the grace period, because some banks charge interest from date of purchase.) By timing your purchases properly, you can maximize your grace period on purchases, as shown in Figure 7.5.

Note your credit cards' billing dates, and time your purchases to maximize the grace period by using the card with the most recent billing date. If necessary, ask the credit card issuer to change the billing date so you have a spread of roughly 15 days between your most frequently used cards' billing dates.

KEY CONCEPT Your Credit Score

When you apply for a credit card, the application form requests the following information:

- Social Security number and birth date.
- Homeowner or renter?
- Length of time at current residence.
- Length of time at current job.
- Family income.

FIGURE 7.5 TIMING PURCHASES PROPERLY.

Transaction	#1	#2
Purchase date	January 1	January 6
Billing date	January 5	February 5
Payment due	January 30	February 28
Days funds available to you	29	52

The creditor to whom you are applying combines this information with the data in your credit report to determine if you are a good or poor credit risk. After gathering the information, the creditor uses a scoring model that is based on historical data to assess you in terms of the "Three Cs":[6]

Character. How long have you lived at your current address and worked for your current employer?

Credit. How much available credit do you have? Do you pay your debts promptly?

Capacity. Does your income allow you to assume more debt?

After considering these factors, the creditor will decide whether to extend credit to you.

You can take several steps to improve your credit score with potential lenders:

- Cancel the credit card accounts that you do not use. Potential lenders consider your *available* credit, not just outstanding balances.

- Reduce the amount of your current debts.

- Make timely payments on your existing accounts.

If your credit history prevents you from obtaining a traditional credit card, consider applying for a secured card. With a secured card, you deposit funds as collateral with the issuing bank. (Most banks pay interest on your deposit.) In turn, the bank will give you a credit card with a spending limit based on the amount of your deposit. Assuming you use the secured card properly and make timely payments, you should be able to qualify for a traditional credit card within a few years. To get a list of secured card issuers, contact the GetSmart card comparison service (800-719-9595) or the Bankcard Holders of America (703-389-5445).

YOUR CREDIT REPORT

 Credit reports are computer files that hold information on your use of credit. Most of your creditors provide regular reports on your account's activity to one or more of the major credit bureaus. The report includes the following items:

- Lender's name and account number.
- Account ownership (single name or joint names).
- Date account opened and date of last activity.
- Account's credit limit.
- Balance outstanding and payment history (on time or late).

When you apply to a new creditor for an account, the creditor will retrieve your credit file and use the information to approve or deny your application.

 It is a good idea to check your credit records for errors every two years, more frequently if you are an active credit user. If you plan to make a major purchase on credit, such as a buying a car or a home, request copies of your credit report several months before applying for the credit. This will give you time to correct (or at least protest in writing) any errors you find in your file. To request your credit history, contact the three major credit bureaus: Equifax (800-378-2732), Experian (800-520-1221), and Trans Union (316-636-6100). The average fee for sending you a copy of your report is $8. If a potential creditor, insurer, or landlord rejects your application because of information in your credit file, you are entitled to a free copy of the report within 60 days of the credit denial. You can also receive a free copy of your report if (1) you are unemployed and plan to apply for a job within the next 60 days, (2) you are receiving public assistance, and (3) you believe your report contains fraudulent errors.

If you find a mistake in your credit report, dispute it *in writing.* After receiving your request for corrections, the credit bureau has 30 days to acknowledge your complaint and respond to you. If the credit bureau ultimately agrees with your dispute, it will remove the information from your report. If the bureau disagrees, you should contact the creditor and ask it to have the erroneous information removed. You also have the right to send the credit bureau a 100-word statement disputing the information you believe is incorrect. That statement will become part of your file, so future creditors who request your file will be made aware that you dispute the item.

RESOLVING DEBT PROBLEMS

Problems with debt repayments can arise from several sources. A CNN/USA Today Gallup poll of individuals who declared bankruptcy in 1996 found that 63 percent of the respondents cited credit card problems, 38 percent blamed a job loss or pay cut, 37 percent blamed mismanagement of personal finances, 28 percent cited medical bills, and 15 percent pointed to problems with a business.[4]

If you become overextended with debt, you must choose a course of action. You can attempt to restructure your debts and negotiate with your creditors, and you can consider bankruptcy. It is possible that no course of action will provide a perfect solution. Each offers specific costs and benefits to you as a debtor. If you fail to act on your debt problems, though, your creditors may eventually force solutions on you that you could have avoided, such as garnishment of your wages or foreclosure on your home. Once you realize that your finances are in crisis, do not delay in considering the steps that follow.

 **Debt Restructuring and Consolidation**

Interest rates on consumer debt, especially credit cards, are frequently higher than 15 percent. If you consistently carry large, high-rate balances on your credit cards, consider paying off those debts by consolidating them into a lower-rate loan. This tactic can significantly lower your monthly payments, especially if you can transfer the balance to a low-rate credit card or home equity loan. Home equity loan rates are usually lower than credit card rates, and equity loans have the additional benefit of being tax deductible in most cases.

 Restructuring your debts by consolidating high-rate loans into lower-rate debt is a sound tactic in many cases, but there are two risks to consider. The first is your *total repayment amount.* You can reduce debt repayments by lowering your interest rate or extending the length of the repayment term. The problem with a longer repayment term is that you while you make smaller payments, you make more of them, which can increase the debt's long-term cost. Estimate the total out-of-pocket cost of the extended repayment schedule before consolidating your debts. The second risk is *continued overspending.* After paying off your high-rate debts, particularly charge cards, you must not return to the spending patterns that originally caused your debt problems. Cancel as many of your charge accounts as possible to reduce the temptation to overspend. If you don't want to give up the convenience of a charge card, switch to a debit card.

Debt restructuring and consolidation can relieve the debt repayment pressure on your cash flow. Once you have solved the short-term repayment problem, you should develop an effective spending plan to avoid future debt crises. Part of your spending plan should include accelerated repayment of any consolidation loan, and you should constantly monitor your debt-to-take-home-pay ratios to avoid disproportionate amounts of debt in the future.

Getting Better Terms

Creditors recognize that consumers today can choose from a wide selection of lenders. This industry competition gives you leverage in obtaining better terms on loans and credit cards, *if you ask for them.* In 1994 a team of 28 reporters from *Money* magazine called the 38 banks that had issued them VISA, MasterCard, and Discover credit cards. Without identifying themselves as *Money* reporters, they asked the banks for better terms on their credit cards. Fully 84 percent of the banks lowered their interest rates, waived their annual fees, or did both.[5] Asking your creditors for better terms is a low-risk strategy—the worst-case outcome is that they reject your request.

Credit Counseling

Instead of dealing with creditors directly, many consumers in recent years have enlisted the aid of credit counselors like the National Foundation for Consumer Credit (800-388-2227). For a modest monthly fee (average $10 per month), counselors at local NFCC offices provide budgeting help and develop payment plans with creditors. Creditors frequently will lower interest rates and suspend finance charges for NFCC clients, giving those clients an opportunity to reorganize their finances while avoiding bankruptcy.

Bankruptcy

The number of personal bankruptcies has grown rapidly during the 1990s. In spite of its increased popularity, declaring bankruptcy is a major financial decision that you should not take lightly. Although bankruptcy can eliminate many of your current debts, it will make it more difficult for you to get a mortgage and other credit for up to 10 years. Also, there are some financial obligations that you must continue to pay even after declaring bankruptcy. You must also consider the cost of bankruptcy: Apart from the legal fees (usually in the $500 to $2,000 range), you can lose many of your assets to settle creditors' claims. Because each person's financial situation is unique, seek the advice of an experienced attorney when you start to consider bankruptcy as an option.

Historically, roughly two-thirds of individuals filing bankruptcy choose Chapter 7 with the remaining one-third applying for Chapter 13. In Chapter 7, also known as a *straight bankruptcy,* the court can seize and sell your nonexempt assets and use those sales proceeds to pay off your debts. In return, most of your debts will be wiped out. A Chapter 13 bankruptcy, or wage-earner plan, takes a less drastic approach. The court appoints a trustee who will supervise the repayment (full or partial) of your debts over a three- to five-year period. At the end of the repayment period, the remaining debt balances are wiped out.

There are several important issues to consider before filing for bankruptcy. At a minimum, you should determine the following:

- Which of your assets will be considered *exempt* in a Chapter 7 filing? There are federal and state bankruptcy laws that determine what you can keep after bankruptcy. You must know which set of rules is applicable to your case before you file, particularly if you have equity in a home.

- Which of your debts will be *forgiven* and which will *remain outstanding* in a Chapter 7 filing? Some debts, such as alimony, child support, and income taxes less than three years past due, are not eliminated by bankruptcy.

To answer these questions, develop a current balance sheet (see Chapter 1) and a projected postbankruptcy balance sheet. That will allow you to see the bankruptcy's impact on your financial status.

If you declare Chapter 7 bankruptcy, don't be surprised if you continue to receive solicitations for credit and credit cards. From a lender's perspective, you are a good credit risk because you can't declare bankruptcy again for another six years. If excessive use of credit caused your bankruptcy, do not make the same mistake again by signing up for new cards and taking on more debt. Use the financial relief that bankruptcy provides to reorganize your finances so you don't repeat your previous mistakes.

END POINT

Debt is a trade-off: In return for receiving the loaned funds today, you give up part of your future income for repayment. If the repayments become too large, your cash flow flexibility is reduced, and at some point you become unable to make repayment. The key to avoiding repayment problems is to closely monitor the amount of debt relative to take-home pay. In particular, you should keep the amount of nonmortgage debt payments below 15 percent of your take-home pay. Experience has shown that exceeding this 15 percent level frequently leads to debt management problems.

Should your debts become difficult to manage, it is important to take a proactive approach to dealing with your creditors. Techniques to consider include debt restructuring, consolidation, negotiation for better terms, working with a credit counselor, and bankruptcy. Each technique has its strengths and weaknesses, but considering the low cost of working with a reputable credit counseling agency, you should consider that method before making any drastic decisions.

Tax Planning

Taxes are injurious to your financial health. The Tax Foundation estimates that in 1997 the average American worked until May 9, or 128 days, to pay his or her tax bills. Individual income tax payments required 44 days, social insurance taxes took 36 days, while property, sales, and other tax bills cost another 48 days.[1] The tax bite has been increasing over recent decades as well. In 1955, the median family with two wage earners spent 28 percent of its income on taxes. By 1996, that figure had risen to an estimated 38.4 percent.[2]

This chapter examines methods for reducing federal and state income taxes. By reducing your income taxes, you keep more of your earnings and send less money to the government, thereby helping you reach your financial goals more quickly.

KEY CONCEPT — EFFECTIVE TAX PLANNING

By the time you sit down to complete your tax return for the previous year, most of your tax planning opportunities are gone. Perhaps you can make deductible IRA or Keogh plan contributions at the last minute, but it is too late to make decisions regarding investments, employer-provided benefits and retirement plans, and other important areas. Effective tax planning requires a long-term perspective. This is especially true for the self-employed, business owners, employees with stock options, two-income families, and investors with substantial portfolios.

You must also integrate tax planning with other financial decisions that might appear to be unrelated to taxes. For instance, if you decide to start a business, what form should the business take: sole proprietorship, partnership, or corporation? If you choose to incorporate, should you have a C or an S corporation? These decisions have income tax implications, in addition to business structure, control, and liability issues. Investment portfolio decisions also affect income taxes. When you shift funds among different investment classes, you must consider the capital gains and losses you will incur (unless the funds are in a tax-sheltered account). Specifically, how can you achieve the desired portfolio allocation with a minimum tax cost? These examples demonstrate that tax planning is not a one-time process. You should consider the tax implications of every financial decision before you commit yourself.

One of the best times for tax planning is early in the year when you complete your return for the prior year. Your records are organized and handy, the numbers are fresh in your memory, and you can measure the impact of different strategies based on last year's numbers. It is also early enough to implement meaningful changes for the rest of the year: Increase retirement plan contributions, make changes to benefit plans, shift assets, and so on. After the plan is in place, you can check your progress in the fall and make any needed modifications.

 ### MARGINAL TAX RATES
After subtracting deductions and personal exemptions from adjusted gross income, you reach your *taxable income.* This is the amount on which your tax liability is based. At this point in the preparation of their tax returns, most taxpayers turn to the tax tables in the back of their instruction booklet and look up their tax liability. Taxpayers whose taxable income exceeds $100,000 are instructed to turn to the tax rate tables. The tax tables simplify calculations, but they obscure the fact that a tax liability is based on a graduated series of rates that range from 15 percent to 39.6 percent. The easiest way to understand these rates, also known as *marginal tax rates* and *tax brackets,* is to think of them as a series of steps. As your taxable income moves to the next higher step, the tax rate of the income *on that step* increases. Figure 8.1 lists the tax brackets for 1997.

TAX-EXEMPT INCOME
If there were an ideal solution to reducing income taxes, you would receive an economic benefit without being required to pay taxes on that benefit. It is possible to achieve that combination, although its avail-

FIGURE 8.1 1997 TAX BRACKETS.

	15%	28%	31%	36%	39.6%
Single	$0–25,350	$25,351–61,400	$61,401–128,100	$128,101–$278,450	$278,451+
Married joint	$0–42,350	$42,351–102,300	$102,301–155,950	$155,951–$278,450	$278,451+
Head of household	$0–33,950	$33,951–87,700	$87,701–142,000	$142,001–$278,450	$278,451+

Source: Kiplinger Tax Letter, December 12, 1997, p. 4.

ability depends on external factors. This section lists the most common forms of exempt income.

- *Municipal bonds.* The interest paid on municipal bonds (described in Chapter 15) is generally exempt from federal income taxes, and certain classes of bonds are also exempt from state income taxes. (States do not tax the interest on their own bonds, but they frequently tax interest from out-of-state bonds.)

- *U.S. government bonds.* Interest paid on bonds issued by the federal government, such as Treasury bills, notes, bonds, and savings bonds, is exempt from state and local income taxes. If you redeem EE savings bonds issued after 1989 to pay for college (or approved vocational school) tuition and fees, the interest on those bonds is tax-exempt provided you meet certain age, ownership, and income tests.

- *Fringe benefits.* Employers frequently provide several benefits to employees. Although the employee receives a direct economic benefit, he or she is not required to pay income taxes on that benefit. These benefits include, among others things, employer-paid medical insurance premiums, group legal plans, group term insurance premiums up to $50,000 coverage, education assistance plans, job placement services, dependent day care services up to $5,000, discounts on company products or services.

If your employer (or your spouse's employer) offers benefits under a cafeteria plan or flexible spending arrangement (FSA), review your use of the plans periodically. Under a cafeteria plan, compare pretax (inside the plan) and after-tax (outside the plan) costs of benefits to determine if you should sign up for a benefit or take the cash. With FSAs, use conservative estimates of your expenses, because you lose any balance remaining in the account at year-end.

CAPITAL GAINS AND LOSSES

KEY CONCEPT

Ordinary income is taxed at ordinary income rates. Net long-term profits on the sale of capital assets, however, are often taxed at lower rates than ordinary income. The term, *capital assets,* is defined broadly. Investments such as stocks, bonds, mutual funds, and land are examples of capital assets. Personal assets such as homes, cars, jewelry, and furniture are also considered capital assets. If you sell a capital asset for more than its cost basis, you have a *capital gain.* If the selling price is below your cost basis, you have a *capital loss.* Generally, your cost basis in an item is the cost you paid, but if you spent money to improve an item, those improvements increase your cost basis.

Before the 1997 Tax Act, figuring the tax on capital gains was relatively straightforward. Short-term capital gains (on assets held less than 12 months) were taxed as ordinary income. If you held a capital asset more than 12 months, it qualified for long-term capital gains treatment. That meant any profits (capital gains) from the asset's sale were taxed at the *lower of* your ordinary income tax rate *or* 28 percent. For example, if you were in the 15 percent bracket, you paid a 15 percent capital gains rate. But if you were in the 39.6 percent bracket, you paid only 28 percent on your net long-term capital gains.

The two tax rates produced significant differences in the after-tax results of earning ordinary income versus long-term capital gains for high-bracket taxpayers. A taxpayer in the 39.6 percent bracket would pay $7,920 of income taxes on $20,000 of ordinary income. But the tax bill for a $20,000 long-term capital gain would be $5,600, a reduction of almost 30 percent. (For high-income earners over the threshold amounts listed in Figure 8.1, the effective capital gains tax would be higher than 28 percent, depending on how much of the personal exemption is disallowed.)

The 1997 Tax Act added several new twists to the treatment of capital gains:

- The Act extends the required holding period for long-term treatment from 12 to 18 months for gains recognized after July 28, 1997.

- The top rate on long-term gains drops to 20 percent from 28 percent.

- Long-term gains for taxpayers in the 15 percent tax bracket are taxed at 10 percent.

- The top rate on gains from collectibles stays at 28 percent.

- The top rate on gains from depreciable real estate is 25 percent.

- Assets acquired on or after January 1, 2001, and held for at least five years will qualify for a reduced long-term rate of 18 percent (8 percent for investors in the 15 percent bracket).

 The new law increases the gap between the higher ordinary income tax rates and the capital gains rates, making capital gains even more attractive than before. The changes also make good record keeping and careful tax planning more important for taking advantage of those lower rates. If you have the opportunity to realize a large capital gain, such as from the sale of appreciated securities or incentive stock options, seek advice from a tax advisor *before* you sell.

Capital losses (selling price below cost basis) are fully deductible against capital gains. If your losses exceed your gains, you can deduct a maximum of $3,000 in a single year. Amounts over the $3,000 limit can be carried forward and used in future years. A loss on the sale of your personal residence is not deductible.

TAX DEFERRAL

Tax deferral allows you to delay taxation until a future date. This delay lets you earn a return on those funds that would have gone to taxes. The following example demonstrates how deferral works. Imagine that you have two bank accounts, both earning 5 percent. One is a regular account whose interest is taxed each year. Each year you withdraw the amount of taxes from the account that must be paid on the interest. (The calculations assume you are in a 30 percent combined tax bracket.) The other account is an Individual Retirement Account (IRA) whose interest is tax deferred. Figure 8.2 shows how the accounts grow.

The tax-deferred account's advantage will continue to increase over time, as the tax savings compound. Tax deferral is *not* the same as tax exemption, however. When the funds come out of the IRA in this example, the interest will be taxed.

FIGURE 8.2 TAXABLE VERSUS TAX-DEFERRED ACCOUNTS.

After Year	Taxable Account Balance	IRA Balance
1	$1,035	$1,050
2	1,072	1,103
10	1,411	1,629

Proponents of using deferral maintain that you (the investor or depositor) can decide when to withdraw funds from deferred accounts. If you are saving for retirement, you can withdraw the funds after you stop working, when presumably you will be in a lower tax bracket. Critics of deferral argue that if tax rates rise, as a retiree you might find yourself in a higher, not lower, tax bracket.

The recent history of tax reform has proven both groups right. After lowering income tax rates in the mid-1980s, the government slowly moved them higher over the following years. But the 1997 Tax Act reduced long-term capital gains rates significantly, and investors who gambled on lower capital gains tax rates and held onto their appreciated assets were rewarded.

If you could project your future tax status with certainty, the tax-or-defer decision would be simple: Defer income in high-bracket years and take income in lower-bracket years. If you lack certainty but reasonably believe that your future tax bracket will be the same or lower than your current bracket, then deferral is a good strategy, particularly when it comes to retirement saving. The major risk in retirement is having insufficient funds; if your deferred accounts contribute to an "excess" of taxable retirement income, congratulations! It is much simpler to deal with too much retirement income than too little.

Retirement Plans

Qualified retirement plans are one of the best vehicles for accumulating the funds needed for a comfortable retirement. In general, employer and employee contributions to the plans are not taxed (and may be deductible), and the growth in the plan's assets is not taxed until withdrawal. There are a variety of retirement plans, including pensions and profit sharing, salary reduction, IRAs and Keoghs, and others. Chapter 20 discusses the role of these plans in retirement planning.

Provided you can create a diversified portfolio within your retirement plans, you should maximize your deductible contributions to these plans. They offer the current advantage of reducing your taxable income, and the long-term tax-deferred growth helps create the funds needed for retirement.

In certain circumstances, you might not want to participate in (or add additional funds to) an employer-sponsored retirement plan. If the plan invests only (or primarily) in your employer's stock, you face the risk of failing to diversify adequately. Another cause for concern is nonprofessional management of the fund's investments. Some business owners, especially among smaller firms, believe their ability to run the business qualifies them as investment managers. They are usually mistaken, and you do not want to pay for this lesson with your retirement assets. In these cases you should look for alternative retirement plans, even if those plans lack some tax advantages of your employer's plan.

New for 1998: The 1997 Tax Act created a new type of IRA, popularly known as the Roth IRA. Starting in 1998, married taxpayers with an adjusted gross income (AGI) of up to $150,000 ($95,000 for single taxpayers) can each make nondeductible contributions of up to $2,000 in a Roth IRA. Although the contributions are not deductible, the account's growth is tax deferred. You can withdraw the funds *tax-free* after the money has been in the account for five years, provided you are age 59½ or older or the funds are being used for a first-time home purchase. Figure 8.3 shows how the Roth IRA compares to a traditional deductible IRA, assuming an 8 percent return on the annual $2,000 contribution for a taxpayer currently in the 28 percent bracket. (Deductible IRA figures assume the taxpayer reinvests annual tax savings in taxable account.)

Conclusion: If you believe your tax bracket will be lower in retirement, you should stick with the traditional deductible IRA. If you believe your tax rate will remain the same or increase, use the Roth IRA.

The 1997 Tax Act provides gradually increased AGI limits for deductible IRAs starting in 1998. By the year 2007, the limits will reach $80,000 for married filing jointly and $50,000 for single status. If you can deduct your IRA, use Figure 8.3 to compare deductible and

FIGURE 8.3 AMOUNTS AVAILABLE AT RETIREMENT.

Years in IRA	5	10	15	20
Roth IRA	$12,672	$31,292	$58,648	$98,845
Deductible IRA:				
Rate at withdrawal				
Drops to 15%	13,849	35,162	63,242	105,182
Stays at 28%	12,446	30,249	55,763	92,401
Rises to 31%	12,122	30,391	54,035	89,451
Rises to 36%	11,581	27,910	51,157	85,533
Rises to 39.6%	11,191	26,795	49,084	80,992

Roth IRAs. If you can not deduct your IRA, the Roth IRA consistently produces greater after-tax returns than *nondeductible* IRAs, however.

Deferred Compensation

In these plans, the employee agrees in advance to defer receipt of part of his or her salary until a future date. If the employee does not have control over the deferred funds, the amount deferred is not taxed until it becomes available to the employee. There is risk in the arrangement for the employee because the employer's promise to pay the funds in the future must be unsecured. The employee can increase the arrangement's security by having the employer place the deferred assets in a nonrevocable trust ("rabbi trust"). The trust's assets are still subject to claims from the employer's creditors, however, if the employer becomes bankrupt or insolvent. Employees (and their beneficiaries) have only the same rights to the assets as other unsecured creditors.

To benefit from a deferred compensation arrangement, your tax bracket must drop significantly between withdrawal and deferral. If you do not anticipate such a drop in tax rates, or if you have any doubts about your employer's financial stability, take your income now and pay the taxes.

Life Insurance Policies and Annuities

Increases in a life insurance policy's cash value and an annuity contract's value are tax deferred. Later chapters discuss life insurance and annuities in more detail, but readers should recognize that the 1997 Tax Act's reduction of capital gains rates diminishes variable annuities' appeal substantially. Variable annuities convert capital gains into ordinary income upon withdrawal, increasing the tax rate on the returns earned in the contract.

INCOME SHIFTING

The concept behind income shifting is straightforward: It is generally advantageous to have income taxed at the lowest possible rate. For example, assume that you are a parent who is accumulating funds for your child's college education. If you are in the 28 percent bracket and keep the funds in your name, you must "give back" 28 percent of the funds' taxable income, not including any state income taxes. In contrast, your child can earn up to $650 of investment (unearned) income without incurring taxes, and the next $650 is taxed at the child's rate, which probably is 15 percent. So while you as a parent would pay $364 on $1,300 investment income ($1,300 × .28), your child would pay only $97.50 ($650 × .15), thus saving $266 in taxes.

There is a critical catch in shifting income to lower-bracket taxpayers, however. You cannot separate income taxability from asset ownership. In other words, the asset's owner is responsible for any taxes on the income the asset produces. You cannot simply tell your bank to report the income on your accounts to your children. If you want to transfer the income, you also must transfer the asset's ownership. At some point between ages 18 and 21 your child can take control of that asset and spend it as he or she wishes.

There are other drawbacks to shifting assets to children. If the child is under age 14 and her investment income exceeds $1,300, any amounts over $1,300 will be taxed at the parents' top rate. This is known as the "kiddie tax," and it negates the income tax savings you sought by transferring the assets to the child. To avoid this tax, give assets that generate little or no current taxable income before the child reaches age 14. These include Series EE savings bonds, growth stocks, and zero-coupon municipal bonds.

A second drawback is the negative impact on college financial aid of shifting assets to children. Under the current (1997) system, the *expected contribution* formulas penalize the student's assets and income more heavily than the parents'. Colleges assess a family's income and assets to determine its expected contribution. Up to 47 percent of the parents' income and 5.65 percent of their assets are assessed, while the student's income is assessed up to 50 percent, assets at 35 percent. A college fund of $40,000 in the parents' name would be assessed up to $2,260 for the student's first year of school. If that same $40,000 were in the student's name, it could be assessed up to $14,000.[3]

You can shift assets to anyone, not just children. For example, if your parents are in a lower bracket than you and they could use additional income, you could transfer income-producing assets to them. Just as gifted assets can backfire on students' financial aid prospects, though, gifted assets can affect retirees' eligibility for financial assistance programs. Evaluate the possible impact of any asset transfers on the recipients' other sources of income before you make them.

If college financial aid or retirement benefits are not issues for the recipients, transferring assets and their income can produce substantial tax savings, particularly within a family. Also, a wide variety of assets can be transferred, depending on the donor's situations. These assets could include shares in closely held businesses, interests in partnerships, appreciated securities, and so on. (Some of these transactions can require the use of a trust to hold the child's assets.) If the arrangement is structured properly, the donor can transfer the asset and its income to a lower-bracket recipient while still retaining effective control of the assets.

If you own a business that can employ your children and pay them a reasonable salary for their services, consider putting them on the payroll. Their wages are a deductible expense for the business, and wages you pay to your children under age 18 are not subject to Social Security or Medicare taxes. The child's income is taxed at his or her rate (after allowing for the standard deduction), and the child can use an IRA to shelter up to $2,000 of earned income.

DEDUCTIONS

A deduction's tax-reduction value is a function of your tax bracket. Taxpayers in the 15 percent bracket reduce their tax liability by $.15 for every deductible dollar they spend; those in the 28 percent bracket reduce their tax liability by $.28 for every deductible dollar they spend; and so on. (Deductions can also reduce state income taxes that are not included here.)

Although deductions have limited tax-reduction value, you should not overlook their role in reducing taxes. First you must determine if you will take the standard or itemized deduction. Claiming the standard deduction has the advantage of reducing the amount of record keeping you must do. But if your itemized deductions exceed the standard amount for your bracket, and you take the standard, you are paying too much in taxes.

Good records are the key to finding and supporting itemized deductions. If you dislike keeping files to track your tax-related expenses, try this approach. Save all your cash-purchase receipts, charge receipts, and canceled checks. Once a month, review these items and identify those that could potentially qualify as deductions. Separate them into the major deductible categories: unreimbursed medical, charitable contributions, taxes, interest, and so on. Repeat the process each month, adding the new documents to the previous months. At year-end, you can add up the amounts in each category to determine if you should claim itemized deductions.

The best place to start looking for deductions is your previous year's return. Reviewing last year's Schedule A (Itemized Deductions) will jog your memory. Here are several important points to keep in mind as you plan your deductions.

1. *Timing.* The general rule of thumb is to accelerate deductions and defer income whenever possible. This statement assumes that your tax bracket the following year will be the same or lower than the current year's. As the year ends, you may be able to control the timing of some deductions so that you claim them in the current tax year. For example, if you have a mortgage payment due in January, by making it in December you can claim the additional month's interest as a current-year deduction. This also applies to any property tax or charitable contribution payments that you planned to make the next year. If you can delay the receipt of income from December to January, the tax due on the income is also delayed.

2. *Donating appreciated assets.* Instead of writing a check to your favorite charity, consider donating appreciated assets like stocks or mutual funds. This increases your deduction and gives the charity a larger contribution. For example, assume that you paid $5,000 for shares that are now worth $10,000. If you sell the shares, you must pay capital gains tax on the $5,000 appreciation, and then you can give the remaining funds to the charity. Your deduction will be the amount of your postsale donation. But if you donate the shares to the charity, you can claim a $10,000 deduction. The charity sells the shares and keeps the full $10,000 because it is not taxed on the gain.

3. *Charitable trusts.* By using charitable trusts, you can benefit a charity while simultaneously reducing your income taxes and potential estate taxes. To understand how these trusts work, you should conceptually separate an asset from the income it produces. With a *charitable remainder trust,* you keep the income, but at your death (or some specified earlier date) the charity gets the trust's principal, or remainder. *Example:* You own a stock that has appreciated considerably over the years but pays only a very small dividend. You are approaching retirement and want to increase your cash flow from investments. If you sold the stock so you could reinvest the proceeds for higher income, you would face considerable capital gains taxes. Instead, you donate the stock to a charity through a charitable remainder trust. The charity sells the stock (without incurring capital gains taxes), reinvests the proceeds

in higher-yielding assets, and the trust pays you the higher income. You receive a deduction for the present value of the remainder, your income increases, and the charity gets the trust's assets at your death.

Charitable lead trusts reverse the process. The charity gets the trust's income, and at the end of the trust's term (a specified number of years), your heirs (not the charity) get the trust's remainder. You can claim a deduction for the present value of the trust's income, the charity receives the trust's income, and your heirs can look forward to the day the trust distributes its assets.

Charitable trusts can be a win-win situation for taxpayers and charities. If you are interested in setting up a trust, contact the charity for details. Most organized charities have access to the legal advice needed to create a trust, and many larger charities actively seek these arrangements with investors.

4. *Home equity loans.*   Personal interest (on auto loans, charge cards, etc.) is no longer deductible, but interest on home equity debt is usually deductible. Some restrictions on the amount of debt include a cap of $100,000 ($50,000 for married filing separately) or the fair market value of the residences (reduced by the amount of acquisition debt) and securing the debt with your first or second home. If you meet these requirements, you can spend the loan proceeds as you choose and the interest will be deductible.

Home equity represents a substantial part of most Americans' net worth. Using that equity as collateral for loans involves some risk. If you default on an auto loan, for instance, you lose the car. If you default on a home equity loan, you risk becoming homeless. Home equity loans make sense for major purchases when you can deduct the interest and the loan offers competitive terms. Do not use a home equity loan for frivolous purchases or luxury items.

 **CREDITS**

Tax credits reduce tax liability dollar for dollar. In other words, a $500 tax credit reduces your tax liability by $500, *regardless* of your tax bracket. Qualifying for credits is usually not discretionary—either you meet the requirements or you do not. This section describes the low-income housing tax credit and several new credits introduced with the 1997 Tax Act.

1. *Child tax credit.*   Beginning with the 1998 return, you can claim a $400 credit for each child under age

17. That amount increases to $500 in 1999, subject to phaseouts for higher-income taxpayers ($120,000 AGI phaseout for married filing joint, $85,000 for singles).

2. *HOPE scholarship credit.* Starting in 1998, you can claim a credit of up to $1,500 for college tuition and fees that you pay for yourself, your spouse, or your children during the first two years of college. The student must be enrolled at least half-time at an accredited institution.

3. *Lifetime learning credit.* You can claim a credit of 20 percent ($1,000 maximum) for education expenses incurred after June 30, 1998. This amount will increase to $2,000 after the year 2002. The credit is phased out for higher-income taxpayers (modified AGI phaseout of $100,000 for joint filers and $50,000 for singles).

4. *Low-income housing investment credit.* To encourage construction of low-income housing, the IRS allows qualified investors to claim a credit in annual installments over 10 years for qualified construction and rehabilitation expenses. Most investors access these credits through partnerships that are sold by securities firms. In return for the initial investment (usually a $5,000 minimum), the investor can receive annual tax credits. The maximum annual credit depends on the amount invested and the investor's tax bracket, ranging from $3,750 for those in the 15 percent bracket to $9,900 for the 39.6 percent bracket. If the partnership's properties generate excess operating cash flow or profits upon sale, the investor can share in those cash flows.

Before investing in a low-income housing partnership, evaluate the projected returns versus the risks. The tax credits are not guaranteed, and there might not be any investment return other than the credits. These partnerships generally project annual after-tax returns of 5 to 7 percent, which is comparable to a tax-exempt bond at current rates.

END POINT

The tax code offers several methods for reducing tax liability. As a taxpayer, you must decide if a particular technique is suitable for your situation. In particular, you should evaluate the costs and risks of any tax-reduction technique before committing funds.

Housing Decisions

Everyone needs a place to live, and that means you will face a series of housing decisions over your lifetime. These decisions can involve large amounts and regular rent or mortgage payments, so they have a major long-term impact on your finances. Housing decisions also require you to evaluate other issues in your life: the need for mobility, stability of your income, and the condition of your credit history, among others. This chapter discusses the factors to consider as you weigh your housing options.

KEY CONCEPT — RENT VERSUS BUY

The first decision many people face is whether to rent or buy. Each approach has its strengths and weaknesses, so the solution is not always clear-cut. Renting offers several advantages:

- Greater mobility than ownership.
- Lower initial costs (no down payments or other closing costs).
- Lower monthly costs.
- No property maintenance chores and expenses.

Proponents of buying point to that method's advantages:

- Increased control of your living space.
- Pride of ownership.
- Home prices have historically increased.

- Part of each mortgage payment increases equity in the property.

- You can lock in a fixed monthly mortgage payment. (Rents typically increase over time.)

- Mortgage interest payments are tax deductible, and up to $500,000 profit from the sale of a residence is excluded from taxation.

- Home equity can be used as a source of credit.

If you face the rent-or-buy decision, consider the following factors:

1. *Duration of residence.* If there is a realistic chance you will be moving within the next three years, renting will be the less expensive option. Buying and selling a home involves substantial costs, and you recoup these costs when the house appreciates in value. Price changes are unpredictable in the short term, and there is no guarantee your home's market value will increase enough to allow you to break even. If you plan to stay in the home for more than three years, consider buying.

2. *Your financial resources.* Even if you buy with a low down payment, buying a home is an expensive transaction. You must factor in closing, moving, fix-up, and furnishing costs. (Of course, you'll also incur some of these costs if you rent.) After you move in, your bills will include the mortgage payment, insurance, property taxes, utilities, and maintenance costs. Although it is common for homeowners to be "house poor" for a period after they buy their homes, that can be an extremely risky position financially. Could you continue paying your mortgage if you (or your spouse) lost your job? If buying a home puts you in a vulnerable position, consider delaying the purchase until you have more resources (savings and predictable income) available.

3. *Your homeowner profile.* Buying a home commits you to maintaining the property. In an apartment, you can call the landlord or maintenance company when you have a problem. But if you own your home, you are responsible for solving the problem or finding someone who can fix it. If you do not want the aggravations of owning property and cannot afford to hire outside help as needed, keep renting.

Because home ownership enjoys substantial tax advantages, you need to compare the after-tax economic costs of renting versus owning. Figure 9.1 shows the calculations for comparing the true costs of each option.

The following assumptions apply in Figure 9.1: Home costs $120,000, purchased with $25,000 down

FIGURE 9.1 THE COSTS OF RENTING VERSUS BUYING.

	Rent	Buy
Cash expenses		
Annual rent or mortgage	$7,200	$ 7,540
Property and liability insurance	200	500
Real estate taxes		2,500
Maintenance		500
Additional utilities		800
Other		
Subtract after-tax interest earned on funds not used for down payment	(1,100)	
Total cash expenses	$6,300	$11,840
Less noncash adjustments		
Loan principal repaid		−$ 1,150
Tax savings on mortgage interest		− 1,688
Tax savings on property taxes		− 700
Appreciation on house		− 3,750
Net annual cost	$6,300	$ 4,552

payment and $95,000 mortgage at 7 percent for 30 years. Savings earn 6 percent. Homeowner is in 28 percent federal tax bracket. State taxes are ignored.

As Figure 9.1 demonstrates, the combination of deductible expenses and appreciation make the after-tax economic cost of owning less than renting, although renting has a significant pretax cash flow advantage.

The current tax laws skew the rent-or-buy argument in favor of home ownership. If you meet the financial and mobility criteria discussed previously, you will benefit more from buying than renting over the long term.

DANGER! There is no guarantee that your home will appreciate in any particular year, and you should not plan on steady increase in your home's value. For example, from the second quarter of 1996 through the second quarter of 1997, the average U.S. home's price increased by 3.6 percent. That average masks the wide variation in regional housing price growth over the period, however. Prices in Alaska *fell* by an average 2.6 percent, while those in the Mountain region increased by 4.6 percent, which included a 6.8 percent gain in Utah.[1]

HOW MUCH HOUSE CAN YOU AFFORD?

To determine how much a home buyer can afford to spend on housing, many lenders use the Federal Housing Administration's formulas. According to these formulas, buyers with other debts can afford to spend up to 29 percent of their gross monthly income on housing, and debt-free buyers can budget as much as 41 percent. Figure 9.2 lists a range of annual incomes, monthly incomes, and 29 percent values.

Figure 9.2 gives you the maximum monthly amount you can budget for housing, but *it does not include real estate taxes or property insurance.* To determine your maximum monthly mortgage payments, deduct realistic estimates for those additional costs from column 3 in Figure 9.2. *Example:* Your gross annual income is $80,000, which gives you a monthly housing budget of $1,933, and you estimate that the property taxes and insurance on your target house would be $400 per month. That leaves you with $1,533 to spend on the mortgage.

Once you estimate your housing budget, use the payment schedule in Figure 9.3 to see how much you could afford to borrow at current interest rates.

Continuing with the previous example, if your mortgage budget were $1,533, with rates at 8.5 percent you could afford up to a $200,000 mortgage.

FIGURE 9.2 INCOME CALCULATIONS.

Annual Gross Income	Monthly Gross Income	Monthly Gross × 29%
$ 25,000	$2,083	$ 604
30,000	2,500	725
35,000	2,917	846
40,000	3,333	967
45,000	3,750	1,088
50,000	4,167	1,208
55,000	4,583	1,329
60,000	5,000	1,450
65,000	5,417	1,571
70,000	5,833	1,692
75,000	6,250	1,813
80,000	6,667	1,933
85,000	7,083	2,054
90,000	7,500	2,175
95,000	7,917	2,296
100,000	8,333	2,417

FIGURE 9.3 MORTGAGE PAYMENTS (30-YEAR FIXED).

Cost	6.00%	6.50%	7.00%	7.50%	8.00%	8.50%	9.00%
$ 60,000	$ 360	$ 379	$ 399	$ 420	$ 440	$ 461	$ 483
70,000	420	442	466	489	514	538	563
80,000	480	506	532	559	587	615	644
90,000	540	569	599	629	660	692	724
100,000	600	632	665	699	734	769	805
110,000	660	695	732	769	807	846	885
120,000	719	758	798	839	881	923	966
130,000	779	822	865	909	954	1,000	1,046
140,000	839	885	931	979	1,027	1,076	1,126
150,000	899	948	998	1,049	1,101	1,153	1,207
160,000	959	1,011	1,064	1,119	1,174	1,230	1,287
170,000	1,019	1,075	1,131	1,189	1,247	1,307	1,368
180,000	1,079	1,138	1,198	1,259	1,321	1,384	1,448
190,000	1,139	1,201	1,264	1,329	1,394	1,461	1,529
200,000	1,199	1,264	1,331	1,398	1,468	1,538	1,609

TIP You are *not* required to borrow the absolute maximum you can on a house unless you cannot find a suitable house for less than that amount. Large mortgage payments can reduce your financial flexibility if your income drops off or you incur unexpected expenses. Also, if you borrow less than the maximum you can redirect your excess cash flow toward other goals such as children's college funds, retirement, and so on.

KEY CONCEPT   MORTGAGES

Once you have identified a price range and home for potential purchase, you must find a lender to give you a mortgage. Fortunately for borrowers, increased competition, low rates, and improved technology have made the mortgage market extremely competitive. Borrowers have considerable clout, and the average up-front fees and charges that previously ranged from 1 to 3 percent of the loan have dropped to less than 1 percent.[2] For buyers who lack the traditional 20 percent down payment, competition is growing among lenders who will accept 10 percent down while waiving the costly private mortgage insurance previously required of these borrowers.[3]

Lenders offer several types of mortgages to appeal to borrowers' needs. These include the following:

Fixed-rate loans. Your rate is locked in for the duration of the loan. Available in 15-, 20-, and 30-year terms.

Adjustable rate mortgages (ARMs). Your interest rate is adjusted periodically to track market rates (i.e., when rates move up, your mortgage rate will increase and vice versa). ARMs offer lower initial rates than fixed-rate mortgages, and some ARMs allow borrowers to convert to fixed-rate loans at certain times during the loan's duration. To protect borrowers against dramatic increases in payments, ARMs include a rate adjustment period and lifetime caps on allowable increases. For example, the maximum increase in a single period could be 2 percent with a lifetime cap of a 6 percent increase.

Hybrid mortgage. Hybrid mortgages start as fixed mortgages, and after a specified period (between 3 and 10 years) they switch to an ARM.

Government loans. Several government agencies offer loan programs to assist home buyers:

- Federal Housing Administration (FHA) (800-732-6643) loans: Allows buyers with modest incomes to purchase homes with down payments of 3 to 5 percent at competitive loan rates.
- Veterans Administration (VA) (800-827-1000) loans: Allows veterans to buy homes with no down payment.
- Rural Housing Service (RHS) loans: Allows moderate-income buyers to purchase homes in rural areas with no down payment at attractive rates.
- State and local programs: Frequently targeted at first-time buyers. Offer attractive rates with smaller down payment requirements.
- Federal National Mortgage Association (FNMA) (800-732-6643): Offers several community-based lending programs for lower-income buyers.

Balloon loans. Offer lower initial rates for first 5 to 10 years. At end of the initial period, outstanding balance must be paid off or refinanced.

 Comparing Mortgages

CONCEPT   Although the mortgage market has become more competitive, you should still compare offers from several lenders, including banks, credit unions, and mortgage companies, before selecting one. In its publication, *Shopping for Your Best Mortgage Deal,* the FNMA suggests you compare the following features:

- Interest rates and points.
- Interest rate lock-ins.
- Required down payments (with and without private mortgage insurance).
- Prepayment penalties.

- Estimated loan processing time.
- Estimated closing costs.

  For ARMS, compare these features:
- Financial index used and lender's margin (percentage markup) over the index.
- Periodic and lifetime rate caps.
- Payment caps.
- Provisions and fees for conversion to fixed-rate loan.

 HSH Associates (800-873-2837) offers mortgage shoppers several useful, inexpensive publications, including a home buyer's mortgage kit. They also provide mortgage rate comparisons for lenders in many parts of the country.

 ### Refinancing an Existing Mortgage

Low rates and increased competition have benefited homeowners as well as buyers. The old rule of thumb, "Consider refinancing if rates are two percentage points below your current rate," has been discarded. Today it makes sense to refinance if rates have fallen one point or more because the costs associated with refinancing are much lower.

The usual method for deciding whether to refinance is to estimate how long it will take to recoup the costs of refinancing. As an example, assume that it will cost you roughly $4,000 to refinance your existing mortgage, and your new monthly payment will be $200 per month lower. Because you pay less interest with the new payment, you will be able to deduct less on your tax return for home mortgage interest with the new loan. This means the after-tax savings from the refinancing are less than the full $200; in this example, the after-tax savings are estimated at $140 per month. Dividing the $4,000 by $140 shows a break-even period of roughly 29 months. In other words, if you stay in the house longer than 29 months, you will recoup the costs of refinancing and benefit from the lower rate.

 You can also refinance for a *shorter term* than the remaining balance on your existing mortgage. If you plan to stay in the house for a long period, shortening your mortgage can save thousands of dollars. *Example:* You have made 36 payments on a 30-year, $100,000, 8.5 percent mortgage with monthly payments of $763.51, and your outstanding balance is $96,840. Figure 9.4 illustrates how much you can save if you refinance with a 7 percent mortgage for 20 years

FIGURE 9.4 SAVINGS FROM REFINANCING WITH SHORTER TERM.

	Current Mortgage	New Mortgage
Balance	$ 96,840	$ 96,840
Payments	763.51	746
Number of remaining payments	324	240
Total of remaining payments	$247,377	$179,040
Savings		$ 68,377

instead of 30. Although your monthly payment falls by only a small amount, your total outlay for the house drops dramatically because you are making 84 fewer payments.

DANGER! Refinancing can increase your cash flow by hundreds of dollars each month. Your goal should be to use that cash productively, either by investing it or reducing other debts. If you merely increase your monthly spending, refinancing will not help you reach your goals any faster. Also, if you stretch out the repayment period each time you finance, you risk significantly increasing the amount you pay for the home over time.

KEY CONCEPT **Mortgage Insurance**

If you make a small down payment (less than 20 percent), many lenders require you to obtain mortgage insurance. The insurance protects the lender, not you. If you default on the loan, the insurance reduces the lender's potential loss if the property's value has decreased. The annual cost for the insurance ranges from roughly .25 percent of the loan balance to .92 percent for the first 10 years, after which the premium falls to the .20 percent range.

Mortgage insurance has helped many homeowners acquire properties for which they lacked a 20 percent down payment. Once your equity in the home reaches 20 percent of the loan, you no longer need the insurance. Government agencies, like the FNMA, require mortgage lenders to cancel the insurance once your equity reaches this level, but you must request cancellation from private mortgage insurers. Unfortunately, many homeowners forget to ask for cancellation and continue to pay for unnecessary coverage. In late 1997 Congress was considering a bill that would require automatic cancellation once the home's equity reached 22 percent, which would save considerable amounts for many homeowners. Until the bill passes, however, you are responsible for monitoring the numbers and asking the insurer to cancel the coverage.[4]

 If it appears you will be required to take out mortgage insurance, ask your lenders about a piggyback mortgage. This package combines a first mortgage for 80 percent of the price plus a second mortgage for the balance that you need after factoring in your down payment. This approach eliminates the need for private insurance on the first mortgage. Crestar Mortgage (800-452-5363) is one national lender that offers this program.

END POINT

The housing decision is important because it represents a long-term cost that probably will total several hundred thousand dollars over your lifetime. Although the tax code and the current environment of low interest rates favor buying a house, you should not overlook the benefits of renting. Once you make the decision to buy, focus your efforts on finding the most favorable mortgage terms that fit your needs.

Risk Management

Disability Income and Long-Term Care Insurance

DISABILITY INCOME INSURANCE

The statistics on disability are disturbing:

- A person age 45 is 3.29 times more likely to become disabled than to die.[1]
- The average duration of a disability lasting over three months for a 45-year-old is three years.[2]
- Over 40 percent of those aged 45 to 54 with disabilities do not return to work.[3]

If you need your earned income to pay bills and save for financial goals, then the loss of that income for a sustained period can be catastrophic. Disability income (DI) insurance is designed to replace part of your income if you should suffer an accident or illness that prevents you from working. This section discusses DI insurance and the role it plays in your risk management program.

KEY CONCEPT — Evaluating the Need

As with any other insurance, you should evaluate your financial exposure from the risk before buying the coverage. In this case, the relevant questions are: (1) What expenses would you incur if disabled? and (2) What sources of income would you have to meet those expenses? Use the worksheet in Figure 10.1 to determine how your current annual expenses would change if you became disabled. You probably will find that there is surprisingly little change in your expenses if you suffer a disability.

FIGURE 10.1 ANNUAL EXPENSE WORKSHEET.

	Current	Disabled
Payroll deductions		
Federal income tax		
Social Security tax		
State income tax		
Medical insurance premium		
401(k) plans		
Total payroll deductions		
Fixed expenses		
Mortgage		
Loan payments		
Utilities		
Insurance		
Property taxes		
Investment plans		
Total fixed expenses		
Variable expenses		
Charitable contributions		
Clothing		
Education		
Food		
Gifts		
Travel/vacation		
Total variable expenses		
Total expenses		

Sources of Replacement Income

If disabled, you may qualify for replacement income from employer programs, social programs, and personal insurance. Use Figure 10.2 to list your current sources of income and the replacement disability income you are qualified to receive.

Use Figure 10.3 to compare your estimated post-disability needs and available incomes. If the analysis reveals that you face the risk of a replacement income deficit, you should consider purchasing private DI coverage.

FIGURE 10.2 ANNUAL INCOME WORKSHEET.

	Current	Disabled
Wages/salary		
Interest		
Mutual fund distributions		
Sale of assets		
From DI insurance		
Employer		
Social Security		
Private disability income		
Other sources		
Total sources		

KEY CONCEPT — Public DI Programs

You may have coverage under one or more public DI programs, including Social Security, workers' compensation, or nonoccupational temporary disability income (TDI) programs. Before factoring a benefit from these programs into the worksheet in Figure 10.2, you should determine both the benefit's availability and amount.

Social Security

To qualify for a disability benefit, you must (1) be insured, (2) be under age 65, (3) have been or expect to be disabled for at least 12 months or have a disability that is expected to result in death, (4) file an application, and (5) complete a five-month waiting period or be exempt from this requirement. In 1997, the maximum allowable monthly disability payment to an individual was $1,547, while the average payment was $705.[4]

The primary obstacle to qualifying for Social Security's benefit lies in the definition of *disability*, which is extremely narrow: "the inability to engage in any substantial gainful activity by reason. . . . A person must not only be unable to do his previous work but cannot,

FIGURE 10.3 NEEDS SUMMARY.

Projected total annual expenses	
Less projected total annual income	−
Difference	

considering age, education, and work experience, engage in any other kind of substantial work which exists in the national economy."[5]

DANGER! If you wish to be conservative in evaluating your sources of disability income, do not include Social Security. Roughly 60 percent of applicants were denied benefits in 1995, and although a rejection can be appealed, there is no guarantee you will receive benefits from the program.[6]

Workers' Compensation

Workers' compensation (WC) covers work-related injury and permanent illness. Each state has its own WC program, and there are separate programs for federal employees, stevedores and harbor workers, and miners. Roughly 90 percent of the employed wage and salary workers in the United States are covered by WC, although there are exempted groups. The programs vary, but the maximum DI benefit is usually 66⅔ weeks of earnings, with a three- to seven-day waiting period before benefits begin.[7] Even if you are covered by a workers' compensation program, you face the risk of suffering a *non-work-related disability*. This is a significant risk, because over 60 percent of disabilities occur off the job and are not covered by WC.[8]

Temporary Disability Insurance (TDI) Plans

Five states (California, Hawaii, New Jersey, New York, and Rhode Island) and Puerto Rico require employers to provide short-term or temporary DI coverage. In contrast to a workers' compensation plan, you can file a claim under TDI for disabilities that are not job-related. Weekly benefits generally replace at least one-half of lost wages for a limited time (26 to 52 weeks), and each plan has a maximum allowable benefit.[9]

KEY CONCEPT Employer-Provided Benefits

Larger employers frequently provide several income-replacement benefits, including sick pay, short-term DI, and long-term DI. That is not true of small employers, however. Less than 20 percent of employers with fewer than 100 employees offer long-term DI as a benefit.[10] Your employer's personnel department can provide details on the benefits, and you should inquire about the following features:

Sick pay and short-term disability. Amount of income replaced; duration of benefits (annual and carryover); qualification requirements.

Long-term disability. Date of eligibility for coverage; definition of disability; length of waiting period and duration of benefit; coordination of benefit with other programs.

Employer-provided plans are an important component in protecting yourself against disability's financial impact, but you should examine the plans carefully. You may find that the benefits' limits are too restrictive and that you need to supplement the coverages with personal insurance. For example, here's a common definition of disability: "You are wholly prevented because of mental or physical disability from performing your regular occupation *or any comparable occupation.*" This language gives the plan administrator considerable flexibility, and you may not agree with his or her definition of a comparable occupation. Also, your employer-sponsored DI benefits may be taxable income. If the coverage pays 60 percent of your recent pretax salary, income taxes on the DI benefit could reduce your income to 40 to 50 percent of your previous gross pay. Finally, ask if your employer's DI benefit covers any bonus or commission income that you earn or if it includes only base salary.

KEY CONCEPT **Private DI Insurance**

If an analysis reveals that you still face a disability income shortage, even after factoring in public and employer-sponsored programs, you should consider private DI insurance. (This section assumes you can purchase private DI coverage. Individuals working in some occupations—authors, for example—may be unable to purchase private coverage because insurers will not issue policies for those occupations.) These are complex policies, and the issuers of private DI insurance have tightened their underwriting practices in recent years, making a good insurance adviser an important ally.[11] Figure 10.4 lists the key features to consider as you examine a company's policy.

Annual DI premiums vary according to the insured's occupation, coverage type and amount, and the inclusion of the features listed in Figure 10.5, which shows the range of annual premiums for a male, age 35, with varying elimination periods. The following assumptions apply to the table in Figure 10.5:

- Insured is in UNUM's AAA category (professionals, executives, business owners).
- *Own occupation* definition of disability used for first 24 months of benefit period; definition switches to *regular occupation* after 24 months.
- Benefit period to age 65.

By modifying a policy's features, you can reduce the annual premiums and customize the coverage. Consider the following:

- Extend the elimination period.

FIGURE 10.4 EVALUATING PRIVATE DI POLICIES.

Policy Feature	Explanation
Coverage amount	Maximum monthly benefit you can receive.
Occupational rating	Your category as an insurance risk.
Elimination period	Required amount of time between disability and first payment. Most policies offer a range of waiting periods from 30 days to several years.
Benefit period	Duration of benefits; coverages range from two years to lifetime; growing number of policies are convertible to long-term care insurance.
Annual premium	Policy's cost for comparable coverages; unisex or gender-based pricing?
Insurance company's rating	Third-party rating of company's financial stability.
Noncancelable	Premiums are fixed for life of contract.
Guaranteed renewable	Insurer can raise premiums for a class of insureds.
Definition of disability	Does policy use *own occupation, modified own occupation, any income,* or a *split* definition?
Partial/residual disability benefits available?	Policy pays a partial benefit if you can return to work, but at a reduced income.
Presumptive disability benefit	Benefit paid if insured loses sight, speech, hearing, limbs.
Exclusions/limitations	Are there circumstances under which the insurer will deny a claim?
Available riders	Cost-of-living adjustments; option to increase coverage; Social Security offset; waiver of premium if collecting benefits; annual renewable premiums (start low, gradually increase with age).

- Include a Social Security rider. This option allows the insurer to reduce your DI benefit if you qualify for Social Security's disability benefit.
- Don't accept the return-of-premium rider.
- Ask if the insurer has an annual renewable policy.

FIGURE 10.5 SAMPLE RATES.

	90-Day Elimination	180-Day Elimination	360-Day Elimination
$2,000/month benefit	$557	$510	$490
$3,000/month benefit	836	765	735

Source: UNUM Life Insurance Company of America.

- Ask about any available discounts, such as reduced rates for nonsmokers.

 **Conversion to Long-Term Care Insurance**

A growing number of companies now offer DI policyholders the option to convert their DI coverage to long-term care (LTC) insurance. For example, the UNUM Life Insurance Company of America, a leading issuer of DI policies, includes the conversion privilege in their Lifelong Disability Protection[sm] plan. The DI policy contract allows the policyholder to exchange the DI policy for an individual LTC policy issued by UNUM when (1) the insured reaches age 61 and is not disabled, or (2) the insured is age 65 or older, disabled, and has received the DI policy's maximum benefits, or (3) the policyholder reaches age 70. The policyholder can convert at these times without submitting evidence of medical or financial suitability. The LTC policy's premium will be the same as the premium paid for the DI policy in the year before the exchange, and the monthly LTC benefit will be based on that premium.

Other DI insurers also offer conversion privileges as part of the basic contract or as a rider, with some offering a reimbursement benefit (benefit paid to health care provider) and others providing an income benefit (paid to insured). Given the increasing cost of long-term care, these options could have considerable value to an insured, especially if his or her health deteriorates and the insured can no longer qualify for LTC coverage when he or she wishes to buy it.

 If you own a small business, you probably need to insure more than your personal income. You have overhead expenses that you must continue to pay, and you may have key employees whose absence would damage your financial results. You may also need DI coverage to fund a buy/sell agreement between you and any other owners or key employees. Schedule a periodic review of your DI policies with an experienced insurance advisor to keep the coverage current.

LONG-TERM CARE INSURANCE

Consumer interest in long-term care insurance is booming. The top 11 sellers of policies reported sales of over 517,000 new policies in 1995, bringing the total number of policies sold by these companies since 1987 to over 4.3 million.[12] This concern with finding protection from long-term costs is understandable. Although average costs vary by region, the financial impact of an extended stay in a nursing home is still substantial in any part of the country. For example, in 1994, costs averaged $154 per day for nursing home care in upstate New York ($56,000 annually) and $205 per day in the New York City metropolitan area ($75,000 annually). Home care services for this same period ranged from an average of $15.50 per hour for personal care to more than $120 per hour for licensed skilled care. If nursing home costs increase annually by 3 percent, a one-year stay in an upstate New York home could cost almost $70,000 by the year 2000.[13] This section discusses the options available for funding long-term care and the role of private LTC insurance.

 Evaluating the Need

The first step in determining the financial exposure you face should you require LTC is to estimate the additional cost that care would impose on your current budget. That cost is determined by type of care and the region in which you live. For example, the national average cost for one year in a nursing home is $40,000. If you receive skilled nursing care at home for six hours per week (three visits of two hours each), the annual cost would be roughly $12,300, while the same amount of personal care from a home health aide would cost you about $8,400.[14] Figures for your region may be higher or lower than the national averages, so you should research local costs to determine more accurate amounts.

Use Figure 10.6 as a starting point for examining your current budget with the projected expense of LTC. You may need to create several worksheets to include the different forms of LTC. If you are married, include your spouse's ongoing expenses and income in the calculations.

 Sources of LTC Coverage

There are several sources of LTC coverage. These include public programs (such as Medicare, Medicaid, and veterans' benefits) and private LTC insurance policies. If you qualify for any of these sources, list the amount on the worksheet in Figure 10.7.

FIGURE 10.6 ANNUAL EXPENSE
WORKSHEET.

	Current	With LTC
Fixed expenses		
Mortgage		
Loan payments		
Utilities		
Insurance		
Property taxes		
Investment plans		
Long-term care		
Total fixed expenses		
Variable expenses		
Charitable contributions		
Clothing		
Education		
Food		
Gifts		
Travel/vacation		
Total variable expenses		
Total expenses		

FIGURE 10.7 ANNUAL INCOME
WORKSHEET.

	Current	With LTC
Pensions/Social Security		
Interest		
Mutual fund distributions		
Sale of assets		
Other sources		
LTC coverage		
Medicare		
Medicaid		
Veterans' benefits		
Private LTC policy		
Total sources		

FIGURE 10.8 **NEEDS SUMMARY.**

Projected total annual expenses with LTC	_____
Less projected total annual income	− _____
Difference	_____

Use Figure 10.8 to compare your expenses and income if you require LTC. If the analysis reveals that you risk incurring a significant deficit, you should consider purchasing private LTC insurance.

KEY CONCEPT **Public LTC Programs**

There are several public programs that can cover LTC expenses. Unfortunately, qualifying for these benefits is difficult.

Medicare

It is estimated that Medicare pays roughly 9 percent of current LTC expenditures, but Medicare and Medicare supplemental insurance are *not* designed to pay LTC expenses. Medicare will cover the cost of some skilled care in limited circumstances, but it does not cover the much more common need for custodial care. Among standardized Medicare supplements, plans D, G, I, and J cover "short-term, at-home assistance with activities of daily living" if you are recovering from illness, injury, or surgery, at home, in a relative's home, or in an institution. The benefit is limited to $1,600 per year, with restrictions on the amount of caregiver visits covered each week.[15]

Medicaid

Medicaid pays for roughly half of all nursing home care, but to qualify for Medicaid, you must meet federal poverty guidelines. This restriction can require you to expend most of your assets on nursing home care until you are poor enough to qualify for benefits. Medicaid is administered by the states, and there are differences among the states' regulations on how much income and assets you can retain while qualifying for benefits. Also, if you plan on transferring assets out of your name so you can qualify for Medicaid without depleting those assets, get qualified advice before you make any transfers. Medicaid can now "look back" up to 36 months for property transfers to individuals and 60 months for transfers to trusts. If your asset transfers are made too close to the Medicaid application date, you will be denied benefits. Also, provisions have been added to the law allowing recovery of benefits from re-cipients' estates.

The Health Insurance Portability and Accountability Act of 1996 introduced criminal penalties for those who dispose of assets in order to qualify for medical assistance. The liability for these acts also extends to anyone who advises a person on these transfers. Although certain transfers are permitted, you should discuss any transfers with an attorney who is experienced with Medicaid before giving away any asset.

Veterans' Benefits

If you are a veteran of a foreign war, you may be eligible for nursing home and home health care benefits. Contact your local VA office or call the Paralyzed Veterans of America (800-424-8200) for more information.

Public-Private Partnerships

Several states (California, Connecticut, Indiana, Iowa, and New York) have introduced programs that encourage residents to buy private LTC insurance. Provided the coverage meets certain standards, the state guarantees that the insured's assets are exempt from Medicaid if the LTC policy's benefits eventually run out. For example, New York requires the policy to have at least a three-year benefit period and a 5 percent compounded inflation benefit, among other features.[16]

These plans offer a strong incentive to buy private LTC insurance. If you reside in a state that offers one of these programs, contact the local Medicaid agency office for specific details on the required coverage.

Employer-Sponsored LTC

In 1995, the employer-sponsored market accounted for nearly 20 percent of LTC sales, with 1,260 employers offering private coverage to their employees.[17] If your employer provides the opportunity for you to purchase LTC through a group plan, you should evaluate the coverage, because group premiums can be 30 to 40 percent lower than those for individual policies.[18] Before signing up for a group plan, however, you should examine the plan's features. Group plans typically lack the degree of benefit customization that you can achieve with a private LTC policy. Use Figure 10.9 as a guide to evaluating the group policy's features.

Review the group plan's portability provisions carefully. If you change employers, you will want the option to maintain the LTC coverage on a private basis without interruption.

FIGURE 10.9 LTC POLICY PREMIUMS.

Company	Benefit Period	Daily Benefit	Waiting Period	Annual Premium Age 60	Age 65	Age 70
American Travelers	3 years	$100	100 days	$ 910	$1,530	$2,120
Bankers Life and Casualty	3 years	100	90 days	856	1,500	2,160
CNA	3 years	100	90 days	856	1,168	1,696
GE Capital Assurance	3 years	100	100 days	1,090	1,480	2,120
John Hancock	4 years	100	100 days	1,320	1,740	2,590
UNUM	3 years	100	90 days	1,875	2,495	3,207

Source: "What the Policies Cost," Kiplinger's Personal Finance Magazine, May 1997, p. 98. Copyright © May 1997 by The Kiplinger Washington Editors, Inc.

KEY CONCEPT — Private LTC Insurance

If the results in Figure 10.9 show that you would face an income shortage if you needed LTC, even after including any public or employer-sponsored benefits, you should consider private LTC insurance. Although these contracts received unfavorable publicity in the late 1980s and early 1990s, today's policies provide a favorable mix of benefits. The primary drawback for most consumers is the coverage's cost. As Figure 10.9 shows, premiums escalate rapidly between ages 60 and 70.

The premiums in Figure 10.9 reflect the likelihood that an insured will use the coverage. Between ages 65 and 69, there is a 10 percent chance you will need to use the coverage. For ages 75 to 79, there is still less than a 20 percent chance. Between ages 85 and 89, however, the probability increases to more than 40 percent. Because older policyholders represent a greater risk, insurance companies charge correspondingly higher premiums.

LTC insurance is complex. You should compare policies from several companies before selecting one, and you can use the information in Figure 10.10 as a starting point. To help prospective insurance buyers perform more detailed analysis, The National Association of Insurance Commissioners (NAIC) provides an outstanding booklet, *A Shopper's Guide to Long-Term Care Insurance.* Federal law requires insurance brokers to give you a copy of the booklet before giving you an application.

KEY CONCEPT — Reducing LTC Premium Costs

If the premiums for traditional LTC insurance will strain your budget, consider alternative sources for

FIGURE 10.10 LTC FEATURES TO REVIEW.

Insurer's financial rating.
Levels of care covered by the policy.
Locations where you can receive care.
Length of benefit period and amounts covered.
Policy's inflation-protection benefits.
Elimination periods/benefit periods.
Under what impairments (physical and cognitive) can benefits begin?
Cost of policy.
Underwriting requirements.

Source: Reprinted by permission of the National Association of Insurance Commissioners.

less expensive coverage. Many associations offer LTC coverage as a benefit to their members. You might also have access to group or individual life insurance coverage that allows you to use part of the death benefit to pay for long-term care expenses. (This reduces the contract's death benefit.) For example, the Golden Rule Life Insurance Company (800-261-3361) offers its Asset Care® policy, which is available as a single-premium or an annual-premium cash value policy. You can buy the coverage on one life or as a second-to-die policy. While living, you can withdraw 2 percent of the policy's face value each month (per insured) for long-term care expenses and up to 1 percent each month for adult day care.

Another option for controlling premium costs is to consider various coverage options. Figure 10.11 shows

FIGURE 10.11 VARYING PREMIUMS.

	Age 55	Age 65	Age 75
Base policy: 　$100 daily benefit; 　4 years' coverage; 　100-day elimination 　period	$ 510	$ 990	$2,830
2 years' coverage	380	720	2,010
$50 daily benefit	410	810	2,350
20-day elimination period	643	1,247	3,566
$200 daily benefit	1,020	1,980	5,660
5% compound benefit 　inflation	1,090	1,740	4,230

Source: Nancy Ann Jeffrey, "Your Needs, Plus Your Budget, Equals What to Pay on Long-Term Care Policy," Wall Street Journal, March 21, 1997, p. C1. Reprinted by permission of the Wall Street Journal, copyright © 1997 by Dow Jones & Company, Inc. All rights reserved worldwide.

FIGURE 10.12 LTC PREMIUM DEDUCTION LIMITS.

Your Age	Limit on Deduction
Less than 40 years old	$ 200
41–50	375
51–60	750
61–70	2,000
71+	2,500

how different coverage options can produce a wide range of annual premiums for an individual policy from the John Hancock Mutual Life Insurance company.

Under tax law changes that took effect January 1, 1997, you might be able to claim part of your LTC premiums as a deductible medical expense, which would help reduce a policy's after-tax cost. To claim the deduction, your itemized medical deductions must be more than 7.5 percent of your adjusted gross income and the LTC policy must qualify. Policies issued before January 1, 1997, qualify automatically, but policies issued on or after that date must be qualified before the premium is allowed as a deduction. LTC insurers are working on qualifying their policies, so ask the agent about the contract's status. Assuming a policy qualifies, the annual deduction you can claim is limited by your age, as shown in Figure 10.12.[19]

END POINT

Most people could not afford to lose their employment income for a sustained period if they suffered a disability. Because of the potentially devastating financial impact disability can impose, it is critical to insure against this risk with disability income insurance. Most retirees cannot afford the additional cost of long-term care for an extended period, creating a need for long-term care insurance. Disability income coverage and long-term care coverage have similar structures, and this chapter's worksheets facilitate the evaluation of both types of insurance.

Life Insurance

L Life insurance can be a critical element in financial planning if used properly. This chapter examines the role of life insurance in financial planning. The material emphasizes the appropriate use of the product and provides guidelines for selecting adequate amounts and types of coverage.

 **WHEN DO YOU NEED**
CONCEPT **LIFE INSURANCE?**

There are several situations in which there can be a need for life insurance:

Expenses at death. Insurance can be used to pay uninsured medical expenses, funeral costs, legal fees, estate taxes, and other estate settlement costs.

Debts. Insurance proceeds can be used to pay your debts.

Survivor benefits. If your dependents rely on your income, life insurance can replace that income until they become self-supporting. The policy proceeds can also be used to fund college expenses or a surviving spouse's retirement needs.

Bequests. You can leave life insurance proceeds to family members, educational and charitable organizations, private foundations, and so on.

Business purposes. Life insurance can fund buy-sell agreements, offset the financial impact of losing a key employee, and serve as part of an employee's benefit package.

 **HOW MUCH INSURANCE DO YOU NEED?**

If your situation indicates a need for life insurance, the next issue to resolve is the amount of coverage you should carry. This section examines that question from a *personal coverage* perspective. If you need insurance for business purposes, consult with an insurance advisor.

You can estimate the amount of required coverage in several ways. There are popular rules of thumb, such as, "Buy an amount that is six to eight times your annual salary." The problem with rules of thumb is that they ignore the differences among individuals. A safer approach is to analyze your life insurance needs based on your personal situation. You'll need to estimate amounts required to pay off debts, settle your estate, and provide for your survivors. Your calculations will not be precise—there are too many unknowns—and you should update the estimates every few years or when your situation changes. The worksheets in this section will help you develop sensible estimates of how much coverage you should carry.

 Married persons or partners should calculate their life insurance needs *individually,* even if one person is not working outside the home. A spouse or partner at home still makes an economic contribution to the household, and it can be surprisingly expensive to replace that person's services. If a mother is at home raising children, she provides child care and other services that could easily cost $25,000 or more per year to replace. You need to examine the economic impact of *both persons' deaths* on the survivors.

The worksheets that follow are designed to help you estimate the amount of life insurance you need based on reasonable assumptions. Begin by working through Figure 11.1a. If you want a more detailed analysis, you can work with an advisor, create a needs analysis spreadsheet, and/or use a personal finance program or an on-line calculator.

Your survivors may qualify for Social Security survivor benefits. There are three types of benefits: (1) a lump-sum death payment of $255, (2) a monthly payment to your surviving spouse for the period when your children are under age 16, and (3) monthly payments to your children during the time they are under age 18 (or age 18 if they are full-time high school or elementary students). Figure 11.1b lists the current Social Security survivor benefits based on 1996 earnings. (The figures are approximate—the actual amount depends on your age and wage history. To get information on your projected Social Security benefits, call 800-772-1213 and request a "Personal Earnings and Benefit Estimate Statement.")

FIGURE 11.1A HOW MUCH LIFE INSURANCE DO YOU NEED?

Step 1: Calculate the expenses your survivors would be required to pay at your death, and list any debts you wish repaid.

Expense	Amount
Uninsured medical bills	
Funeral	
Legal fees and probate costs	
Estate taxes	
Debts	
Mortgages	
Auto loans	
Other debts	
Total	

Step 2: Estimate your survivor's annual income needs. Review the cash flow worksheets in Chapter 1 for additional categories. If your heirs will repay debts, remember to subtract the debt payments from their expenses.

Expense	Amount
Food	
Clothing	
Mortgage/home insurance/taxes	
Utilities	
Car expenses	
Child care/tuition	
Other expenses	
Total	

Step 3: Estimate the annual income your family will receive after your death.

Source	Amount
Spouse's after-tax income	
After-tax survivor benefits from your employer	
Social Security benefits (see Figure 11.1b)	
Other sources (investments, royalties, etc.)	
Total	

Step 4: Compare survivors' total annual income and expenses.

Annual income (from step 3)
Less annual expenses (from step 2)
Difference (+/−)

FIGURE 11.1A (Continued)

If deficit, number of years additional
   income will be needed   _____
Number of years times annual deficit   _____

If your survivors' income exceeds their projected expenses by a comfortable margin, and that margin will exist for the foreseeable future, then you do not need insurance to help fund their current needs.

Step 5: Your survivors may face needs beyond paying their bills. For example, you might wish to create a paid-up college fund for your children in the event you or your spouse died. You might also want to set aside funds that can be invested to supplement your spouse's eventual retirement.

Other Needs	Amount
College funds	_____
Investment account	_____
Other needs	_____
Total	_____

If you are comfortable with time-value-of-money calculations, you can create detailed college-cost estimates by projecting inflated college costs and discounting those numbers at an assumed rate of return. A less accurate but much simpler method is to assume that the insurance proceeds earmarked for college earn the same after-tax return as the college-cost inflation rate. In other words, if college costs increase by 5 percent each year, your survivors' college investment fund will earn 5 percent after taxes, and so on. With this assumption, you can reasonably use the average total costs for college as your funding needs. In 1997, the average total four-year costs were roughly $30,000 for a public college and $85,000 for private.

Step 6: Add up the resources your survivors currently would have to meet their needs. Include only those assets that are actually available. If your family plans to stay in your current home, for example, do not count your home equity as an asset.

Resources	Amount
Bank and other liquid accounts	_____
Existing life insurance	_____
Investments	_____
Retirement plans (after taxes)	_____
Total	_____

Step 7: Compare your survivors' total resources with their total needs.

	Amount
Total resources (from step 6)	_____
Less final expenses (from step 1)	− _____

FIGURE 11.1A (Continued)

Less current income needs
(from step 4) —_____

Less special needs (from step 5) —

Additional insurance needed
(if negative) _____

FIGURE 11.1B SOCIAL SECURITY SURVIVOR BENEFITS (APPROXIMATE).

Deceased Worker's 1996 Earnings

	$20,000	$30,000	$40,000	$50,000	$62,700+
Spouse and 1 child	$1,194	$1,594	$1,844	$2,030	$2,184
Spouse and 2 children	1,459	1,874	2,152	2,370	2,549
1 child only	597	797	922	1,015	1,092
Spouse at age 60*	569	760	879	968	1,041

*1996 dollars; future benefits would be adjusted for inflation.

KEY CONCEPT — TYPES OF COVERAGE

After estimating the amount of life insurance you need, you must choose the appropriate type. There are two generic categories of life insurance policies: *term* and *cash value*. Term life insurance provides a death benefit if the insured dies while the policy is in force. If the insured fails to renew the policy by non-payment, the coverage lapses. A term policy has a predetermined term, as the name implies. Annual-renewal term insurance must be renewed annually, a five-year term policy has a five-year term, and so on.

Cash value life insurance also provides a death benefit, but it offers the policyholder benefits while living. The first benefit is that part of each premium payment is credited to a "savings account" within the policy. (Technically, the funds are not in a savings account, but the analogy is useful.) The insured has access to the funds, known as the policy's *cash value,* via policy loans, and if the policy is surrendered, the insured receives the policy's cash value. Under current tax law, the policy's cash value growth is tax deferred, and in most cases policy loans are not considered taxable income. Also, cash value policies do not have fixed terms—they generally provide coverage to age 100 without requiring renewal. There are several varieties of term and cash value policies. Figure 11.2 lists the

FIGURE 11.2 BASIC FEATURES OF LIFE INSURANCE POLICIES.

Policy	Description	Death Benefit	Premium	Cash Value
Term policies				
Annual renewable term	Death benefit only; contract renewable each year.	Level for duration of contract.	Fixed; increases each year as insured ages.	N/A
Level term	Death benefit only; contract renewable each year.	Level for duration of contract.	Fixed for life of contract, which ranges from 5 to 20 years.	N/A
Decreasing term	Death benefit only; contract renewable each year.	Decreases each year.	Fixed for life of contract.	N/A
Cash value policies				
Whole life		Level for life of contract.	Fixed for life.	Fixed with a guaranteed minimum return.
Adjustable life	Gives policyholder increased flexibility with living and death benefits.	Adjustable.	Adjustable.	Basic contract cash value is fixed with a guaranteed minimum return; can vary with changes to premium.
Universal life		Flexible; policyholder has choice of level or increasing benefit.	Flexible.	Policy earn higher of a guaranteed rate or market rate.
Variable life	Policyholder controls investment of cash values.	Offers a guaranteed minimum that can increase with positive investment results.	Fixed.	Varies with policy performance.
Universal variable life	Offers features of both universal and variable life contracts.	Adjustable.	Flexible.	Varies with amount of premium, death benefit, and policy performance.

main features of the different coverage types of term and cash value policies.[1]

If the premiums for term and cash value policies were equal, the cash value policies' living benefits would give them a distinct advantage over term policies. The premiums for cash value policies are substantially higher than those for term, however, which makes the selection between the two types more difficult. *In many cases there is no single correct type of policy*—you may find that several different policies fit your needs and budget. Figure 11.3 lists representative first-year premiums for different types of policies that provide a $250,000 death benefit.

There are several factors you should consider in selecting a policy type[2]:

- How long you will need the coverage?
- Do you need the living benefits that cash value policies offer?
- Which policy best fits your budget?
- Do you want a guaranteed death benefit and cash values or are you willing to accept variability in policy values?

Leimberg[3] offers the following rules of thumb for selecting an appropriate policy:

1. If you need coverage for less than 10 years, term insurance is usually less expensive.
2. For 10- to 15-year coverage periods, either type of coverage, or a mix of both types, can be appropriate.

FIGURE 11.3 FIRST-YEAR PREMIUMS.

Male/ Age	Annual Renewable Term	10-Year Term	20-Year Term	Universal Life	Whole Life
30	$210	$ 240	$ 340	$1,000	$2,000
40	250	350	535	1,500	3,250
50	385	700	1,170	2,600	5,500
60	830	1,560	2,600	4,900	9,600

Female/ Age	Annual Renewable Term	10-Year Term	20-Year Term	Universal Life	Whole Life
30	$185	$ 210	$ 300	$ 800	$1,700
40	225	285	420	1,300	2,750
50	315	510	790	2,200	4,500
60	565	950	1,590	3,900	7,600

Source: From Marshall Loeb's Lifetime Financial Strategies (cloth) by Marshall Loeb. Copyright © 1998 by Marshall Loeb Enterprises, Inc. By permission of Little, Brown and Company.

3. For 15-year or more periods, cash value policies are usually more cost effective.

4. If you want maximum control over your policy's benefits, consider variable life and universal variable life.

James Hunt of the Consumer Federation of America published an interesting study of cash value policies in 1997. He found that the rate of return on a cash value policy depended on the source of the policy (whether sold by a commissioned agent) and the length of time the policy is held. Figure 11.4 summarizes the results.[4]

NO-LOAD AND LOW-LOAD POLICIES

A growing number of companies offer insurance policies that charge significantly lower sales commissions than traditional contracts. By lowering commissions, the policies can offer the policy owner lower costs or faster cash value buildup. Figure 11.5 lists several of these insurers. (A company may offer both no- and low-load products, and some may sell only through financial advisors.) Note that Figure 11.5 lists two types of coverage that were not discussed previously: *first-to-die* and *survivorship* (also known as *second-to-die*). These policies provide coverage on two lives. First-to-die insurance pays the policy's death benefit upon the death of either insured, and second-to-die coverage pays upon the second death. These policies can offer substantial premium savings over traditional single-life coverage.

If you are a healthy nonsmoker, the market for term insurance is extremely competitive. Figure 11.6 lists several companies that act as national brokers for term insurance. Each provides a comparative shopping service that can save you considerable time in looking for a low-cost policy. Several of these companies also have Web sites where you can price policies on-line.

FIGURE 11.4 SAMPLE POLICY RATES OF RETURN.

Years Policy Held	Sold by Commissioned Agent	Low-Load Policy
5	−14.5%	6.7%
10	2.3	6.9
15	5.1	7.2
20	6.1	7.2

FIGURE 11.5 NO- AND LOW-LOAD INSURERS.

Insurer/Telephone	Insurance Products
American Life Insurance Company of New York 800-957-5432	Term; variable universal
Ameritas Life Insurance Corporation 800-255-9678	Survivorship; term; universal; variable universal
Federal Home Life 800-887-1211	First-to-die; term; universal
First TransAmerica Life Insurance Company 800-544-0506	Term; survivorship; universal
John Alden Life Insurance Company 800-327-7012	Disability income; universal; survivorship; term
Life Insurance Company of the Southwest 800-228-4579	Term
Security Benefit Life Insurance Company 800-888-2461	Universal; variable universal
Southland Life Insurance Company 800-872-7542	Survivorship; universal

FIGURE 11.6 TERM INSURANCE QUOTE SERVICES.

Company	Telephone
Direct Quote	800-845-3853
InsuranceQuote Services	800-972-1104
InstantQuote	888-223-2220
QuickQuote	800-867-2404
Quotesmith	800-431-1147
Quicken's Insure Market	800-695-0011
Select Quote	800-343-1985
TermQuote	800-444-8376
Wholesale Insurance Network	800-808-5810

SELECTING A POLICY

Once you have identified an appropriate amount and type(s) of coverage to consider, you must select a specific policy. You should consider the following factors in your selection:

1. *Insurance company's financial condition.* Several firms rate insurance companies' financial conditions. The rating agencies include A.M. Best Company (900-555-2378), Duff & Phelps (312-368-3100), Moody's (212-553-5377), Standard & Poor's (212-208-1527), and Weiss Research (800-289-9222). Each company uses its own rating scale, but the scales generally run from multiple-A grades (AAA, A+, etc.) to failing grades (C or F, depending on the rating service). You should buy from insurers that have top ratings to reduce the risk that your insurer will experience financial problems.

2. *Policy guarantees and projections.* Insurance policy illustrations, particularly for cash value policies, can be difficult to decipher. Leimberg[5] recommends the following "critical questions":

   • What do you pay each year—compared to what you get if you live and what your heirs receive if you die?

   • What portion of those amounts is guaranteed and how much is projected (not guaranteed)?

   • What assumptions are built into the projections?

Most consumers need help in understanding life insurance illustrations. Unfortunately, the most convenient source of aid is usually the salesperson who stands to benefit from your purchase of the coverage. If you are concerned that this conflict of interest is tainting the salesperson's advice, consider having an independent advisor review the illustration. You will pay a fee for this service, but it could prevent you from buying inappropriate insurance. Sources of noncommissioned insurance advisors include the Fee Insurance Alliance (800-874-5662) and the Life Insurance Advisers Association (800-521-4578).

Don't buy a life insurance contract that you do not understand. If the policy illustration confuses you, find an advisor who can explain it to your satisfaction. Hunt estimates that 30 percent of agent-bought policies are terminated within five years.[6] As Figure 11.4 illustrated, you must hold an agent-bought cash value policy for a fairly long period to earn a reasonable return on it. If you do not understand your policy, or if the coverage is inappropriate, you are more likely to surrender it in the early years and incur a financial loss.

Certain types of specialized life insurance are frequently a waste of money. These include the following:

- *Credit life insurance.* A study from the Consumer Federation of America and the U.S. Public Interest Research Group found that most credit life insurance was extremely expensive for the limited coverage it provided.[7] Although there are exceptions, particularly with the insurance issued by credit unions to members, most credit life is overpriced and should be avoided.

- *Limited-coverage policies.* Some policies provide benefits only for specific illnesses, while other policies are marketed to older consumers through "guaranteed acceptance" advertising. These policies offer limited benefits compared to traditional life insurance. For example, if you die within two years of buying a "guaranteed acceptance" policy, the policy may only return your premiums plus a small amount. Your heirs will not receive the promised death benefit until you own the contract for more than two years.

VIATICAL SETTLEMENTS

In some cases, life insurance policy owners would like to use their policy's death benefit while they are still living. There may be medical bills or other debts that the insured would prefer to pay before his or her death. Although the insured who owns a cash value policy can borrow or withdraw funds from that cash value, the amount available for loan or withdrawal is usually much less than the policy's death benefit. Term policies lack cash values, so this option is not available to term insurance owners.

Viatical settlements allow you to sell your policy while living. In return, you receive a percentage, usually 50 to 80 percent, of the policy's *death benefit,* not its cash value. These settlements are available to insureds with limited life expectancies—typically less than two years. The company buying the policy views it as an investment. It buys the policy, makes the premium payments while the insured is living, and collects the death benefit upon his or her death. Provided the insured is certified as terminally or chronically ill, the settlement is not subject to federal income taxes. (This favorable tax treatment also applies to accelerated death benefits that are included with some life insurance policies.) The number of insureds using viatical settlements is growing rapidly, with projected volume approaching $1 billion by 1998.[8]

FIGURE 11.7 NAIC VIATICAL SETTLEMENT GUIDELINES.

Insured's Life Expectancy	Minimum Percentage
Less than 6 months	80%
6 to 12 months	70
12 to 18 months	65
18 months to 2 years	60
More than 2 years	50

Source: Kiplinger's Personal Finance Magazine. Copyright © March 1997 by The Kiplinger Washington Editors, Inc.

Viatical settlements can convert an illiquid asset (a policy's death benefit) to a liquid asset. If you or a family member could benefit from a settlement, start your research by contacting the Viatical Association of America (202-429-5129). The VAA can provide information to guide your search for a company. Also be sure that the insurer's offer meets the National Association of Insurance Commissioners' (NAIC) settlement guidelines, which are listed in Figure 11.7.

END POINT

Life insurance is a critical element in the foundation of every personal financial plan. Although it is tempting to apply rules of thumb to determine how much and what type of insurance you need, these rules do not apply to all situations. A more prudent method is to determine how much (if any) insurance is required for your needs, followed by a review of the policy types and insurers. You probably will find that several types of policy from multiple insurers can meet your needs.

Health Care Insurance

The need for medical care can cause extensive damage to your finances, with total charges for extended hospital stays easily reaching tens of thousands of dollars. Because these costs are potentially unlimited, you should not overlook the need to protect yourself against the financial impact of medical expenses. This chapter focuses on the use of health care insurance to protect your assets.

 **EMPLOYER-PROVIDED INSURANCE**

Several factors are likely to influence the health insurance options available to you. If you work for a small company, you are less likely to receive health insurance as a benefit. In 1995, among firms with less than 10 employees, only 25.8 percent provided insurance coverage. At larger firms with more than 1,000 employees, that percentage increased to 68.5 percent.[1] Employers in the Northeast tend to offer a larger selection of plans than employers elsewhere. According to a 1997 survey by KPMG Peat Marwick, 29 percent of Northeast employers offered employees one plan, 27 percent offered two plans, while 44 percent allowed employees to choose from three or more plans. In contrast, only 24 percent of employers in the South offered three or more plans.[2]

There are three primary types of employer-provided health insurance plans: traditional fee-for-service plans, health maintenance organizations (HMOs), and preferred provider organizations (PPOs). In 1980, fee-for-service plans dominated the health insurance market, enrolling almost 100 percent of full-time employees at privately held medium and large companies. By 1995, the fee-for-service plans had less than 40 percent of this same employee group. HMOs' market share had grown to over 30 percent and PPOs' share was slightly below 30 percent.[3]

Besides having more choices among coverage providers, you probably are paying at least part of the premium out-of-pocket for your employer-provided health insurance. The KPMG study found that average employee contribution to fee-for-service premiums was $29 per month for single coverage and $108 for family coverage. Single HMO members paid an average $37 per month while families paid $125.

 Comparing Plans

If you have a choice between two or more plans, you should compare the plans' features and costs to determine which best matches your needs. Figure 12.1 lists several of the features you should compare.

 Figure 12.1 is only a partial list of the range of medical services. You should compare each insurer's coverage for the services you use to determine the lowest-cost option that still meets your requirements.

FIGURE 12.1 COMMON FEATURES TO REVIEW.

General costs
Out-of-pocket premiums
Annual deductibles (in network and out of network)
Office visit co-payments
Maximum lifetime benefits
Charges for specific services
Physical, speech, and occupational therapy
Private duty nursing
Durable medical equipment
Home and hospice care
Routine eye exams
Lab procedures and X rays
Prescriptions
Mental health and substance abuse
Maternity/well baby care
Dental care
Prescriptions

This chapter does not discuss the issue of evaluating the *quality* of medical care—that is a book-length topic in itself. *The absence of that discussion does not imply that the issue is unimportant.* It is certainly a critical factor in choosing health care providers, but it is beyond the scope of this book. A good source for publications on evaluating health care providers is Castle Connolly Medical Ltd. (212-980-8230). Among its books is *How to Find the Best Doctors, Hospitals and HMOs for You and Your Family.*

DANGER! Check each plan's maximum lifetime benefits and out-of-network procedure limits. A common lifetime limit is $1 million, but a plan with unlimited benefits is preferable. An estimated 10,000 people will reach their policies' maximums between the years 1995 and 2000, with medical problems ranging from chronic diseases to catastrophic illnesses.

KEY CONCEPT — HEALTH INSURANCE PORTABILITY

When you leave an employer (voluntarily or otherwise), you should ensure that your health insurance coverage continues without interruption. There are two important laws affecting your benefits in this situation: the Consolidated Omnibus Budget Reconciliation Act of 1985 (COBRA) and the Health Insurance Portability and Accountability Act of 1996 (HIPAA). COBRA allows you (or your spouse and dependents) to continue coverage under your former employer's health insurance plan for at least 18 months, and possibly up to 36 months, after your employment ends. You will pay the premiums out-of-pocket, but your cost will be the employer's group rate plus up to a 2 percent surcharge.

Under HIPA, if you change jobs, your new employer must provide coverage to you and your family members who were covered under the previous employer's plan. If you have a preexisting health problem, the new plan cannot impose a waiting period of more than one year before covering that problem. The waiting period may be shorter, however, if the conditioned was covered under your previous employer's plan. HIPAA also prevents employer plans from considering pregnancy as a preexisting condition, and the plan cannot exclude newborns or adopted children.

Do not assume that HIPAA fills all the possible coverage gaps that a job change can impose, however. For instance, if you leave a company with no health plan to start your own business, the regulations do not apply, and you are not guaranteed coverage from an insurer. Also, if you want to shorten the waiting period with the new employer for any preexisting conditions, you must not have gone without group coverage for more than 63 days.[4]

Many companies impose waiting periods on new employees before they can enroll in the group health plan. If you encounter this requirement, or if your previous plan provided better coverage than the new plan, consider using your COBRA coverage to stay in the previous plan.

PRIVATE COVERAGE

There are times when you may not have access to employer-provided coverage: Your employer may not offer coverage; you may be between jobs and post-COBRA, self-employed, or retired but too young for Medicare. There are an estimated 10 to 11 million people in these situations who buy their own health insurance. If you need to buy individual or family health coverage directly, consider the following sources.

Local insurers. This group includes the Blue Cross and Blue Shield and any HMOs and PPOs in your region. These organizations may offer direct-pay plans with a variety of deductibles and benefit limits to control the cost.

National insurers. Several firms, including Golden Rule Insurance (317-297-4123) and Time Insurance (800-800-1212), offer a variety of individual policies, including short-term and comprehensive major medical coverage.

Associations. Alumni, consumer, and other membership associations frequently offer medical insurance plans to their members. The Federation of American Consumers and Travelers (FACT) (800-872-3228) offers coverage from Golden Rule insurance.

Business groups. If you are self-employed, check with your local Chamber of Commerce and other business membership organizations, such as the National Association for the Self-Employed (800-232-6273) and USA for Health Care (800-872-1187), to learn if they offer group-rate plans from local insurers.

Medical savings accounts (MSAs). If you own a small business (less than 50 employees) or are self-employed or unemployed, consider opening an MSA. Congress authorized a limited number (roughly 750,000 by the year 2001) of these accounts with the 1996 HIPAA legislation. As of late 1997, an estimated 150,000 participants had opened MSAs. To open an MSA, you must first purchase health insurance with a high deductible: $1,500 to $2,250 for single coverage and $3,000 to $4,500 for family. This policy serves as your safety net in the event you incur a large medical expense. With this policy in place, you are allowed to make *deductible* contributions into a medical savings account, up to 65 percent (single) or 75 percent (family) of the policy's deductible. You can then make *tax-free* withdrawals from the account for qualifying medical expenses. Unused balances in your account earn tax-deferred interest, and unused funds can remain in the account and accumulate, tax deferred, each year. Figure 12.2 compares the net cost for a traditional low-deductible ($500) policy with a high-deductible ($4,500) policy and MSA for a family with modest annual medical expenses of $500.

The MSA market is still developing, so the number of insurers offering policies is growing, and the policies are not approved for sale in all states. Figure 12.3 lists details on four policies for a 35-year-old male (nonsmoker) with a wife and two children living in a suburban area.[5]

Shopping for medical insurance can be time-consuming, and it is easy to overlook potential insurers. Consider using an independent insurance agent or broker to help you identify policies that will meet your needs. An experienced agent may also suggest strategies for reducing your premiums.

***FIGURE 12.2* TRADITIONAL PLAN VERSUS MSA.**

	Low-Deductible Policy	High-Deductible Policy + MSA
MSA contribution	$ 0	$3,375
Deductible	500	0 ($500 withdrawn from MSA)
Premium	4,225	2,280
Gross outlay	$4,725	$5,655
Less tax savings	0	−1,148*
Net dollar outlay	$4,725	$4,507
Less MSA balance	0	−2,875
Year-end cost	$4,725	$1,632
Savings with MSA		$3,093

*34 percent combined tax rate.
Source: Time Insurance Company.

FIGURE 12.3 MSA COMPARISONS.

Company	Monthly Premium	Interest Rate on Savings	Fees	Account Access	Telephone
Golden Rule	$109	4%	$10 setup/ $3 month	Checkbook	317-297-4123
Medical Savings of America	149*	4.5	$12 setup/ $2 month	Checkbook or debit card	800-853-7321
Time Insurance	110	4.5% on balances of $750+	None	Submit claims	800-800-1212
Mellon Bank or debit card	137*	4% on balances of $4,000+	$12 setup/ $3.50 month†	Checkbook	888-200-0515

Blue Shield policy.

†*Fee waived if account balance exceeds $3,000.*

Source: Kiplinger's Personal Finance Magazine. Copyright © October 1997 by The Kiplinger Washington Editors, Inc.

KEY CONCEPT

MEDICARE

Medicare is a federal health insurance program available to people age 65 and older, disabled, or with permanent kidney failure. The insurance provides two types of benefits: hospital insurance (Part A) and medical insurance (Part B). Part A covers inpatient hospital care, skilled nursing care, home health services, and hospice care. Part B covers physician services, outpatient hospital care, and medical equipment and supplies.

To cover the co-payments and deductibles in Medicare, many consumers purchase Medigap insurance or enroll in Medicare HMOs. In addition, the Balanced Budget Act of 1997 introduced several new options that are being referred to as the "Medicare+Choice" program. These options will become available in 1998.

DANGER!

The following review of Medigap policies, Medicare HMOs, and Medicare+Choice focuses on the financial elements of selecting coverage. The material does not discuss health care quality, selection of physicians, and other critical health-related issues. It would be foolish to select an insurer or health care provider on the basis of cost alone. Use the information in this section to compare the financial aspects of the options available to you, but cost should be only one element in comparing plans. *Do not sacrifice medical care quality to save premiums.*

Medigap policies

Medicare Supplemental Insurance, usually referred to as "Medigap" coverage, is available in 10 approved forms, A through J. Figure 12.4 lists each form's coverages.[6] All plans provide a level of basic benefits:

- *Hospitalization:* Part A coinsurance plus coverage for 365 additional days after Medicare benefits end.
- *Medical expenses:* Part B coinsurance (generally 20 percent of Medicare-approved expenses).
- *Blood:* First three pints of blood each year.

Medicare HMOs

Medicare HMOs are becoming more popular. As of early 1997, roughly 13 percent of Medicare recipients had joined HMOs, and that number is predicted to reach 25 percent within the next few years.[9] Medicare

FIGURE 12.4 STANDARD MEDICARE SUPPLEMENT PLANS.

Benefit	A	B	C	D	E	F	G	H	I	J
Basic	X	X	X	X	X	X	X	X	X	X
Skilled nursing facility		X	X	X	X	X	X	X	X	X
Part A deductible	X	X	X	X	X	X	X	X	X	X
Part B deductible			X			X				
Part B excess charges						X*	X*		X*	X*
Foreign emergency care			X	X	X	X	X	X	X	X
At-home recovery care				X			X		X	X
Basic drug benefit								X	X	X
Preventive screening					X					X
Average annual cost[7]	$528	$838	$908	$872	$870	$1,117	$1,050	$1,203	$1,344	$1,811
Percentage of sales[8]	5.1%	17%	21%	8.4%	0.8%	29.7%	2.2%	2.7%	5.9%	6.9%

*Policy benefits can vary.

Source: 1996 Guide to Health Insurance for People with Medicare.

HMOs frequently charge lower premiums, co-payments, and deductibles than Medigap plans, and they offer greater convenience in the form of less paperwork. Use Figure 12.5 to compare the costs of Medicare HMOs.

Medicare+Choice

The Medicare+Choice program will offer additional health care options starting in November 1998. The new options include Medicare preferred provider organizations (PPOs), provider-sponsored organizations (PSOs), medical savings accounts (MSAs), private fee-for-service plans, and private contracts. As of late 1997, it is difficult to predict how these options will develop. From a planning perspective, your best strategy will be to wait until details are available, then evaluate your options using the criteria discussed in this section.

K·E·Y CONCEPT   **FINANCIAL DISPUTES**

Insurance companies and policyholders seem to battle constantly over two areas: billing errors and service coverage. In both cases, the end result can be increased out-of-pocket expenses for you. Because medical care charges can be very expensive, you should review bills diligently and be prepared to dispute denied services.

1. *Billing errors.*   These errors can come from several sources: procedure and diagnostic coding errors, duplication, redundant charges, unrequested items, and human error, among others. You have a stronger negotiating position if you contest a charge before you pay it, so request itemized bills from

---

FIGURE 12.5 COST REVIEW FOR MEDICARE HMOS.

Monthly premium
Preventive care
Visits to primary care physician
Visits to specialists
Prescription drugs
Emergency room visits
Hospital stay
Mental health care
Dental care
X rays and tests
Prescription eyewear and hearing aids
Durable medical equipment
Care outside the plan area

---

providers and explanation-of-benefit forms (EOBs) from insurers before you make payment.

2. *Denied services.* As managed care becomes more prevalent, consumers frequently find themselves arguing with their insurer or HMO over covered services. If your request for a procedure or claim for its payment are denied, you should take the following steps:

- Learn why the request or claim was denied. If it was due to a coding error, that can be resolved fairly easily.
- Appeal the decision within the insurer or HMO.
- Contact your state's insurance commissioner.
- Bring a lawsuit against the insurer or HMO.

END POINT

The high cost of medical care, even for routine procedures, makes adequate medical insurance critically important. In particular, you must have coverage for the catastrophic expenses that can wipe out your accumulated assets very quickly. Your choices of medical insurance may be limited to the options that your employer provides. If you do not have employer-provided coverage, you should examine the various private coverages that are available. Your goal is to find acceptable coverage at a reasonable cost.

Asset Protection

PROPERTY AND LIABILITY INSURANCE

Your activities and your ownership of property expose you to two types of financial risk. The first is the expense of repairing or replacing your property when it is damaged. The second risk, and the more critical of the two, is the liability you face if your actions injure another person or his or her property. According to Jury Verdict Research, 8 percent of the 4,000 judgments against individuals in 1995 resulted in awards of $1 million or more.[1] Although it is unlikely you will ever experience a judgment of that magnitude, you should not overlook the risk. This chapter describes methods for protecting yourself against property and liability losses through the proper use of homeowner's, auto, and liability insurance.

KEY CONCEPT   Homeowner's and Renter's Insurance

Homeowner's and renter's insurance provides multiple coverages within one policy. Homeowner's policies cover the following:

Part I. Your property.

Part A: Damage to dwelling. At a minimum, you need to insure 80 percent of the home's value to avoid coinsurance problems. If your insurer offers replacement-cost coverage, this coverage protects you against cost increases if the property needs to be rebuilt.

Part B: Damage to other structures. This section covers structures that are not attached to the home, such as detached garages, up to 10 percent of the coverage amount in Part A.

Part C: Damage to personal property. The standard policy limit is 50 percent of Part A's amount, although you can obtain replacement-cost coverage for personal property as a rider.

Part D: Loss of use. Covers expenses if you need to stay in another location because of damage to your home.

Some specific items, such as cash, jewelry, and collectibles, usually have low limits under a standard policy. Most policies also limit coverage of computer equipment and peripherals to $2,500. If you have any of these items or other valuables, purchase extended coverage through a policy rider.

Part II. Your liability.

Part E: Personal liability. If someone is injured on your property, or is injured by you or a member of your family, or if you (or a family member) damage another person's property, this section covers the cost of the damage and legal fees. (This assumes the act that caused the damage was unintentional.) Suggested minimum for this coverage: $300,000.

Part F: Medical payments to others. If a person, other than a resident, is injured on your premises, the policy will cover medical expenses up to the per-person limit.

Renter's insurance will not cover the dwelling and any attached structures—those are the building owner's responsibility. If you are renting, however, you still need the other coverages, which are part of a renter's insurance policy.

There are several types of homeowner's insurance, which are also known as *forms.* Renter's coverage is provided on form HO-4, condominium owner's on form HO-6, while many homeowners use form HO-3. The standard version of each form offers specific coverages and exclusions, limits, and so on. A property and casualty insurance agent can tell you which form is most appropriate for your situation.

Homeowner's insurance does not cover every risk. Floods and earthquakes are two prominent examples of natural disasters that are not covered. You must purchase flood and earthquake insurance separately. Your insurer can provide details and cost estimates on these coverages. You can also call the

National Flood Insurance Program (800-427-4661) for information on flood insurance.

There are several techniques for reducing homeowner's insurance premium costs (ask your insurance company how much each strategy could save on your policies):

- Raise your deductibles.
- Install smoke detectors, fire extinguishers, burglar alarms.
- Avoid filing small claims too frequently.
- Compare rates from several insurers.

Auto Insurance

Similar to homeowner's policies, auto insurance provides several coverages in one policy. Standard coverage includes the following:

Part A: Liability. This section covers damages you cause to other people and their property, and it is one of the most important parts of your auto policy. The liability coverage maximum can be stated as a single amount per accident (e.g., $300,000 per accident) or in split amounts (e.g., 250/500). This split limit provides coverage of $250,000 per person in an accident and $500,000 total per accident. Suggested minimum: $300,000 total coverage.

Part B: Medical payments. Pays for injuries suffered by you and others in your vehicle. It also provides coverage to you as a pedestrian if you are struck by a vehicle.

Part C: Uninsured/underinsured motorists. This section is your coverage for bodily injury you suffer in an accident caused by an uninsured or underinsured. This is another critical component of your coverage. Suggested minimum: $300,000.

Part D: Damage to your auto. This coverage has two parts:

Collision. Insures your vehicle against damages caused by collision with another vehicle, trees, or other objects.

Other than collision. Covers damage from theft, breakage, fire, hail, and so on.

There are several techniques for reducing auto insurance premium costs (ask your insurance company how much each strategy could save on your policies):

- Check insurance rates before you buy a vehicle.
- Raise your deductibles.
- Drop collision and other-than-collision on older cars.

- Install antitheft alarms, tracking systems (Lojack), antilock brakes.
- Maintain a clean driving record. Avoid moving traffic violations.
- Avoid filing small claims too frequently.
- Compare rates from several insurers.
- Combine homeowner's and auto coverage with one insurer.
- Inquire about discounts for completing driving safety courses, low-mileage vehicles, and so on.

The Consumer Federation of America (CFA) has published several reports on auto insurers, *Auto Insurer Efficiency, Price and Customer Service: The Best and the Worst* and *Auto Insurer Efficiency Rankings of 496 Leading Companies.* These are valuable references as you compare auto insurers, and you can order copies by calling the CFA at 202-387-6121. If you want to save time with your comparison shopping, contact *Consumer Reports* about its Auto Insurance Price Service (800-808-4912) or Progressive Insurance (800-AUTOPRO) for its rate-comparison service.

KEY CONCEPT · Personal Excess Liability Insurance

These policies, known popularly as "umbrella" policies, offer additional liability protection over the amounts provided with homeowner's and auto insurance. Umbrella policies gained national attention in early 1996 when it was revealed that President Clinton's policy had paid almost $900,000 to defend him against Paula Jones's sexual harassment allegations.[2]

An umbrella policy acts as backup insurance if a judgment against you exceeds the amount of your auto or homeowner's policy liability limit. Some policies cap the amount of covered legal fees at the policy's limit, while others do not cap the legal expenses. The cost for a $1 million policy is usually less than $200 per year.

Umbrella policies are an inexpensive technique for protecting yourself against the expense of a potentially catastrophic lawsuit. You should carry *at least* a $1 million policy.

ADVANCED STRATEGIES

Carrying adequate insurance coverage, particularly liability coverage, is an important element of your asset-protection plan. There are additional steps you can consider, however, and this section reviews several of these more advanced strategies.

An Integrated Approach

KEY CONCEPT

Asset-protection planning encompasses a range of activities and techniques. Barry Engel, a highly regarded Denver attorney who specializes in asset-protection planning, offers the following definition. "It (asset protection) is the process of planning to protect against those risks that threaten accumulated wealth. To be effective, it must be implemented in advance of a particular risk materializing rather than after it has occurred."[3]

A sound asset-protection plan requires an integrated, balanced approach so that costly gaps don't occur. The following steps illustrate a systematic approach to developing the plan.

Step 1. Identify your risk exposures.
The first step in developing an asset plan is to identify the risks that pose a threat to your wealth. These risks include the following:

- Illness and accident (medical expenses and lost income).
- Need for nursing home care (depletion of income and assets).
- Premature death (final expenses, loss of decedent's income for dependents, disruption of family-owned business, estate taxes).
- Property loss (destruction of personal property and loss of its use).
- Property-related liability (liability for damages to other persons or their property).
- Business and professional activities (general and professional liability, bankruptcy).

These are general categories—your personal situation determines the risks you face.

Step 2. Determine available response time.
After identifying your exposures, you must determine if any assets are at immediate risk. For example, if you are on the verge of declaring personal or business bankruptcy, or if you believe you are about to be sued, you have fewer options than you did six months ago. In general, a longer planning period gives you access to more asset-protection techniques. Advance planning and implementation also increases the likelihood that any protective measures you take will survive challenges.

Step 3. Evaluate and select the appropriate protection strategies.

Some asset-protection measures, such as buying excess personal liability insurance, are relatively easy and inexpensive to implement. Other decisions are more complex, though, and they require in-depth evaluation. Examples of these measures include selecting the proper forms of business and asset ownership, asset transfers to avoid creditors, and the use of U.S.-based and foreign trusts.

The risk management strategies in Chapters 10 through 12 provide a foundation for a sound asset-protection plan, but this is one area where a do-it-yourself approach can backfire. If you have substantial assets or if your work exposes you to liability suits, consult a financial planner or an attorney who is experienced in asset-protection planning.

 Asset Ownership

Properly structuring title to property can be a simple and inexpensive method for protecting assets. This is particularly true for married couples if one spouse has a significantly greater liability exposure. By shifting property to the less exposed spouse, the couple can reduce the amount of assets that creditors or claimants can reach.

There are several forms of property ownership, which include the following:

Sole Ownership: One Person or Entity

Advantages. Simple to create; sole owner has complete control over property.

Disadvantages. Creditors have easier access to solely owned property unless that property is exempted from claims under federal or state law.

Strategy. Consider transferring nonexempt property to lower-risk spouse. There are potential drawbacks to this strategy, however. The lower-risk spouse is not immune to lawsuits; he or she has complete control over the transferred assets; and the transfer could have estate planning or divorce proceeding implications.

Joint Ownership

1. Tenants in common

   Advantages. Simple to create; gives each owner a separate partial interest in the property.

   Disadvantages. Cotenants cannot act for each other; creditors have access to a tenant's interest in the property; cotenants do not automatically inherit the other tenant's interest in the property.

Strategy. Tenancy in common has limited asset-protection value.

2. Joint with right of survivorship (JWROS)

Advantages. Avoids probate upon death of an owner; ownership passes in full to survivor.

Disadvantages. More difficult to create than tenancy in common—most states have requirements that must be met or ownership defaults to tenants in common.

Strategy. Although the JWROS form has little formal asset-protection value, it can discourage creditors from seizing an asset because of the difficulty of reselling a single joint tenant's interest. But if both joint tenants are liable for the same debt, the creditor will have a claim against both interests.

3. Tenants by the entirety

Advantages. Property protected from creditors' claims against one spouse—creditor must have a joint claim against both spouses.

Disadvantages. Available only to married couples; not recognized in every state; frequently limited to personal property and real estate.

Strategy. Depending on applicable state law, consider moving assets from high-risk spouse into tenancy by the entirety.

4. Community property. Nine states have community property laws: Arizona, California, Idaho, Louisiana, Nevada, New Mexico, Texas, Washington, and Wisconsin. If you are married and reside in one of these states (or if you acquired property while living in one of them), you face a different set of laws than those in the other states and the District of Columbia. From an asset-protection perspective, creditors can reach a spouse's separate property, and in some states they have access to the couple's community property. One possible strategy is to convert community property to separate property, but this action can have unintended implications for estate planning and divorce proceedings. Alternative strategies include transferring property to family limited partnerships or trusts.

KEY CONCEPT   **Marital Property Agreements**

Prenuptial and postnuptial agreements frequently appear in news reports when wealthy and high-profile couples divorce. Apart from these highly publicized cases, these agreements can serve a valuable role in reorganizing the ownership of a couple's current and future assets. Most states impose a set of conditions on these agreements before accepting them as valid. These conditions typically include the following[4]:

- Agreement made in writing.
- Agreement signed by both spouses and notarized.
- A fair agreement (at time of signing) that both spouses accept voluntarily.
- Full financial disclosure between spouses.
- Full understanding of legal impact of the agreement.
- Agreement filed in local records office.

Marital agreements are useful in changing community property, which is available to creditors, to separate property, which can shift assets from the high-risk spouse to the lower-risk spouse.

Do not agree to sign a pre- or postnuptial agreement without having *independent* legal advice. You should have a lawyer (*not* your spouse's lawyer) review the document and explain its short- and long-term implications to you.

Choosing a Business Form

If you plan to start a business, or already own one, selecting the proper business form is a critical component in your asset-protection plan. Each form has advantages and disadvantages that you should consider. The forms include the following:

Direct Ownership

1. Sole proprietorship

   Advantages.   Easy to create, maintain, and dissolve.

   Disadvantages.   The sole proprietor assumes unlimited personal liability for the business's debts or any other obligations.

   Strategy.   Avoid sole proprietorship if the business faces any potential liabilities from its products or other sources, including employees' actions.

2. Partnerships

   Advantages.   Easy to create, maintain, and dissolve. Limited partnerships offer increased asset protection.

   Disadvantages.   In a traditional general partnership, each partner is liable for claims against the partnership.

   Strategy.   If partners wish to reduce their liability exposure, a limited partnership (LP) is an attractive alternative. In an LP, the limited partners are not active in the business's management, and their liability is limited to their investment. The LP's general partner has control of the partnership and unlimited liability.

Indirect Ownership

3. C, S, and qualified small business corporations

Advantages. Increased liability protection to owners (shareholders).

Disadvantages. Must meet state regulations regarding creation and maintenance; more complex to dissolve than sole proprietorship or partnership; courts can ignore corporate status in some cases.

Strategy. If the business increases your liability exposure, incorporation is a sound strategy. Other factors, such as the number of shareholders and tax treatment of business income, will determine which form you should select.

4. Limited Liability Corporations (LLCs)

Advantages. LLCs offer a combination of the S corporation's advantages (limited liability, flow-through taxation) and a partnership's flexibility.

Disadvantages. Must meet state regulations regarding creation and maintenance; states' laws differ on certain aspects of LLC formation.

Strategy. If multiple owners plan to participate in the business's management, consider using an LLC instead of a general or limited partnership.

 Family Limited Partnerships (FLPs)

Similar to a limited partnership (LP) created for business purposes, an FLP consists of general and limited partners, and the FLP's general partner assumes unlimited liability for the partnership's debts. In contrast to a business LP, the FLP's partners are almost always members of the same family. FLPs also offer significant estate planning advantages.

In the typical FLP, one or both parents assume the role of general partner(s) with their children and other family members as limited partners. The parents transfer assets to the FLP to fund it. The IRS (and state law) require that the FLP have a business purpose, and avoiding creditors' claims is not considered an acceptable purpose for establishing the FLP. The following assets usually meet this business requirement test:

• Businesses.

• Publicly traded securities (stocks, bonds) and cash.

• Real estate.

• Life insurance policies.

Some assets are inappropriate for FLPs, including commonly owned assets such as personal residences and qualified retirement plans. Discuss any transfers with your accountant or lawyer *before* you change the asset's title to the FLP.

The FLP is an effective asset-protection device because creditors are restricted in their actions against a limited partner. Specifically, the creditor can reach the partner's interest in the FLP, but *not* the FLP's assets. The creditor may also be able to claim the limited partner's share of any distributions from the FLP, but the general partner controls the distributions. As a result, the creditor may see little, if any, cash from the claim. The practical effect is that the creditor's bargaining position is diminished relative to the limited partner, possibly forcing the creditor into a settlement that favors the partner.

It is possible to build multiple layers of asset protection around the FLP. For example, the general partner can be a corporation that is controlled by the parents. Also, you can create multiple FLPs to hold different assets. Finally, the partnership agreement can contain restrictive clauses to further reduce the likelihood that a creditor will receive any funds.

The FLP will not work as intended if the courts determine it does not serve a valid business purpose or if it was created solely to avoid creditors. Obtain qualified legal advice on the FLP's viability and any asset transfers from the earliest stages.

Domestic (U.S.-Based) Trusts

Trusts have an important role in estate planning (see Chapters 20 and 21 for details), but they are also a valuable asset-protection tool. Three parties are needed to create a trust:

- *Grantor.* Person who establishes the trusts and transfers assets into it.

- *Trustee.* Person or organization responsible for managing the trust's assets.

- *Beneficiary.* Person(s) or organizations that receive distributions from the trust.

A trust's flexibility stems from the potential relationships among these parties. A person can serve in one role (grantor), two roles (grantor and trustee, grantor and beneficiary), or all three roles. From an asset-protection perspective, a trust is useful because creditors can reach only trust assets that the debtor owns or controls. In other words, (1) if you cannot retrieve the trust's assets, (2) if you name an independent trustee, and (3) if the trust's beneficiaries do not have an absolute right to the trust's distributions, then the beneficiaries' creditors cannot reach the assets.

The trust must meet the following key tests to thwart creditors:

- If you wish to protect the trust's assets from *your* creditors, the trust must be *irrevocable* and you cannot be a beneficiary.
- There must be an independent trustee with discretionary control over trust distributions.
- Beneficiaries should have only limited control (if any) over the trust's assets.

Spendthrift trusts can help prevent a beneficiary's creditors from attaching trust assets. Most states allow a trust to use spendthrift provisions; ask your attorney if any trust you are considering would benefit from these provisions.

Before you transfer assets into an irrevocable trust, review the transfer's impact on your current and projected financial needs and your estate plans. Asset protection is an important goal, but it must be coordinated with the other aspects of your finances.

Foreign Trusts

Foreign, or offshore, trusts are receiving increasing attention as asset-protection techniques. In one highly publicized case, a wife charged that her ex-husband, owner of a financial services firm, had moved 90 percent of their assets to a trust in the Cayman Islands. Because the Cayman's laws are designed to protect these trusts, it is expensive and extremely difficult (with no guarantee of success) to reach such assets. As a result, the ex-wife in this case settled for considerably less than she believed she would otherwise have received.[5]

The wife's decision to settle in this case illustrates a key advantage of offshore trusts. Even if a creditor *could* eventually reach the trust's assets, the expense and aggravation of the effort are prohibitive unless very large sums are involved. When faced with the challenge of reaching the offshore trust's assets, a creditor will probably be inclined to settle more quickly and more favorably to the debtor. According to Denver attorney Barry Engel, roughly 5 percent of the over 1,000 offshore trusts his firm has created have been challenged, and the average settlement was for 15 cents on the dollar.[6]

Several countries have established laws that are favorable to trusts from U.S. citizens, including the

Bermuda, Barbados, the Bahamas, and the Cook Islands. Although these countries may also be known as tax havens, an offshore trust does not avoid income taxes, and you must report the trust to the IRS. Although each country has its own laws, benefits of offshore trusts generally include the following:

● Ability to create a spendthrift trust, in which the grantor is also the beneficiary. This is prohibited in the United States.

● Offshore courts do not recognize a U.S. court's judgment against the trust.

● Shorter periods (statute of limitation) during which creditors can discover and challenge the trust.

● Requirement that creditors must use local (offshore) attorneys to challenge the trust in the offshore location.

There are drawbacks to establishing an offshore trust, however. They are expensive, with typical setup fees starting around $20,000 and annual fees of $3,000.[7] You also need to create the trust before a divorce, lawsuit, or bankruptcy is filed or it may be too late to shelter assets effectively.

 Before creating an offshore trust, carefully weigh its costs and advantages against the less exotic alternatives described in this chapter. You may find that you can accomplish many of the same asset-protection goals with these other techniques. In particular, ask your attorney if you should consider establishing trusts in Alaska or Delaware. These states passed laws in 1997 that are designed to replicate many of the offshore trusts' benefits at a substantially lower cost.

 Bankruptcy

Chapter 7 discussed bankruptcy from the personal credit perspective, but bankruptcy also can serve as an asset-protection strategy, especially if you have sufficient lead time. The goal is to emerge from the bankruptcy proceedings with the greatest amount of assets that you retain legally. This requires an understanding of the *exemption* and *fraudulent transfer* laws.

 Even if you understand the bankruptcy laws thoroughly, do not underestimate the value that an experienced attorney can bring to your case. A competent attorney can help you maximize your postbankruptcy wealth and prevent you from making detrimental errors in presenting your case.

Federal and state bankruptcy laws allow debtors to *exempt* specified types and amounts of property from creditors' claims. A major goal of prebankruptcy planning is to shelter your wealth in exempt assets. Under federal law, the following assets are exempt[8]:

Homestead (residence up to $15,000).

Automobile (one vehicle, $2,400 maximum value).

Jewelry ($1,000 total value).

Tools of trade ($1,500 total value).

Prescription health aids.

Qualified retirement plans (not including IRAs).

Life insurance contracts (including annuities).

State bankruptcy laws frequently have different limits than federal law, and *you must know which limit applies in your case.* For example, some states have extremely liberal homestead exemptions, while others offer no exemption. The exempt amount on a life insurance policy's cash value also varies, with most states capping it at roughly $5,000.

The second critical concept you must understand for effective bankruptcy planning is *fraudulent transfer.* If a court decides that a transfer was fraudulent, your asset-protection plans probably will fail. Deciding if a transfer was fraudulent is difficult, because it requires proof that the person making the transfer was attempting to defraud the creditor. Keller[9] lists two typical conditions of these transfers:

> *Usually, fraudulent transfers are characterized by a lack of adequate consideration (the transferor does not receive value equal to the value which he transfers) or an attempt by debtors to place their property beyond the reach of creditors with the intent of impairing the ability of the creditor to collect a debt.*

DANGER! Some transfers are obviously fraudulent, even to a nonprofessional. Other transfers may qualify, however, even though they were made before the debtor considered bankruptcy. This risk of unintentional fraud is another reason you should consult a qualified attorney before you file for bankruptcy.

END POINT

Accumulating wealth is not sufficient in today's litigious society—you must also plan to protect that wealth. Having adequate insurance coverage is an important first step, but it may be insufficient. In particular, if your business or professional activities create liability, you should consider the more advanced strategies described in this chapter. These measures may include creation of corporations, trusts, and other limited liability entities to make it more difficult for others to reach your assets.

PART 3

Investments

14

Investment Fundamentals

In an ideal world, you would be able to place your funds in guaranteed, tax-exempt, inflation-adjusted accounts that earned high rates of return. No matter what happened to the economy or the investment markets, your money would be protected from taxes, risk of loss, and inflation. Because there is no single risk-free account that can accomplish every investment goal, you must choose among investments that combine varying degrees of risk and return. This chapter looks at the basic principles of developing an investment plan to help you reach your financial goals. The chapters that follow will examine specific investments in more detail.

ASSET CLASSES

KEY CONCEPT

There are thousands of different investments available. Later chapters describe some of them in more detail, but a brief review of the three major categories is helpful at this stage.

- *Stocks.* Common stocks are *equity securities* that represent ownership (equity) in a corporation. Corporations issue *shares* as evidence of ownership of the business's assets and profits. Shares in *publicly traded* corporations can be bought and sold by investors, while shares in *privately held* corporations do not trade among the general public. Stocks may pay *dividends* (income distributions), but these are not guaranteed. The goal of buying common stock is to profit from dividends (if any) and a potential increase in the stock's price per share.

- *Bonds.* Bonds are *fixed-income securities* that represent loans to a business or government. Bondholders receive periodic *fixed-interest payments* during the life of the bond, and at the bond's *maturity* they receive the bond's principal, or face value, usually $1,000 per bond.

- *Cash.* The term *cash* is somewhat deceptive. Investors avoid holding cash because it earns no interest. Instead, they invest cash in short-term fixed-income securities (such as Treasury bills or money market mutual funds) that earn interest.

Stocks, bonds, and cash are considered to be the foundation investment classes for most portfolios. When Wall Street investment strategists discuss "asset allocation," they usually state it in terms of the target percentages for each class. For example, a strategist might recommend a portfolio mix of "10 percent cash, 30 percent bonds, and 60 percent stocks."

 **COORDINATING GOALS AND INVESTMENTS**

The first step in selecting investments is to set specific financial goals. Once you develop a timetable and funding plan for your goals, you can evaluate the suitability of different investment classes. For instance, assume that over the next two years you want to accumulate $15,000 for your child's wedding. You are considering two accounts for your savings plan. The first is a money market fund that has a current yield of 5 percent. You must deposit $593 each month to accumulate $15,000 in two years. The second account is a mutual fund that invests in very risky stocks, but it has earned 25 percent each year recently. If you can earn that return over the next two years, your required monthly savings drops to $478.

You choose the stock fund and it performs as expected for the first few months. Then the market begins falling and your fund account's value drops by 15 percent, and it stays at this depressed level for the next year. Instead of having $15,000 available after two years, you have only $12,000, and you must use other assets to make up the $3,000 shortfall.

 Do not overlook the time horizon as you select investments. Short-term goals should be matched with short-term, low-risk investments; for long-term goals, where the benefit of time is on your side, longer-term, riskier investments are appropriate. Figure 14.1 lists the historical results for the major investment classes over the period January 1926 through August 1996.

FIGURE 14.1 INVESTMENT RESULTS: JANUARY 1926 THROUGH AUGUST 1996.

Asset Class	Average Compound Annual Return
Small company stocks	12.5%
Real estate	11.1
Dow Jones Industrials	10.0
Bonds	5.2
Treasury bills	3.7
Inflation	3.1

Source: Wall Street Journal, *October 1, 1996, p. C1. Reprinted by permission of the* Wall Street Journal, *copyright © 1996 by Dow Jones & Company, Inc. All rights reserved worldwide.*

Be very careful about projecting an investment's historical results into the future. It is common for volatile investments to produce outstanding results one year followed by below-average results in future years. Even long-term historical results have very little value for predicting the immediate future.

 **OVERCOMING INFLATION AND TAXES**

If investment results are unpredictable, at least in the short run, why bother taking risks with your money? Wouldn't it be more sensible to keep your funds in guaranteed accounts? Yes, it would—*assuming taxes and inflation were irrelevant to your situation.* For most investors, however, taxes and inflation are serious impediments to accumulating wealth. Assume that your combined federal and state tax bracket is 32 percent and the annual inflation rate is 3 percent. If you have $10,000 in a taxable account that earns a guaranteed 4 percent, or $400, you will suffer a *loss,* even though the account's principal is guaranteed. Here are the calculations: $400 interest minus $128 taxes equals a $272 after-tax yield. The purchasing power lost on $10,000 due to 3 percent inflation is $300. The combined loss from taxes and inflation is $428, producing a net *real* return of –$28. You won't see that loss if you look at your account statement, of course, but you cannot avoid the economic impact.

Focus on an investment's *real* (after-tax, after-inflation) return, not its nominal, or stated return. If you evaluate your account's real return, you probably will discover that you need to have at least part of your funds in higher-risk, potentially higher-yielding investments.

Although you probably must accept some investment risk to meet your goals, you do not need to take excessive risk. For example, if you can reach your targets with a 5 percent real return, do not place all your funds in higher-risk investments that offer potentially much higher returns. There is a close link between risk and return, and the prospect of higher returns means you generally must incur higher risk.

RISK TOLERANCE

Unlike the characters in movie or television scenes who wager large amounts of money without exhibiting the slightest nervousness, most investors experience anxiety at the prospect of losing money, especially in amounts that would affect their financial well-being. Understanding the amount of investment risk you can tolerate is an important step in selecting investments. If you choose investments that are too conservative (for you), your returns will be lower than they could have been. But if you choose investments that are too risky, your discomfort with those investments' volatility may cause you to sell at an inappropriate time.

The T. Rowe Price investment management company has developed a questionnaire to help investors match risk-tolerance levels and time horizon goals with suitable investments. Use Figure 14.2 to identify your risk tolerance.

After identifying your risk profile and time horizon goals, the next step is to develop an initial portfolio strategy. You can do that with Figure 14.3 by finding the intersection of a goal's time horizon and your risk-tolerance level for that goal.

The next section discusses the portfolios' performance, and you should note how each portfolio's mix changes as risk tolerance or time horizon changes. A longer time horizon allows an investor to take greater risk, as does a higher risk tolerance. Shorter time horizons or a lower risk tolerance call for less aggressive investment policies.

There are many varieties of risk questionnaires, and most financial advisors and mutual fund companies can supply you with one. Even if you are an experienced investor with a good intuitive grasp of your risk tolerance, completing and scoring a questionnaire can give you additional insight into your investing personality.

PERFORMANCE AND RISK

Figure 14.4 shows how the portfolios in Figure 14.3 performed over the period from 1950 to 1994. Notice how the performance varies as you move from

FIGURE 14.2 RISK TOLERANCE DESCRIPTIONS.

Instructions: After deciding on your goals and time horizons, check the box that most appropriately describes your risk tolerance for each goal.

Short-term goals (3–5 years)

☐ Low risk — I'm uncomfortable with price volatility, and I'm willing to give up the possibility of higher returns in order to keep my principal intact. I am satisfied with an investment that stays ahead of inflation.

☐ Moderate risk — I expect the value of my investments to fluctuate, but not drastically. I could potentially suffer a 3 percent loss or more in a single year, but I'm willing to assume this risk for the opportunity to earn higher returns.

☐ High risk — Capital growth is my goal. During this short investment period, I hope to earn superior returns. However, I could experience a loss from 5 to 13 percent or more in a single year from which I might not fully recover.

Intermediate-term goals (6–10 years)

☐ Low risk — I'm willing to accept short-term fluctuations in the value of my investments to earn the returns that should protect my money from the effects of inflation.

☐ Moderate risk — Although my investment might suffer a 5 to 13 percent decline or more in a single year, my intermediate time horizon gives my money time to recover losses and potentially earn moderate returns.

☐ High risk — I'm willing to risk a double-digit drop in my investment for the opportunity to achieve superior growth. I plan to hold my investment for 6 to 10 years and I should have time to recover a loss.

Long-term goals (11+ years)

☐ Low risk — It's important that my investment provide healthy returns over time to stay ahead of inflation. Therefore, I'm willing to accept moderate fluctuations in the value of my investment, which should allow me to achieve modest growth.

☐ Moderate risk — I'm investing for the long term and can withstand considerable fluctuation in the value of my investment. I may suffer a loss of 7 to 20 percent or more in a single year, but as a long-term investor, I should recover from these temporary setbacks over time.

☐ High risk — I have the conviction necessary to hold onto my investment during those years when it could drop in value by 25 percent or more. My goal is to earn superior returns, so I'm willing to assume a high degree of risk.

Source: The T. Rowe Price Personal Strategy Planner, p. 9.

FIGURE 14.3 MODEL PORTFOLIOS.

Your Time Horizon	3–5 years	6–10 years	11+ years
High risk tolerance	10% cash 30% bonds 60% stocks	20% bonds 80% stocks	100% stocks
Moderate risk tolerance	20% cash 40% bonds 40% stocks	10% cash 30% bonds 60% stocks	20% bonds 80% stocks
Low risk tolerance	35% cash 40% bonds 25% stocks	20% cash 40% bonds 40% stocks	10% cash 30% bonds 60% stocks

Source: The T. Rowe Price Personal Strategy Planner, p. 13. Categories: 30-day Treasury bills (cash), intermediate government bonds (bonds), S&P 500 Stock Index (stocks).

the most conservative (100 percent cash) to the most aggressive (100 percent stocks). The riskier portfolios earn higher returns, but they also experience greater losses in down years. (The term *risk* is used in a general sense to signify a negative investment return or loss of principal.)

KEY CONCEPT — DIVERSIFICATION

If you knew with certainty which individual stock would earn the highest return over the next year, you would invest every dollar you could find in that stock. Similarly, if you knew with certainty which asset class (stocks, bonds, or cash) would have the best per-

FIGURE 14.4 PORTFOLIO PERFORMANCE.

Portfolio No.	1	2	3	4	5	6
Allocation	100% cash	35% cash 40% bonds 25% stocks	20% cash 40% bonds 40% stocks	10% cash 30% bonds 60% stocks	20% bonds 80% stocks	100% stocks
Average annual returns	5.2%	7.5%	8.6%	9.9%	11.1%	12.1%
Best year	14.7%	20.7%	22.5%	32.5%	42.6%	52.6%
Worst year	0.9%	−1.5%	−6.7%	−13.4%	−20.0%	−26.5%
Number of down years	0	3	8	8	10	10
Average loss in down years	NA	−0.7%	−2.0%	−5.0%	−6.5%	−9.6%

Source: The T. Rowe Price Personal Strategy Planner, p. 14.

formance, you would shift all your funds to that class. Because people lack that knowledge of the future, they can only make uncertain projections based on their best analysis. This uncertainty introduces risk: What if you choose the wrong stock or the wrong asset class?

This unknown future performance causes investors to *diversify* their holdings by owning stocks in different companies, industries, and even countries. You can extend the diversification to holding several asset classes, as Figure 14.3 demonstrated. Spreading your investments among different assets and classes takes advantage of the fact that most assets' price changes are not perfectly *correlated* over long periods. For instance, if interest rates are rising, the returns on cash holdings will increase. Bond values certainly will drop, and stock prices probably will go lower. In a period of falling rates, cash accounts will earn less, while bond (and probably stock) prices will go higher. By spreading your funds among several asset classes, you can adjust the risk-versus-return profile of your portfolio.

There is an alternative to diversification: *concentration* (or nondiversification), which means holding a small number of assets. A diversified portfolio follows the advice, "Don't put all your eggs in one basket." If you decide to concentrate your investments, you *are* putting all your eggs in one basket, so you will need to watch the basket carefully. Concentrated investing can be a very successful strategy, but it is generally riskier than a diversified approach and therefore requires extra diligence.

A portfolio can be less diversified than it might appear to be. For example, if you own several stocks in computer-related industries, those stocks could all be influenced by the same computer hardware industry trends. A portfolio of mutual funds, each of which is highly diversified, can also be less diversified than imagined if the funds themselves own many of the same securities. Also, the correlation between assets can change, especially during periods of market volatility.

INVESTMENT RETURN

The term *return* has several meanings, and it is important to distinguish among them.

- *Bond yield.* The (annual) interest paid on each bond divided by the bond's current market value. *Example:* $50 annual interest paid on a bond with a current market value of $950 per bond produces a yield of 5.26 percent ($50 ÷ $950 = .0526, or 5.26%).

- *Dividend yield.* The (annual) dividend paid on each share of stock divided by the stock's price. *Example:* A $1 annual dividend paid on a stock with a current market value of $50 per share produces a 2 percent dividend yield ($1 ÷ $50 = .02, or 2%).

- *Capital gain.* The increase in a security's value. *Example:* If you buy a stock for $25 per share and its price increases to $30, you have a capital gain of $5 per share, or 20 percent ($5 ÷ $25 = .20, or 20%). A *capital loss* is a decrease in value from your purchase price.

- *Total return.* The combination of any income received from dividends or interest plus any capital gain or loss. *Example:* You buy a stock for $30 per share. During the next 12 months you receive $.60 in dividends per share and the share price increases to $33. Your total return is ($.60 + $3) ÷ $30 = 12 percent.

Focus on total return when you evaluate investments. Naive investors frequently choose investments solely on the basis of yield, but this method overlooks the important role of capital gains. A 12 percent yield sounds attractive, but if the asset suffers a 10 percent capital loss, the total return is only 2 percent.

THE INVESTMENT MARKETS

You probably hear and read news reports about the financial markets every day: "The Dow was up 30 points today," "The NASDAQ index dropped 4 points," "The long bond gained 4 ticks on good inflation news." If you are unfamiliar with investment jargon, these statements have little meaning, but each is simply a summary about a particular investment market's performance. The following is a brief introduction to the various U.S.-based investment markets and the indexes used to track those markets. Later chapters explore these topics in more detail.

Stock Markets

Stocks trade in many locations throughout the United States. Some trading locations are centralized in *stock exchanges,* such as the New York Stock Exchange (NYSE) and the American Stock Exchange (Amex). Some stocks do not trade in one central location. Instead, the brokerage firms that trade the stocks are linked via computer networks to the National Association of Securities Dealers Automated Quotation (NASDAQ) over-the-counter market.

Investors track the aggregate performance of the markets by following market *indexes*. The Dow Jones Industrial Average (DJIA), or the Dow as it is frequently called, is an index used to measure the price performance of 30 large U.S. companies' stocks. These companies are all well known: American Express, AT&T, and General Electric, among others, are in the DJIA. Even if you do not follow the markets, you cannot avoid hearing news reports when the Dow makes new records or experiences large fluctuations.

The Standard & Poor's 500 Index (S&P 500), is another frequently quoted index that tracks 500 stocks: 400 industrial companies, 40 public utilities, 40 financial companies, and 20 transportation firms. Because it tracks a larger number of stocks than the DJIA, the S&P 500 is considered a more accurate index of overall market activity. The New York Stock Exchange Composite Index (NYSE Composite) includes all the common stocks listed on the NYSE, while the NASDAQ indexes use over-the-counter stocks.

Bond Markets

Most bond trading takes place over telecommunications links between securities firms' bond trading departments. Investors use several indexes to track specific segments of the bond market. These include the Lehman Brothers T-Bond Index, Lehman Brothers Corporate Bond Index, Ryan Labs Treasury Index, and the Bond Buyer Municipal Bond Index, among others. In financial news reports, however, you are most likely to hear about changes in short- and long-term Treasury bond rates. Three-month and six-month Treasury bills are tracked as indicators of short-term rates, while the 30-year Treasury bond (the "long bond") tracks long-term rates.

Commodity Markets

Markets exist for a variety of commodities: precious metals, agricultural crops, oil products, and so on. Activity in these markets is reported by changes in the commodity's price: dollar cost per ounce of gold or cost per pound of coffee, for instance.

It may seem obvious, but it is inadvisable to invest in something that you don't understand. In particular, you should understand how you can profit from an investment *and* how you can lose money. Many Americans seem to be investing on blind faith, however. A 1997 John Hancock–Gallup survey of 800 participants in 401(k) retirement plans determined the following[1]:

- Almost half the respondents didn't know that it is possible to lose money in a bond mutual fund.
- Almost two-thirds of respondents didn't know that it is possible to lose money in a government bond fund.

As any investor with bond fund experience will tell you, it certainly is possible to lose money in these funds. The moral: Understand the potential rewards and losses of any investment before you commit your money.

END POINT

The basic principles of investing are straightforward. Investors should consider their goals' time horizons and risk tolerance before selecting asset classes. Once the portfolio's initial allocation is in place, diversifying among different investments is a prudent policy for most investors.

Investing in Bonds and Stocks

For most U.S. investors, stocks and bonds are the primary financial assets for building a portfolio. When Wall Street strategists discuss their outlooks for the markets, they often refer to model portfolios that are comprised of stocks, bonds, and cash: 50 percent stocks, 40 percent bonds, and 10 percent cash, for example. An analyst who sees improved prospects for one asset class relative to the others will increase that asset's weight in his or her model portfolio.

The cash asset class usually consists of short-term (30- or 60-day) Treasury bills or money market mutual funds. Defining the bond and stock classes is more difficult, however, because each class consists of thousands of issues with a wide range of characteristics. This diversity may create an overabundance of choices, but it also allows investors to build portfolios that can meet a variety of financial needs. This chapter provides an introduction to bonds and stocks, focusing on direct investment where the investor buys individual securities.

BONDS

A Conventional Bond's Timeline

Bonds represent a borrower's promise to pay interest and principal; they are an IOU issued by U.S.-based and foreign corporations, national governments and government agencies, and local governments. When you invest in a bond, you lend your money to a borrower. With most bonds, that borrower agrees to pay you periodic interest, and when the loan's term ends, the borrower will repay the loan principal. The following example demonstrates the process.

XYZ Corporation needs funds to build a new factory. It decides to raise $50 million by selling bonds that will pay 6 percent annual interest for the next 10 years. XYZ will pay that interest each year in two semiannual payments of 3 percent. Each bond sells for $1,000, and you decide to buy 10 bonds for a cost of $10,000. As long as you own the bonds, you will receive an interest payment of $300 every six months ($10,000 × 3%). If you still own the bonds when they mature in 10 years, XYZ Corporation will redeem them from you for $1,000 each, or $10,000 total. Figure 15.1 shows a timeline illustrating the bond's history.

You are *not* required to hold the bond for the full 10-year term. You can sell it at any time to another investor, but your selling price is unpredictable: It may be more or less than the original $1,000 cost. This is a key point with bond investments: If you hold the bond to maturity, you receive its full payoff value. But if you sell before maturity, you may receive more or less than you paid, as will be illustrated shortly.

Investors, especially those over age 60, often object to buying long-term bonds. They make statements such as, "The bond probably will outlive me." The objection is humorous, but it assumes that the investor must hold the bond to maturity. The reality is that the investor can sell the bonds at any time, although the selling price will fluctuate from the cost. Even if the bond does outlive the investor, the estate can sell the bond and distribute the proceeds to the heirs.

FIGURE 15.1 A BOND'S TIMELINE.

```
|————|————|————————————————————————————————|
1    2    3                                4
```

Date 1 (time = 0). XYZ issues the bonds and you buy 10 for $1,000 each.

Date 2 (time = 6 months). XYZ pays you $30 interest per bond.

Date 3 (time = 12 months). XYZ pays you $30 interest per bond.

(Payments for intervening years not shown.)

Date 4 (time = 10 years). Bonds mature. XYZ sends you the final $30 interest payments and pays off each bond for $1,000.

‹DANGER!› Bonds offer predictable income and fixed value at maturity, *but they are not risk-free.* Bond prices fluctuate between the date the bond is issued and its maturity. Even bonds that are fully backed by the U.S. government can experience dramatic price fluctuations. In some circumstances, bond prices can be more volatile than stock prices—a fact that might surprise an unsuspecting investor.

Some bonds have different payment streams than standard bonds. *Zero-coupon bonds* do not pay interest before maturity. The investor buys them for less than $1,000, and at maturity the bond is worth $1,000. *Example:* Investor pays $558.39 today for a zero-coupon bond that matures in 10 years at $1,000. If the investor holds the bond to maturity ($1,000 value) he or she will earn a 6 percent yield. *Adjustable-rate bonds* pay a variable interest rate that is reset periodically to track an interest rate index. The Treasury's new inflation-protection bond, discussed later in the chapter, is an example of an indexed bond.

KEY CONCEPT ### Bond Terminology

The previous example introduced the basic principles of bond investing. This section defines those concepts more formally.

- *Issuer.* Organization that borrows funds from investors by selling bonds.

- *Par value.* The bond's value (in dollars) at the time of issue and maturity.

- *Coupon rate.* Annual interest rate paid on bond's par value.

- *Term.* Number of years until issuer redeems bond.

- *Maturity date.* Date when bond comes due and current owner receives par value.

- *Secondary market.* Market in which bonds trade among investors after issue; most bonds trade over the counter (i.e., not on organized exchanges).

- *Yield.* Coupon rate divided by bond's current market price.

- *Discount.* If a bond's market price drops below its par value, the bond is said to be "trading at a discount." *Example:* $1,000 par value – $960 market value = $40 discount.

- *Premium.* If a bond's market price rises above its par value, the bond is said to be "trading at a premium." *Example:* $1,040 market value – $1,000 par value = $40 premium.

- *Yield to maturity.* Yield calculation that accounts for any premium or discount paid to buy bonds.

KEY CONCEPT

Types of Bonds

There is a wide variety of bonds available to investors. Here are the major categories:

1. *Corporate bonds.* Issued by U.S. and foreign corporations. The primary types are *debentures* (backed by corporation's good faith and credit), *collateralized bonds* (secured by a lien on property), *convertible bonds* (can be converted into the company's stock), *high-yield bonds* (high yield but lower quality), and *asset-backed bonds* (backed by pools of assets such as car loans).

2. *U.S. government and government agency bonds.* These include U.S. Treasury notes and bonds, Government National Mortgage Association (GNMA, or Ginnie Mae), Federal Home Loan Mortgage Corporation (FHLMC, or Freddie Mac), and the Federal National Mortgage Association (FNMA, or Fannie Mae), among others. Treasury notes and bonds are backed by the U.S. Treasury, as are GNMAs. FNMAs and FHLMCs are backed by their issuing institutions, but are still considered very safe bonds.

3. *Municipal bonds.* State governments, agencies, and local municipalities also borrow to fund their operations. Bonds sold by governmental units at the state level and below are known as *munis.* The interest paid on municipal bonds is generally exempt from federal income taxes and from most state and local income taxes in the state of issue. (Some municipal bonds are considered taxable when calculating the alternative minimum tax, but most municipal bonds avoid this treatment.) There are several types of municipal bonds; *general obligation* (backed by issuer's taxing authority), *revenue bonds* (backed by a specific project), and *insured municipals* (carry third-party insurance to guarantee interest and principal payments).

If you are in the 28 percent marginal tax bracket or higher, consider municipal bonds. Because these bonds offer federal, and possibly state, income tax exemption, their after-tax equivalent yields can be very competitive with those of taxable bonds. To calculate the taxable equivalent yield of a municipal, divide the bond's tax-free yield by 1 minus your tax rate. *Example:* You are in the 28 percent federal tax bracket and can choose between a 5 percent municipal bond or a fully taxable 6.5 percent corporate bond. The muni's taxable equivalent yield is .05 ÷ (1 − .28) = .0694, or 6.94

percent, so the municipal has the higher equivalent yield. You can calculate a taxable bond's tax-exempt equivalent yield by reversing the process: Taxable yield × (1 – tax rate) = tax exempt yield. Using the same numbers, .065 × (1 – .28) = .0468, or 4.68 percent.

KEY CONCEPT — Pricing Bonds

A bond's price is the present value of its future interest payments and principal payoff. Because present value calculations use interest rates, this introduces the major source of variability in bond prices: changing interest rates. To calculate a present value for a future sum, you discount it back to today using a *discount rate*. Here is an example. If you assume a 6 percent interest rate, the present value of $1,000 to be received in one year is $1,000 ÷ 1.06 = $943.40. In other words, the future amount of $1,000 is worth $943.40 today. If you raise the discount rate to 7 percent, the present value of the (future) $1,000 falls to $934.58 ($1,000 ÷ 1.07). If the discount rate falls to 5 percent, the present value of the (future) $1,000 increases to $952.38.

This discounting process is applied to a bond's future interest payments and its final principal payoff. It leads to several important implications for bond investors:

- Prices of long-term bonds change more than those of short-term bonds for a given change in interest rates.
- Prices of zero-coupon bonds change more than those of standard bonds that make regular interest payments.

Because long-term bonds are more volatile than short-term bonds, investors usually demand a higher yield for longer maturities.

KEY CONCEPT — Risks of Bond Investments

Several risk factors can prevent bond investors from receiving the return they expect in the form of cash flows. A discussion of each follows.

Default

If the bond issuer fails to make timely interest and principal payments, the issuer is in default. Some bond issuers buy insurance from third parties to make these payments if the issuer cannot, but most bonds are uninsured, so the investor must rely on the issuer's creditworthiness. Several firms, including Standard & Poor's and Moody's, rate the ability of bond issuers to repay their debts, using a rating scale to evaluate firms. Standard & Poor's uses the following rating scale:

AAA (best quality).

AA (high quality).

A (high-medium quality).

BBB (medium quality).

BB (some speculative element).

B (able to pay now, but some risk of default in the future).

CCC (poor quality).

CC (highly speculative).

C (lowest rated).

Moody's rating scale is similar, ranging from Aaa for top quality to D for bonds in default. Yields increase as bond ratings drop—in other words, investors in lower-rated bonds require a higher return to compensate for the greater risk that the issuer might default.

Unless you have access to research about a bond issuer's financial status, restrict your direct bond investments to higher-quality issues. The first four categories (AAA to BBB) are considered *investment grade* issues, and you should be able to find suitable bonds in those categories. If you decide to invest in lower-rated issues, use a mutual fund or bond investment firm that specializes in these bonds.

Higher Rates

All bond investors face this risk. If rates move higher, the value of your bonds will drop. A bond's *duration* measures its sensitivity to changes in interest rates. As an example, a bond with a duration of 5 will drop 5 percent in price if interest rates move up by 1 percent. Conversely, if rates fall 1 percent, that same bond's price will rise 5 percent. If you plan to hold a bond until it matures, however, interest rate changes during the intervening period are much less important. By holding the bond until it matures, you receive its par value, avoiding the problem of selling the bond when it might be trading at a discount.

Unless yields on long-term bonds are significantly higher than those on short- and intermediate-term issues, it usually makes sense for the individual investor to avoid the longer-term issues. This is *not* because of the pseudorisk mentioned earlier: "The bonds will outlive me." Shorter-term bonds are less volatile than longer-term issues, and the yield differential between them is often quite small. Why accept the additional volatility of long-term issues unless they offer a substantially higher yield?

Inflation

Even if interest rates remain steady, inflation is a serious problem for bond investors and all other fixed-income investors. The interest payments from most bonds are fixed, and the payoff at maturity is generally limited to the bond's par value. But inflation and prices are not fixed, which means that each year the bond's interest payment can buy less. The impact is even more dramatic for principal payments that are in the distant future. For example, if inflation averages 2.5 percent, an item that costs $1.00 today will cost $1.45 in 15 years. Approaching it from the another perspective with the same inflation rate, a bond's $1,000 par value will have the purchasing power of just $690 in 15 years. You should evaluate bonds on the basis of their *real* (after-tax, after-inflation) return.

 Do not confuse a guarantee of *principal* with a guarantee of *purchasing power.* As the inflation illustration shows, bonds offer little protection against inflation. A bond will return your principal at maturity, but that principal probably will buy less than it did when the bond was issued. Most investors need to offset inflation's impact with other assets, such as stocks and real estate.

 ### Investing in Bonds

Individuals who want to invest in bonds directly face several challenges. First, most bonds trade over the counter and are *not* listed in the financial pages, making it difficult to price an issue accurately. Also, if a bond has not traded recently, the broker can give only an approximate price, unless a very similar bond is in the broker's inventory. Second, among dealers, bonds trade in large blocks. In some institutional bond markets, trades of $1 million are considered the minimum. At the retail level, bonds usually move in minimum blocks of five, or $5,000 par value, although most dealers prefer larger multiples of 5 ($15,000, $25,000, etc.). This emphasis on large transactions can create a liquidity problem for small investors by making it more difficult or costly to trade small numbers of bonds.

The institutional nature of the bond market has led many financial publications and advisors to recommend that investors avoid direct bond investments and use indirect methods such as mutual funds. Direct bond investments have several advantages, however:

1. *Control.* Direct investors choose the issues that meet their yield, maturity, and quality specifications. In a mutual fund, that control is handed over to the fund manager. While the direct investor may be forced to compromise on some details if the dealer

cannot locate a particular bond, a close substitute usually can be found.

2. *Costs.*   Direct investors usually pay commissions to buy and sell bonds, but they do not pay annual fund management fees. Over the long term, these management fees will be substantially higher than any buy-sell commissions.

3. *Liquidity.*   There is a popular notion that small lots of bonds (less than $20,000) are difficult to buy and sell. Small-block liquidity is influenced by several factors, including the state of supply and demand in bond dealers' inventories. These inventories change daily, and if a particular dealer has a large number of bonds like yours, the price he or she offers for your bonds will fall. If the dealer has low inventory and needs bonds, you will see a better offer for your bonds.

4. *Diversification.*   If you invest in high-quality or insured bonds, you can minimize the risk of default. For example, if you have $20,000 to invest, you could spread the funds among four issuers at roughly $5,000 per bond. While a small number of bonds will not give you the same degree of diversification as a mutual fund that might hold over 100 bonds, it will serve as a good foundation for building a bond portfolio. As the dollar amount of your bond portfolio grows, you can easily diversify your holdings even more.

Because bond dealer's inventories are constantly changing, working with a good broker is an invaluable aid to finding the right bonds. A broker can alert you when a suitable bond comes into inventory and can keep you abreast of new issues. If possible, work with more than one broker, because the depth and quality of dealers' inventories can vary considerably, depending on the resources the firm devotes to retail bond trading. Commissions and price markups also vary among firms, so ask how much it will cost you to buy a bond before you commit any funds.

Some bonds are very complex, and you should not invest in them directly unless you have a thorough understanding of the security and the market. These categories include high-yield junk bonds, collateralized mortgage obligations (CMOs), and foreign bonds. Access these markets through mutual funds or bond account managers.

KEY CONCEPT   **Inflation-Indexed Bonds**

In early 1997 the U.S. Treasury began offering 10-year-maturity Treasury inflation-protection securities (TIPS), with plans to introduce five-year notes later in the year. As previously discussed, inflation reduces the real return on bonds significantly. TIPS are designed to protect the investor against inflation by providing a periodically adjusted (every six months) return that will reflect changes in the Consumer Price Index (CPI). Every six months, the TIPS' principal is adjusted by an amount equal to the CPI. Figure 15.2 compares a traditional (nonindexed) 10-year bond with a 5.60 percent coupon to a 3 percent TIP with 2 percent inflation. Although both bonds pay interest semiannually, the illustration assumes annual payments.

There is a drawback to TIPS that makes them better suited for tax-deferred accounts such as IRAs and other retirement plans. Investors receive cash payments based on the bond's fixed interest rate. The inflation adjustments on the principal, and the resulting increase in interest payments, are accrued until the bond matures, at which time they are paid out. In a tax law quirk, however, income taxes must be paid on *total changes* in the bond's value, not just on the cash received. If the bonds

FIGURE 15.2 CONVENTIONAL BONDS VERSUS INDEXED BONDS.

Conventional Bonds

Year	Nominal Value of Principal	Real Value of Principal	Nominal Interest Payment	Real Interest Payment
1	$1,000	$980.39	$50.60	$49.61
2	1,000	961.17	50.60	48.64
10	1,000	820.35	50.60	41.51

Indexed Bonds

Year	Nominal Value of Principal	Real Value of Principal	Nominal Interest Payment	Real Interest Payment
1	$1,020.00	$1,000	$30.60	$30.00
2	1,040.40	1,000	31.21	30.00
10	1,218.99	1,000	36.60	30.00

Summary Comparison

	Conventional Bond	Indexed Bond
Total nominal receipts	$1,506.00	$1,554.07
Real value of principal at maturity	820.35	1,000.00

Source: "Inflation-Indexed Bonds: How Do They Work?" FRB Philadelphia Business Review, Jeffrey W. Wrase, p. 5.

are held in a tax-deferred account, this taxation of "phantom" CPI-related income will not be a problem. If the CPI drops, your bond's principal will also fall, but not below the bond's face value.

 Several mutual fund groups, including Dreyfus, PIMCO, and Twentieth Century/Benham have announced plans to offer TIPS mutual funds. If you plan to buy and hold these bonds, especially in a retirement account, you can avoid the funds' management fees by buying from the Treasury through a Treasury Direct account. Call the Federal Reserve office nearest you for details on opening an account, or contact the Bureau of Public Debt at 202-874-4000 to request the paperwork.

Inflation reduces municipal bonds' purchasing power just as it does with taxable bonds, so it is natural to assume that muni investors would be interested in inflation indexing. In early 1997, two Florida municipalities, Orlando and Gulf Breeze, introduced inflation-indexed municipal bonds modeled after the TIPS. The 10-year Orlando bonds pay an adjustable tax-exempt rate of 1.25 percent plus the rate of inflation over the preceding six months. It remains to be seen if other municipalities will also experiment with inflation indexing.

STOCKS

It is safe to assume that the average investor who thinks about the investment markets thinks first of the stock market. The stock market no longer concerns only the wealthy; employees whose retirement plans are invested in stocks track the market as well. This focus on stocks is understandable when you consider the U.S. stock market's performance in recent decades. Over the period from 1977 through 1997, the Standard & Poor's 500 Index increased *almost 1,000 percent.* That means a $1,000 investment in the index made in early 1977 was worth over $9,300 by September 1997. The same $1,000 investment made in 1987 would have grown to almost $6,500. Compare that performance to the results earned from investing in gold, whose price peaked in 1980 at $900 per ounce. A $1,000 investment in gold grew to only $1,570 over the years 1977 to 1997, and if you had bought $1,000 of gold in 1987, it would have been worth only $834 in 1997.[1] This section provides an introduction to stocks, focusing on direct investment where the investor buys individual securities.

A Common Stock's Timeline

KEY CONCEPT

Stocks represent partial ownership (equity) in a corporation. If you own 20 percent of a corporation's stock, you have a claim to 20 percent of the company's assets and profits. If you own more than 50 percent of the stock, you have effective control of the business. Unlike an investment in bonds, owning stock does not mean you will receive regular income. Another difference between stocks and bonds is that common stock has no maturity date. While the company can buy back shares and retire them, there is no predetermined maturity date for the shares. So you cannot plan on a date when the company will redeem your shares and return your original principal to you.

It is important to recognize that the stock market's performance over a period, as measured by an index such as the S&P 500, does *not* mean that all stocks have done as well as the index. While the overall market saw outstanding results between 1977 and 1997, some stocks performed poorly and other companies went bankrupt. An index measures some form of weighted performance for a large number of stocks, not individual issues.

Don't assume that the market's strong performance since 1977 has always seen a steady increase in stock prices. On October 19, 1987, the market, as measured by the Dow Jones Industrial Average, dropped 23 percent *in a single day.* Ten years later, in late October 1997, the Dow fell by 554.26 points, losing 7.18 percent of its value. When viewed from a long-term perspective, the stock market has done very well. In any given short-term period, though, its performance can be very choppy.

Stock Terminology

Stocks have their own language, and if you don't understand the phrases, it is difficult to track the markets. Here are the key terms used to describe stock investing:

- *Bear market.*   An extended period of declining stock prices.
- *Bull market.*   An extended period of rising stock prices.
- *Blue chips.*   Largest, most widely recognized publicly traded companies.
- *Correction.*   A brief period of declining stock prices.
- *Dividends.*   Distributions of earnings (usually in cash) to shareholders. Larger companies frequently pay quarterly dividends.
- *Earnings per share (EPS).*   Net income available to shareholders divided by the number of common stock shares outstanding.

- *Initial public offering (IPO).* A company's first-time sale of shares to investors.
- *Price-to-earnings ratio (P/E ratio).* A company's price per share of common stock divided by its earnings per share.
- *Penny stock.* A stock that sells for less than $1 per share.
- *Rally.* A brief period of rising stock prices.
- *Round lot.* Stocks usually trade in multiples of 100 shares. Trades that are not a multiple of 100 shares are called odd lots.
- *Stock split.* An increase in the number of a corporation's shares with no change in the overall value of the shares.

Types of Stocks

Stocks are frequently grouped into several major categories, as follows:

- *Consumer stocks.* Companies that make products for consumers. Consumer *durables* are products with long lives (such as home appliances). Consumer *nondurables* have short lives (cosmetics and food, for example).
- *Cyclical stocks.* Company stocks that closely track the economy (for example, hotel stocks, because in a healthy economy, people tend to travel more, increasing the demand for hotel rooms, and vice versa).
- *Growth stocks.* Companies with above-average growth of sales and earnings (such as stocks of successful high-tech companies).
- *Income stocks.* Companies that pay above-average dividends (utilities, for example).
- *Large caps (large capitalization).* Companies whose stock value (number of outstanding shares times price per share) is greater than $1 billion.
- *Mid-caps.* Stock value from $500 million to $1 billion.
- *Small caps.* Stock value less than $500 million.

Risks of Stock Investments

Several factors can cause a stock to underperform. Some of these causes relate directly to company performance while others reflect the influence of the economy and the markets.

1. *Earnings disappointment.* Analysts at brokerage firms predict quarterly earnings for the stocks they cover. If a firm fails to produce the expected earn-

ings, investors frequently sell their shares after the earnings announcement, causing a sharp drop in the stock's price.

2. *Currency fluctuations.*   Many firms sell much of their output to buyers in overseas markets. If these sales are denominated in foreign currencies, changes in those currencies can affect the U.S.-based firm's performance. For example, a rise in the dollar's value relative to a foreign currency makes dollar-denominated goods more expensive in the foreign market.

3. *Changes in interest rates.*   Stock investors pay close attention to interest rates because higher interest rates can slow the economy, which translates to lower sales and profits. If you listen to or read the financial news, you frequently will find statements such as, "The stock market followed the bond market higher today." Changes in interest rates affect an investor's outlook for the markets, and this outlook influences all stock prices.

4. *Changes in industry outlook.*   Stocks are grouped by industry: personal computer software, oil drilling, and so on. Good or bad news about a prominent stock in an industry often has a spillover effect on the other stocks in the group. For example, if the major firm in a group is the first to report its earnings, and those earnings are above expectations, analysts frequently increase their estimates for the group's other stocks, leading to price increases.

5. *Changes in the overall market.*   In the short term, it is difficult for a stock to go against a strong trend in the market. If 90 percent of stocks fall on a particular day, it is more difficult for a stock's price to increase than it would be on a day when 90 percent of all stock prices rise.

The traditional measure of a stock's risk, or volatility, is *beta,* which is a statistic that indicates how closely a stock's performance tracks the S&P 500. Stocks that follow the S&P 500's changes very closely will have a beta of roughly 1.0. If a stock's price changes relatively less than the S&P 500's change, the stock's beta will be less than 1.0, and if the stock's price moves more than the S&P 500's change, its beta is greater than 1.0. Stock advisory services such as Value Line and Standard and Poor's also provide measures of a stock's risk, usually based on a relative scale of low to high risk.

While it is important to recognize the volatility of an individual stock, a more valuable measure is the stock's impact on your overall portfolio's risk level. It is likely that a stock's contribution to your portfolio's volatility will be considerably less than you might assume, even for very volatile stocks.

KEY CONCEPT **Investing in Stocks**

It is easy for the individual investor to buy stocks. Open an account with a brokerage firm and you are ready to trade. You can also contact a growing number of firms that sell their shares directly to investors. After investing, you can track most stocks' prices on-line or through the newspaper.

Some advisors recommend that small investors avoid direct stock purchases and place their funds in the market through mutual funds. The arguments in favor of mutual funds are professional management and instant diversification. This is good advice in many situations, particularly for foreign stock markets or if the investor does not have the time or inclination to research individual stocks. The diversification issue is particularly important, because it generally takes at least 15 to 20 separate issues for a stock portfolio to achieve adequate diversification.

Assuming you have the resources to build a diversified stock portfolio, however, direct stock investments have several advantages:

1. *Control.*   The direct investor chooses the issues that meet his or her specifications. In a mutual fund, that control is handed over to the fund manager. The investor also decides when to sell individual stocks and therefore has more control over the tax impact of the transaction.

2. *Costs.*   The direct investor usually pays commissions to buy and sell stocks, but does not pay annual fund management fees. Over the long term, these management fees will be substantially higher than any buy-sell commissions.

3. *Diversification.*   The mutual-fund-or-direct-stock-purchase decision does not require an either-or response. By combining the two methods, a direct stock investor can achieve greater diversification, even in the early stages of building a portfolio. For example, assume that you have $20,000 available to invest, which is a small account by most standards. You could divide the funds among a broad-based index fund (discussed in Chapter 17) and individual stocks. In a 50/50 split, you would invest $10,000 in the index fund and $10,000 in several moderately priced stocks (less than $40 per share, for instance). This solution does not offer the same diversification as investing 100 percent in mutual funds, but it does improve the portfolio's overall mix. Also, don't overlook your retirement plan investments when evalu-

ating your portfolio. If those assets are diversified, you may have more freedom to invest more aggressively in your direct stock purchases.

As will be discussed in later chapters, PC-based investment management software and the growth of on-line research and trading have benefited the small investor tremendously. There is a wealth of powerful, relatively inexpensive tools available today to help investors who want to make their own investment decisions.

Don't underestimate the potential volatility of individual stocks, especially those in high technology or other hot areas that trade over the counter. To convince yourself just how volatile stocks can be, look at the *Wall Street Journal*'s "Price Percentage Losers" column for the NASDAQ market. You are likely to find several stocks that lost 20 percent or more of their value *in a single day.* If you decide to buy stocks directly, be prepared for sudden price movements—up or down.

END POINT

Bonds and stocks traditionally have formed the foundation for most U.S.-based investors' portfolios. Given the size and diversity of the markets for these securities, an experienced investor can design a portfolio to meet almost any investment need. For the novice investor, it's important to recognize the potential risks of investing in these securities. It is easy to get swept up in the enthusiasm of the bull markets that have prevailed in the United States in recent years, but you must understand and accept the risks that accompany those returns.

16

Other Investments

The previous chapters in this section focused on the traditional asset classes of stocks, bonds, and cash. While these assets form the foundation of many portfolios, there are other asset classes and investments available. This chapter briefly reviews several of those alternative investments and discusses the pros and cons of each.

VARIABLE ANNUITIES

KEY CONCEPT
Technically, variable annuities (VAs) are not a distinct category of investments; they are essentially mutual funds wrapped inside an insurance company contract. VAs have become very popular in the 1990s, with sales of roughly $70 million for 1996.[1] It is easy to understand VAs' attractiveness: All investment gains in the contract's value grow tax deferred until withdrawal, at which point any growth is taxed as ordinary income. Traditional mutual funds can generate substantial tax liabilities, even when the investor reinvests all distributions, but the growth in VA accounts enjoys the same tax-deferred treatment as IRAs and other retirement plans.

Proponents of VAs point to several benefits that the contracts provide investors[2]:

- *Tax-deferred growth.*
- *Tax-free switching* among the funds in the VA.
- *Unlimited contributions.* There are no annual limits as with IRAs and pension plans.

- *Asset protection* from creditors in many states.
- *Guaranteed death benefit.* Many contracts guarantee that the beneficiaries will not receive less than the original investment.
- *Expenses are fixed* for life of contract.
- *Proceeds avoid probate* because investor names a beneficiary.
- *Tax-favored distributions.* Part of distributions is considered return of principal and is not taxed.

Critics point to several drawbacks of VAs:

- *Marketing costs.* Many VAs are sold by commissioned salespeople, which increases the contract's expenses.
- *Mortality charges.* Issuers charge an annual insurance premium against each contract to pay for the guaranteed death benefit.
- *Early withdrawal penalty.* Investors under age 59½ may be subject to a 10 percent penalty on withdrawal of gains.
- *Surrender charges.* Many VAs charge investors a surrender fee if they withdraw more than 10 percent of the account's value in the early years.
- *Loss of capital gains.* All growth withdrawn from the VA is treated as ordinary income, even if the growth was generated by capital gains in the account's funds.
- *Loss of basis step-up.* At the investor's death, all gains remaining in the annuity are treated as ordinary income. In contrast, traditional mutual funds can receive a step-up in basis, which is beneficial to the heirs.
- *Limited choice of investment selections.* VA investors can select only from the funds offered in the contract. Traditional fund investors can choose from a much wider selection.

The analyses to decide if a VA is more appropriate than a traditional mutual fund depend on the investor's situation and the assumptions used in the analyses. These assumptions include the investor's pre- and postretirement tax rates, the amount and type of fund distributions, the amount and timing of annuity withdrawals, and so on. In some cases the VA's benefits outweigh its drawbacks, but in other cases a traditional fund is the better selection. Two recent events have reduced the VA's attractiveness considerably, however: the emergence of tax-managed funds and the lower capital gains rates introduced by the 1997 Tax Act.

TAX-MANAGED FUNDS

Mutual funds report their returns on a pretax basis, but investors in nonqualified accounts (i.e., outside of retirement plans) must pay income taxes on fund distributions. These after-tax returns are roughly 15 percent lower than pretax returns, with the results varying by fund category.[3]

In response to fund investors' concerns over taxes' impact on net returns, several fund companies have developed tax-managed funds. By using a combination of accounting and investment strategies, these funds aim to minimize realized gains, which are taxable to shareholders, while maximizing unrealized gains, which are not taxable. Figure 16.1 compares the performance of a $10,000 investment in a tax-managed fund and a non-tax-managed fund, using the following assumptions[4]:

1. Funds return 10 percent annually (7 percent price appreciation and 3 percent taxable dividends).

2. Distribution: 50 percent taxed as ordinary income; 25 percent taxed at 28 percent rate; remaining 25 percent taxed at long-term 20 percent rate.

3. Investors in 28 percent federal tax bracket.

Figure 16.1 demonstrates how a tax-managed fund can benefit long-term investors, who are the target market for variable annuities. In practice, several tax-managed funds offered by Charles Schwab & Co. (800-266-5623) and the Vanguard Group (800-635-1511) have avoided paying *any* distributions to investors in recent years, despite earning solid returns. Each firm offers several tax-managed funds with different investment objectives.

To date, these funds have produced tax-deferred gains while avoiding the VAs' fees and withdrawal restrictions. More important, though, shareholders in these funds will benefit from the 1997 Tax Act's reduction in long-term capital gains rates when they sell their shares. Depending on the fund investor's tax bracket at the time of sale, he or she will pay a *maximum* of 20

FIGURE 16.1 THE VALUE OF TAX EFFICIENCY.

	5 years	10 years	20 years	30 years
Tax-managed fund	$14,743	$22,094	$51,150	$120,950
Non-tax-managed fund	14,523	21,247	46,154	101,348
Tax-managed advantage	$ 220	$ 847	$ 4,996	$ 19,602
Tax-managed advantage (%)	1.5%	4.0%	10.8%	19.3%

percent on long-term gains, while taxpayers in the 15 percent bracket will pay just 10 percent. (Those rates fall to 18 percent and 8 percent, respectively, for assets acquired after January 1, 2001, and held for at least five years.) Although future tax rates are unpredictable, VA investors will pay the ordinary income rate for their bracket when they make withdrawals. This combination of lower capital gains tax rates and the emergence of tax-managed funds significantly reduces VAs' relative attractiveness. Unless a VA meets an investor's non-tax-related needs in some truly unique fashion, there are no longer compelling reasons to invest in a VA.

The T. Rowe Price company offers a free software program (The T. Rowe Price Variable Annuity Analyzer) that lets investors compare VA investments with traditional mutual fund accounts. The program is easy to use, and it allows the user to create multiple scenarios for analysis. You can request a copy by calling 800-469-5304.

INVESTMENT REAL ESTATE

Real estate has made many investors wealthy. Contrary to what some investors believe, however, it is possible to lose money in real estate. Although property values might not experience the daily volatility of the securities markets, real estate prices can drop for extended periods. This section reviews the basic methods of real estate investing and examines the benefits and risks of each method. The material covers *direct investments,* in which the investor holds some form of title to an investment property, and *indirect investments,* such as real estate investment trusts (REITs), real estate mutual funds, and limited partnerships.

Direct Real Estate Investment

In a direct investment, the investor holds title to a property as evidence of ownership. Investors typically own property either *individually, jointly* with other owners, or through a *partnership.* General categories of investment property include land, residential (single- and multiple-family dwellings), and commercial.

Direct real estate investments offer several potential benefits:

- Potential increase in value.
- Benefits of leverage. Using borrowed funds can increase the return on the property owner's invested (nonborrowed) funds.
- Favorable tax treatment. The IRS allows real estate investors to depreciate, or write off, part of their in-

vestment in a property (not including land). This reduces the property's taxable income, even though depreciation is a noncash expense. Investors can also deduct mortgage interest and property taxes.

- Potential for positive cash flow.
- Investor's ability to add value to a property.

Figure 16.2 offers a simplified example of the potential tax and cash flow benefits from an investor's second year of owning residential real estate. The example assumes that the rental property cost $100,000, of which $15,000 is attributable to the land's value. The investor borrows $70,000 on a 15-year mortgage at 8.5 percent, resulting in monthly mortgage payments of $684. In the mortgage's second year, roughly $5,604 of the total payments will be interest expense, which is deductible. The IRS allows investors to depreciate the building over 27.5 years, which works out to 3.636 percent of the building's value per year. This allows the investor to claim a $3,091 depreciation expense each year. Finally, the property generates $9,600 of rental income and an additional $3,000 of expenses (taxes, insurance, maintenance, etc.).

The example in Figure 16.2 is simplistic, but it illustrates several key points. For tax purposes, the property creates a deductible loss of $2,095. If the investor is in the 28 percent bracket, this loss results in a tax savings of $587 ($2,095 × .28). But the economic reality is that the property generated a positive cash flow of $996. The combined effect of the tax savings and the positive cash flow produces a net benefit to the investor of $1,587. (The annual IRS allowance on rental real estate tax losses as demonstrated in this example is $25,000. That amount is phased out as the investor's modified adjusted gross income increases from $100,000 to $150,000. Also, the investor must *actively participate* in the property's management to claim the loss.)

A return of $1,587 on a $100,000 property may not seem impressive, but that figure does not include the

FIGURE 16.2 REAL ESTATE INVESTMENT.

	Tax Return	Cash Flow
Rents	$9,600	$9,600
Less depreciation	– 3,091	– 0
Less interest	– 5,604	– 5,604
Less other expenses	– 3,000	– 3,000
Net	–$2,095	$ 996

property's appreciation and the impact of leverage. Recall that the investor used only $30,000 of personal funds to buy the property—the balance was mortgaged. If you assume the property's value increased by 3 percent ($3,000) over the year, the return on the *investor's funds* becomes: (tax savings + cash flow + appreciation) ÷ investment, or ($587 + $996 + $3,000) ÷ $30,000, which equals 15.3 percent.

Cash flow and appreciation from real estate investments are *not* guaranteed. Rents may be lower than expected, expenses may be higher, and in a weak market, a property's price can decrease. As with stock investments, real estate investors benefit from a long-term perspective that recognizes the short-term uncertainty of the property's return.

Direct real estate investments also have disadvantages:

- *Complexity.* Properly evaluating an investment in property requires effort and knowledge of the local markets. Owners of residential or commercial rental properties must also deal with local regulations and other legal issues.

- *Size of initial investment.* Down payments, closing costs, and other start-up expenses frequently total $25,00 or more. While it may be possible to reduce the initial cash outlay by borrowing additional funds, using greater leverage increases the investment's financial risk.

- *Management.* Managing property to maintain its value requires time and additional funds. The investor can hire a manager, but that increases expenses, reducing net income from the property.

- *Risk.* Several variables affect a real estate property's return: cash flows (rent and expenses), appreciation, tax laws (which are subject to change), and local property values. Unexpected changes in these variables will change the property's return.

- *Lack of liquidity.* In contrast to traded securities, it is much more difficult to sell property on short notice without accepting a reduction in price. Even in good market conditions, property transactions can require several months.

Among direct real estate investments, purchasing undeveloped land is the most speculative method because the investment usually results in a negative cash flow. Nonagricultural land generates no cash income but continues to incur property taxes. Occupied rental property is less risky, since the rental incomes are predictable for at least the term of the leases.

This section provides a very brief introduction to the potential risks and benefits of direct investments in real estate. Should you decide to investigate real estate, plan on substantial research to determine a property's value, its economic potential, and the pros and cons of ownership. If you do not have sufficient time for property evaluation and management, consider working with an experienced investor as a partner. Teaming up with another investor could speed your learning process considerably. Whatever method you take, be cautious. You can sell most securities immediately after purchasing them if you decide you've made a mistake, but unloading a bad real estate investment is not that simple.

Indirect Real Estate Investments

The three major categories of indirect real estate investments are *limited partnerships, real estate investment trusts* (REITs), and *real estate mutual funds.* These investments add some of real estate's diversification benefits to a portfolio without requiring the investor to take an active role in property selection and management.

Limited partnerships (LPs) are an investment form in which the investors act as limited partners. A general partner, usually a subsidiary of a real estate investment and management company, controls the partnership's investment decisions. Investors buy their partnership interests through a securities firm, and large LPs can have thousands of individual investors. LPs developed a poor reputation in the 1980s when many programs failed to return their projected results. As a form of investment, however, the LP is still viable. Its advantages include the following:

- *Small initial investment.* Investors can buy partnerships units for a modest investment, with minimum initial investments often starting at $5,000 or less.

- *No property management required.* The general partner is responsible for all aspects of property selection and management.

- *Limited legal liability.* The LP format limits an investor's potential liability to the amount he or she has invested.

- *Professional management.* The general partner usually has substantial experience with real estate investing.

- *Diversification.* A large LP may buy over a dozen properties in different real estate markets.

Real estate LPs have several disadvantages:

- *Lack of control.* The investor has no influence in property selection and management decisions.

- *Fees.* LPs are sold by commissioned salespeople, and the general partner charges ongoing management fees and takes a percentage of profits. These commissions and fees reduce the investor's return.

- *Loss of tax benefits.* LPs are considered passive investments, and current tax law limits deductible losses from passive (versus active) real estate investments.

- *Lack of liquidity.* Most LPs sell at steep discounts in the secondary markets—if a market for the LP exists at all. Investors who decide to sell their LP units before the partnership terminates its activities may suffer substantial losses.

- *Investment risk.* Professional management and diversification do not guarantee profits.

Because it lacks liquidity, a limited partnership is a long-term investment, and you should plan on a 5- to 10-year (or longer) commitment of your funds. Focus your preinvestment research on the LP's management and the investment's fees and profit-sharing arrangement. Because you will not have an active voice in the LP's operation, you want an experienced and successful real estate company selecting and managing the partnership's properties. Also check the LP's fees, including sales representatives' commissions, ongoing management fees, and the division of cash flow and profits among limited and general partners. Lower commissions and fees do not guarantee a successful investment, but they increase your share of the LP's cash flows.

Real estate investment trusts (REITs) are another indirect real estate investment. Like LPs, REITs own a collection of professionally selected and operated properties. In contrast to LPs, REIT investors can trade their ownership shares on stock exchanges, giving REITs a significant liquidity advantage. As of late 1997, there were 200 publicly traded REITs, divided among three major categories[5]:

- *Equity REITs* own real estate; their revenue comes principally from rents.

- *Mortgage REITs* loan money to real estate owners. Their revenue comes principally from interest earned on their mortgage loans. Some mortgage REITs also invest in residuals of mortgage-based securities.

- *Hybrid REITs* combine the investment strategies of both equity REITs and mortgage REITs.

FIGURE 16.3 NAREIT TOTAL RETURN INDEXES FOR PERIOD ENDING SEPTEMBER 30, 1997.

	Year-to-Date	1 Year	3 Years	5 Years	10 Years
Equity	18.20%	40.47%	22.61%	18.76%	12.79%
Mortgage	13.90	34.04	33.77	19.51	8.48
Hybrid	11.21	29.84	20.24	19.13	7.13
S&P 500 Index	29.64	40.45	29.87	20.74	14.72

Source: Reprinted with the permission of The National Association of Real Estate Investment Trusts, Inc.®

REITs have generated solid results for investors in recent years, as Figure 16.3 illustrates.

Selecting REITs is similar to choosing non–real estate stocks. You should consider the management team's qualifications and the REIT's performance relative to other stocks in its group. Many brokerage firms have REIT analysts whose reports can help you identify suitable stocks.

Real estate mutual funds invest in shares of REITs and in companies with real estate operations. Many of these funds have started operating in only the past few years, making it difficult to judge their long-term performances, although the category returned an average 31 percent in 1996 and 16 percent through October 1997.[6] As with other fund investments, the critical variables to consider are risk-adjusted performance, fund management's experience, fund fees, and shareholder features.

UNIT INVESTMENT TRUSTS

KEY CONCEPT

Unit investment trusts (UITs) are fixed (non-traded) portfolios of securities, usually stocks in a specific industry or with a specific investment theme. A brokerage firm buys the targeted shares, places them in a trust, and sell units (ownership interests) in the trust to investors. The stocks are held until the trust's termination date, which is set for one to five years. UITs have become very popular in recent years, with sales of almost $25 billion for the first eight months of 1997.[7] Investors can choose from a variety of investment themes, including the "dogs of the Dow" (10 DJIA stocks with highest dividend yields), biotech companies, and top-ranked analysts' favorite stocks, among others.

UITs offer a convenient and inexpensive method for investing in specific themes by eliminating the need to buy the trust's stocks individually. (Investment minimums for IRAs start as low as $250.) The main drawback has been the trusts' fees: most brokerage firms charge a 1 percent sales load and 1.75 percent in annual management fees. Those fees appear to be headed lower, however—both Charles Schwab & Co. and Smith Barney have announced plans to introduce lower-cost UITs.

A potential drawback for UIT investors is the lack of a secondary market for the trusts. Although the selling brokerage firms claim a willingness to buy back the units from investors, this offer has not been tested in a market correction where numerous investors decide to cash out simultaneously.

CONVERTIBLE SECURITIES

Convertible securities offer features of both bonds and stocks. Like bonds, convertibles pay a fixed coupon rate and have a predetermined maturity date. During its life, the convertible can be exchanged for a fixed number of shares of the issuing company's common stock. Their risk/return profile reflects this mix of characteristics, as convertibles' average return and volatility fall between the comparable measures for traditional bonds and stocks. You can invest in convertibles through direct purchase or mutual funds.

Welder (1997) discusses several advantages and disadvantages of investing in convertibles.[8] The advantages are as follows:

- Lower volatility than common stocks.
- Higher income than stocks.
- Occasional market pricing inefficiencies.
  Disadvantages include the following:
- Less price appreciation than common stocks.
- Sensitivity to increasing interest rates.
- Less research available than for stocks and bonds.

Convertibles are more complex than traditional stock and bond investments because they combine characteristics of each. If you are unwilling or unable to research individual convertibles, invest through a mutual fund that specializes in these securities.

Convertibles are exposed to the risks that affect both the bond and stock markets. Convertibles pay fixed yields, so their prices fall when interest rates rise; because they can be converted into common stocks, their prices fall when stock prices drop. In a period of rising interest rates and falling stock prices, this can produce the worst of all possible combinations for convertibles.

COMMODITIES

Commodities are raw materials: metals, agricultural and petroleum products, and so on. These commodities trade in the *futures markets,* such as the Chicago Board of Trade, which also offer contracts on interest rates and stock indexes. Buyers and producers of these commodities use the futures markets to hedge against unexpected price changes, while investors who wish to speculate on these price changes can invest in futures contracts.

Futures contracts are *obligations* to buy or sell a commodity on a specific date for an agreed-upon price. The contracts allow investors to use a large degree of leverage, which magnifies the profit or loss on an investment. The commodities market is a professional's market, and the individual investor should not speculate in commodities without extensive research.

In late March 1997 the Oppenheimer fund company launched the Oppenheimer Real Asset Fund (800-255-2750). The fund plans to invest in notes whose prices are linked to commodity prices and indexes. As the commodities' values change, the fund's price will move in tandem. Because of its recent inception date, the fund lacks a long-term track record, but it has the potential to offer small investors ($1,000 minimum) access to the commodities' markets. Previously, the usual method for participating in professionally managed commodities funds often required a minimum investment of $50,000. The fund advisors also charged high fees and took up to 20 percent of an account's profits.

Because futures contracts have predetermined expiration dates, they should *not* form the core of your investment portfolio. Securities' prices are unpredictable in the short term, even when they follow a long-term upward trend. By investing in short-term, finite-lived contracts, you cannot rely on long-term trends to salvage your investment. You must be right about the direction of the security's moves *and* the timing of those moves. Limit investments in futures and options to disposable funds so that any losses will not reduce your net worth significantly. As an alternative to speculating with these contracts, consider a gambling vacation to Las Vegas or Atlantic City—there you can at least see a show while losing your money.

END POINT

It is possible to build a portfolio using only the traditional categories of stocks, bonds, and cash. But other investments, particularly real estate, can diversify the traditional portfolio while offering excellent potential returns. You should limit the funds you allocate to alternative investments (speculative options and futures positions) to small amounts that you can afford to lose.

Mutual Funds

When financial market historians look back at the 1990s, it would not be surprising if they classify the span as the "mutual funds decade." The U.S. stock market's strong performance benefited both the fund industry and fund investors. By late 1997, the number of funds had grown to almost 10,000, and investors frequently placed over $15 billion of new money into stock funds *in a single month.*[1] Even though numerous funds failed to match the overall market's performance, the average fund in many categories still produced an impressive performance, with the average growth generating an annualized three-year return of 25.18 percent through the third quarter of 1997. Those investors smart (or lucky) enough to be in the top-performing funds saw incredible results, with dozens of funds generating *50 percent* returns and higher for the 12 months ending with the third quarter of 1997.[2]

DANGER! Montgomery Asset Management, a San Francisco fund company, surveyed 750 fund investors in mid-1997. The survey revealed that those investors anticipated average annual returns of 34 percent on their investments over the next decade.[3] While such high returns are possible, they are extremely unlikely, considering that the average annual return for stocks has been closer to 12 percent for the past 60 years. *Do not make this mistake of assuming that stock funds' recent high returns will continue indefinitely.* If you plan for more realistic long-term average returns in the 8 to 12 percent range, for example, you are less likely to be disappointed if the market fails to maintain its torrid pace.

K E Y
CONCEPT

HOW FUNDS WORK

A mutual fund is a company that pools investors' funds with the goal of investing for a specific purpose. As an investor, you receive shares in the fund that represent your claim to a fraction of the fund's assets, liabilities, profits, and losses. In an *open-end fund,* investors buy shares directly from the fund itself, and the fund also redeems shares directly from investors who wish to sell their shares. This means that the number of shares in an open-end fund will fluctuate. A *closed-end fund* issues a fixed number of shares at its inception through an initial public offering (IPO). After the IPO, the fund's shares trade on a securities market. Investors who wish to buy shares must purchase them from a current shareholder in the market, and shareholders who wish to sell must offer their shares to another investor in the market as well.

All funds hire a portfolio manager (or multiple managers) who buys and sells the appropriate securities for the fund. The fund's goals determine the manager's investments: aggressive growth, income, stability of value, and so on. For providing these services, the fund charges its shareholders several fees, typically ranging from .50 to 2 percent in total.

You can profit from a fund investment in several ways, as the following illustration from the Vanguard Group shows. Assume that you buy shares in a fund for a cost of $50 per share. Over the next year the fund pays an income distribution of $1 per share and a capital gains distribution of $2 per share, and the value of each share increases from $50 to $52. Your *total return* per share is: (income + capital gain + appreciation) ÷ original purchase price, or ($1 + $2 + $2) ÷ $50 = 10 percent.

Distributions and price appreciation are *not* guaranteed, however. Even if the fund pays regular income distributions, capital gains and price appreciation are unpredictable, and if the fund's price per share drops, you can experience a loss.

K E Y
CONCEPT

Advantages of Funds

In addition to their recent strong performance, mutual funds offer investors several well-known advantages:

- *Professional management.* Fund companies are staffed by full-time investment managers and analysts whose goal is to find the best investments to meet the fund's objectives.

- *Diversification.* Many funds hold over 100 securities, providing instant diversification, even for small accounts.

- *Ease of management.* Fund companies have made it convenient to open accounts and make additional investments. They also provide summaries of transactions, which can be very helpful for filing tax returns.

- *Liquidity.* Investors can sell some or all of their shares on any business day, and they can move money among funds easily, usually with a single phone call.

Disadvantages of Funds

In spite of their booming popularity, funds have some drawbacks:

- *Loss of investment control.* Investors realize that they have no control over the investments that the fund manager selects, but they select a fund based on its stated investment objectives. Those objectives are generally broad enough, however, to give the manager considerable flexibility in choosing specific investments. A fund may own moderate-risk stocks when the investor first buys shares. If the manager chooses to increase the amount of high-risk stocks in the portfolio, the investor has no control over this decision. In fact, the investor may not know about the shift until several months after it has happened. This change in a fund's investment mix is known as *style drift* and is discussed in more detail later.

- *Less control of tax timing.* Fund investors do not control the timing of income or capital gains distributions. If the fund generates distributions, investors are responsible for the income taxes on their own shares, even if they reinvest the distributions.

- *Expenses.* Funds' annual fees range upward from .20 percent, with most stock funds falling in the 1 to 2 percent range. Although this cost may seem small, especially when the markets are performing well, these fees add up over time, reducing investment returns.

CLASSIFYING FUNDS: TRADITIONAL METHOD

There are several methods available for categorizing funds. The basic method is by general asset class: cash, bonds, or stocks. These classes can be further refined by the source of the securities (U.S. or foreign), issuer type (government or corporate), maturity, and risk level. Another method for classifying funds is to match the investor's investment goals with an appropriate fund class, given the investor's risk/return preferences. Figure 17.1 is an example of this classification method.

FIGURE 17.1 TYPES OF FUNDS.

Objective	Fund Type	Fund Holds	Growth Potential	Income Potential	Stability of Principal
Current income, stability of principal	Money market	Money market instruments	None	Moderate	Very high
Tax-free income, stability of principal	Tax-exempt money market	Municipal money market instruments	None	Moderate	Very high
Current income	Taxable bond	Government and corporate bonds	N/A	Moderate to high	Low to moderate
Tax-free income	Tax-exempt bond	Municipal bonds	N/A	Moderate to high	Low to moderate
Current income, capital growth	Balanced	Stocks and bonds	Moderate	Moderate to high	Low to moderate
	Equity income	High-yielding stocks, convertible securities	Moderate to high	Moderate	Low to moderate
	Growth and income	Dividend-paying stocks	Moderate to high	Low to moderate	Low to moderate
Capital growth	Domestic growth stocks	U.S. stocks with high growth potential	High	Very low	Low
	International growth stocks	Stocks of companies outside US	High	Very low to low	Very low
Aggressive growth of capital	Aggressive growth	Stocks with very high growth potential	Very high	Very low	Very low
	Small capitalization	Stocks of small companies	Very high	Very low	Very low
	Specialized	Stocks of industry sectors	High to very high	Very low to moderate	Very low to low

Source: Reprinted from Mutual Fund Basics, *p. 7, with permission of The Vanguard Group, 1998.*

THE MORNINGSTAR METHOD

The traditional method of classifying funds is a useful starting point, but as noted previously, funds usually state their investment policies in broad language. Using broad investment categories gives the fund manager flexibility, but it also makes it more difficult for investors to classify the fund properly. Funds in the same general category can have very different portfolios and risk levels, which in turn makes a direct comparison of results difficult. To help investors classify funds more accurately, *Morningstar,* the respected Chicago-based provider of mutual fund, stock, and variable insurance information, classifies funds by their investments. Stock funds are placed in a "style versus size" equity style box; municipal bond funds use a "duration versus credit quality" box; and taxable open-end bond funds have a "maturity versus quality" fixed-income style box. Figure 17.2 shows the stock fund box as it would depict a medium-cap value fund. The bond fund box in Figure 17.3 depicts a low-quality, long-duration municipal bond fund. An explanation of the style box's classes is included with each table.

SELECTING A FUND

With so many funds available, you need to develop a fund-selection strategy before you start your research or you risk being overwhelmed. The following steps will help you reduce the number of funds you should consider to a more manageable level.

Step 1. Consider your investment objectives' time horizons and your risk tolerance.
Longer time horizons and greater risk tolerance allow you to consider more aggressive funds. Use Figure 17.1 to identify appropriate categories of funds for your goals.

Step 2. Evaluate the amount of time you want to spend on your fund investments.
Mutual funds are marketed as tools for simplifying your financial life. But selecting the right funds deserves considerable attention, because the long-term impact of choosing a fund that performs poorly can be substantial. If you want to minimize the amount of time you spend selecting and managing your portfolio, consider index funds or life-cycle funds.

Index Investing

Investors track the financial markets with indexes: The Dow Jones Industrial Average and the

FIGURE 17.2 MORNINGSTAR'S EQUITY STYLE BOX.

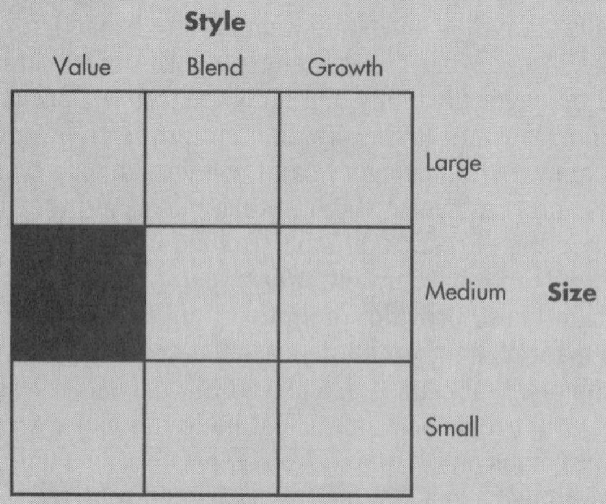

Style

Value   Blend   Growth

Large

Medium   **Size**

Small

Source: Morningstar.

Explanation of terms

Investment Style

Value: Relative price/earnings ratio plus relative price-to-book-value ratio less than 1.75.

Blend: Relative price/earnings ratio plus relative price-to-book-value ratio between 1.75 and 2.25.

Growth: Relative price/earnings ratio plus relative price-to-book value greater than 2.25.

Size

Small: Invests in companies with market capitalizations less than $1 billion.

Medium: Invests in companies with market capitalizations between $1 billion and $5 billion.

Large: Invests in companies with market capitalizations greater than $5 billion.

Standard & Poor's 500 Index are examples of two widely cited stock market indexes. Other indexes track different stock market segments, such as mid-caps, small caps, foreign stocks, or different markets, including bonds and commodities.

Indexes provide performance benchmarks. Large-cap stock funds' performances are compared to the S&P 500 index; small-cap investors compare their funds' results to the Russell 2000 Index, and so on. Many investors look for a fund that will earn better results than its comparative index—after all, fund shareholders are paying a fee for professional manage-

FIGURE 17.3 MORNINGSTAR'S FIXED-INCOME STYLE BOX.

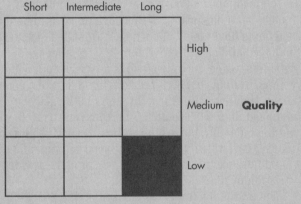

Source: Morningstar.

Explanation of terms

Quality
Low: Securities rated BB or lower.
Medium: Securities rated BBB through AA.
High: Securities rated AA or higher.

Duration (muni bond funds)
Short: Less than 3.5 years.
Intermediate: Between 3.5 and 6 years.
Long: Greater than 6 years.

Duration/maturity (taxable open-end funds)
Short: Less than or equal to 4 years.
Intermediate: Between 4 and 10 years.
Long: Greater than 10 years.

ment. Surprisingly, though, many mutual funds frequently earn lower returns than the index for their category. Much of this underperformance can be explained by the funds' expenses—management fees and trading costs, for instance. In defense of actively managed funds, there are periods when the majority of funds outperform their respective indexes. For the period from the mid-1980s to present, however, most actively managed funds' returns have trailed the indexes.

Investors' frustration with below-index results from actively managed funds has led to a boom in *index investing.* Index funds are designed to closely track the performance of a particular index. In contrast to actively managed funds, index funds use a *passive* approach in which the managers rarely trade securities; instead, they buy and hold the securities that comprise the index. This passive strategy gives index funds a significant cost advantage over actively managed funds. As an illustration of this advantage, assume that two funds hold identical portfolios. One fund is actively managed and charges investors 2 percent for its expenses, while the other fund is a passive index fund with an annual cost of .3 percent. If the portfolio generates a 10.5 percent return, investors in the actively managed fund will see an 8.5 percent return (10.5 – 2), but the index fund investors will realize a 10.2 percent return.[4] Given the impact of long-term compounding, that difference in annual results will produce a wide variation in shareholders' accounts.

The first index funds were based on the S&P 500, and that market continues to draw the largest amount of investor funds. The Vanguard Group's Index Trust 500 was the fastest-growing mutual fund in 1996, and in October 1997 the fund held over *$46 billion* of investors' assets.[5] Investors are not limited to large-cap stock index funds, though. By 1997 investors could choose from over 125 index funds that tracked over 20 stock and bond indexes.

Index funds continue to proliferate because indexing produces very respectable results in most markets, but indexing your entire portfolio is not always the best solution. There is evidence that actively managed funds regularly beat the indexes for small-cap and foreign stocks.[6] Also, investing solely in large-cap index funds that track the S&P 500 ignores the basic principle of diversification among asset classes. Index funds are an excellent foundation for any portfolio, but you should not overlook the value actively managed funds can add.

All index funds are not created equal—their expenses can vary considerably. Because funds that track the same index invest in the same securities, lower expenses will produce higher returns for investors. Use the Vanguard Group's index funds for cost benchmarks, because their index funds have some of the lowest expense ratios in the industry.

 ### Life-Cycle Funds

Another alternative to selecting and managing funds is to invest in a fund where the fund manager invests in other funds. The investment allocation is based on your selection of a broad investment goal. For example, the T. Rowe Price Spectrum Funds offer a choice of a growth, an income, or an international fund. Investments in those funds are then divided among other T. Rowe Price funds that have similar investment objectives, subject to minimum and maximum investment allocations in each subfund. The Vanguard LifeStrategy Portfolios take a similar approach. Investors can choose from four portfolios: Income, Conservative Growth, Moderate Growth, and Growth. In both cases, the life-cycle funds do not charge additional management fees above those already charged by the funds in which they invest.

KEY CONCEPT — RESEARCHING FUNDS

It is not an exaggeration to state that the amount of information available to fund investors is potentially overwhelming. As the amount of assets invested in funds has grown, so has the fund advisory and analysis business. Sources of information include newspapers, magazines, books, pamphlets and fund research publications. If you have a computer, you can use analytical fund software and visit on-line fund-selection sites. Whatever resource you use, you should focus on finding the following information:

- *Fund's investment strategy.* The fund's strategy should match the strategy you are following to reach your goals.

- *Fund's investment style.* As discussed previously, check the fund's investment style to avoid style drift.

- *Fund's risk-adjusted performance.* It is not enough to focus solely on a fund's return—you must also evaluate the amount of risk the fund manager took to achieve that return.

A fund's performance is cited for a particular time period, and changing the period can alter that performance substantially. Figure 17.4 shows how funds' 10-year records improve once the October 1987 stock market crash is dropped from the calculations.[7]

- *Volatility of fund performance.* Ideally, you want to invest in a fund that places consistently in the top half of its peer group. Also, don't overlook the fund's performance in down markets—you want a fund that holds up relatively well when the market pulls back.

- *Fund management.* Rookie fund managers can occasionally produce excellent results for their investors. But these managers frequently lack the experience of more seasoned fund managers who have experienced and survived weak markets. Stick with experienced managers unless you have a specific reason for investing with a newcomer.

- *Fund fees.* It is easy to overlook fund fees of 1 to 2 percent when you are earning high returns. That's

FIGURE 17.4 ANNUALIZED RETURNS.

Fund	9/30/87 to 6/30/97	10/31/87 to 6/30/97
American Century—		
20th Century Vista	10.6%	15.4%
Brandywine	16.2	21.6
CGM Capital Development	16.9	22.0
Delaware Trend (A shares)	14.9	20.1
Fidelity Select Brokerage	13.9	19.7
Invesco Strategic Technology	18.1	24.0
Nicholas-Applegate Growth		
Equity (A)	11.6	16.4
Oberweis Emerging Growth	14.2	19.1
Oppenheimer Capital		
Appreciation (A)	13.2	18.4
Parnassus	11.4	16.1

Source: Reprinted by permission of the Wall Street Journal, copyright © 1998 by Dow Jones & Company, Inc. All rights reserved worldwide.

unfortunate, because the long-term impact of fund fees is substantial. Figure 17.5 lists the various fees that mutual funds can charge.

Don't ignore fund fees—they reduce your net return directly. You can find information on a fund's fees from research services such as Morningstar or in the fund's prospectus in the "Fund Expenses" section.

Your research should include a review of either the *Morningstar Mutual Funds* publication (800-735-0700) or the *Value Line Mutual Fund* (800-833-0046). These publications contain a wealth of information you can use to evaluate funds. For example, the Morningstar publication contains details on the following:

- Fund performance records.
- Risk analysis.
- Portfolio analysis.
- Investment style (current and historical).
- Details on fund fees and management.
- Commentary from Morningstar analyst.

Morningstar also ranks each fund's risk-adjusted performance with its well-known star rating system. Ratings range from one star (lowest) to five stars (highest). While the star ratings cannot predict a fund's performance, they do provide insight into the fund's past performance.

FIGURE 17.5 MUTUAL FUND FEES

Type	Description
Sales charges	
Front-end load	Paid on purchase of new shares and possibly with reinvested dividends. Range from 1% to 8.5%.
Back-end load	Charged when shares are redeemed. Frequently starts at 5% or 6% and decreases by 1% each year.
Level loads	Paid annually on a continuing basis; less than 1%.
Operating expenses	Includes advisory fees paid to investment manager, administrative expenses, and marketing/distribution (12b-1) fees.
Other fees	
Exchange fees	Charge to exchange shares between funds in a fund family.
Account maintenance fees	Usually charged against small accounts.
Transaction fees	Charged on purchase or redemption of shares (not paid to sales staff).

Source: Reprinted from Mutual Fund Costs *with permission of The Vanguard Group, 1998.*

Annual subscriptions to *Morningstar Mutual Funds* and the *Value Line Mutual Fund Survey* are expensive: $425 for Morningstar and $295 for Value Line. Those prices are reasonable if you are an active fund investor with a large portfolio, but they represent an annual cost of 3 to 4 percent on a $10,000 portfolio. As an alternative to an annual subscription, take advantage of each firm's trial subscription offer, which lets you order a three-month trial subscription to each publication for about $50. Many public libraries also subscribe to one or both publications.

KEY CONCEPT FUND SUPERMARKETS

Until 1992, mutual fund investors faced a potential snag in moving money from one fund to another. While it was relatively easy and inexpensive to switch between funds within the same fund company, moving to a fund outside the company was more difficult. Some funds charged sales or redemption fees, and even when there were no fees involved, switches meant dealing with multiple fund companies, multiple transactions, and multiple statements.

Charles Schwab & Co. eliminated that problem with the introduction of its OneSource service. The OneSource program allowed investors to buy and sell over 80 funds from six fund companies at net asset value, generally without commissions, sales loads, or transaction fees. Today over 70 companies participate, and investors can choose from roughly 600 funds. Not all fund companies participate in the OneSource program, however, and transaction fees apply to some funds and short-term trades (less than 91 days). The OneSource program took the convenience of fund investing to a new level, and competitors have followed Schwab's lead. In particular, Fidelity Investment's discount brokerage arm and the Jack White & Co. brokerage firm offer a wide range of no-transaction-fee funds.

The key to selecting a fund supermarket is to evaluate it based on the criteria that are important to you:

- Availability of the funds that interest you.
- Account minimums: initial and subsequent investments.
- Automatic investment programs available?
- Costs to buy funds outside the no-fee network?
- Is buying on margin permitted?
- Is short selling permitted?
- Can you receive reports and analyses on network funds?

If you plan to invest in a fund that is part of a funds supermarket, buy it through the supermarket. It won't cost you any more than investing directly with the fund, and you also receive the additional benefits that the supermarket provides.

 **DOLLAR COST AVERAGING**

If you have a large sum available for investing, you face a decision: Should you invest in one lump sum, or should you take an installment approach where you spread the investment over time? The latter technique is known as *dollar cost averaging,* and for most investors it is the preferred method for fund investing. With dollar cost averaging you ignore the fund's price and make a regular series of investments (monthly, quarterly, and so on). This allows you to buy more shares when the price is low and fewer shares when the share price is high. Figure 17.6 shows a hypothetical example from 1987, when the stock market dropped sharply in October. The example assumes a $200 monthly investment in the S&P 500 index from January through December.

FIGURE 17.6 DOLLAR COST AVERAGING.

	Investment	S&P 500 Price	Shares Purchased	Total Shares	Total Market Value
January	$200.00	$274.08	0.7297	0.7297	$ 200.00
February	200.00	284.20	0.7037	1.4334	407.38
March	200.00	291.70	0.6856	2.1191	618.13
April	200.00	288.36	0.6936	2.8127	811.05
May	200.00	290.10	0.6894	3.5021	1,015.95
June	200.00	304.00	0.6579	4.1600	1,264.63
July	200.00	318.66	0.6276	4.7876	1,525.61
August	200.00	329.80	0.6064	5.3940	1,778.95
September	200.00	321.83	0.6214	6.0155	1,935.95
October	200.00	251.79	0.7943	6.8098	1,714.63
November	200.00	230.30	0.8684	7.6782	1,768.29
December	200.00	247.08	0.8095	8.4877	2,097.14

Source: T. Rowe Price, Dollar Cost Averaging.

In spite of the S&P 500's sharp drop in October, the investor suffered a relatively smaller loss. This example illustrates that dollar cost averaging can produce favorable results, even when the market (or fund) drops. Dollar cost averaging has the added benefit of reducing novice investors' nervousness about the markets. By investing gradually, these investors gradually raise their comfort level with the investment's changing prices.

KEY CONCEPT — CLOSED-END FUNDS

When investors redeem shares in a traditional open-end fund, they sell the shares back to the fund for their net asset value (NAV). In contrast, closed-end fund investors must sell their shares to other investors via the stock market, and they may receive more or less than the shares' NAV. This tendency for closed-end funds' market prices to vary from their NAV, and particularly the tendency to sell below NAV, has discouraged many prospective investors. That is an unfortunate reaction, because closed-end funds offer several potential benefits that fund investors should consider:

- *A variety of investments.* In the past, most closed-end funds invested in municipal bonds. Today there are roughly 500 closed-end funds with a much wider range of investments, including foreign stocks.[8]

- *Bargain prices.* When you buy a fund at a discount to its NAV, you are acquiring bargain-priced shares. For example, if a fund is trading at a 10 percent discount to its NAV, you are paying just $.90 for each $1 of fund assets.

- *Conversion feature.* The Securities and Exchange Commission now allows a closed-end fund to change status to open-end fund if it trades at a 5 percent (or higher) discount for 15 consecutive days.

- *Available research.* You can obtain research reports on closed-end funds by contacting Morningstar (800-735-0700), which has a software program that covers roughly 600 funds. The *Closed-End Fund Investor* organization (626-441-0320) also produces research reports on these funds, as does Thomas J. Herzfeld Advisors, Inc. (305-271-1900).

Besides the possibility of trading below NAV, there is another drawback to closed-end funds. Investors give up the benefits of working with an open-end fund family (automatic investment and distribution plans, switching privileges, and so on). A lack of liquidity also can be a problem if the fund does not trade very frequently in the secondary market.[9]

 CONCENTRATED FUNDS

The average stock fund holds over 125 securities, which enables the fund to offer investors instant diversification. In contrast, concentrated, or nondiversified, funds invest in 20 or fewer positions. The result is a fund that has above-average profit potential if the manager picks the right stocks—or above-average losses if the manager is wrong.

A small number of funds take the concentrated approach. These funds include Clipper (800-776-5033), Oakmark Select (800-625-6275), Sequoia (800-686-6884), Vonotobel U.S. Value (800-527-9500), and Yacktman Focused (800-525-8258).

END POINT

The stock market's strong performance since the October 1987 crash has increased the popularity of mutual funds, leading fund companies to introduce an increasing number of funds. Funds offer several advantages to investors, but they are not the ideal solution to every investor's needs. A fund's advantages and its performance record should be evaluated in light of the risks, costs, and drawbacks of investing through funds versus direct investments.

PART 4

Retirement and Estate Planning

CHAPTER

Building Your
Nest Egg

RETIREMENT REALITY

According to a 1997 survey conducted for Fidelity Investments by the Public Agenda research group, 30 percent of the respondents ages 51 to 61 have saved *less than $10,000* for their retirement.[1] Fortunately, other recent surveys have found some recent improvement in savings habits. According to the 1997 Merrill Lynch Baby Boom Retirement Index(sm), baby boomers as a group are saving 38.5 percent of the amount they will need to maintain their current standard of living when they retire. That result is an improvement of the 1996 survey's index of 35.9 percent.[2]

One reason that partly explains the difficulty in saving adequate retirement funds is the increase in life expectancies, which in turn leads to more years spent in retirement. When the Social Security Act was passed in 1935, men had an average life expectancy of 60 years and women 63 years. In contrast, a 65-year-old today can look forward to spending almost 15 years in retirement, to age 80.[3] Longer retirements require greater amounts of money, increasing the risk of underfunding.

THE BASIC STRATEGY

When you stop working, you must replace part of your salary so you can maintain your desired lifestyle. That means you must project the amount of income you will need and the amount you will have available in retirement. Unfortunately, it is difficult to make precise projections about several critical aspects of retirement:

- *Retirement expenses.* Short-term estimates (less than five years) of expenses can be reasonably accurate. Beyond that time horizon, however, estimates become less reliable.

- *Available retirement income.* The same logic applies here. If you retire next year, both the Social Security agency and your employer can give you reliable estimates of your pension benefits. For a 40-year-old, those projections are much less valid because of Social Security's instability and potential job changes over the next 20 years.

These examples illustrate the challenge of retirement planning. You will not know for certain how much income you need until you retire. But if you wait that long to project and plan for your needs, it will be too late to take corrective action. Because of the inherent uncertainty in retirement planning, you should adopt a flexible, defensive strategy. Specifically, you should (1) maintain some flexibility in terms of your desired retirement income, and (2) attempt to accumulate more assets and income than you believe you will need. This approach allows you to combine a lower-cost lifestyle with an aggressive funding approach to increase your margin for forecasting error.

 **PROJECTING RETIREMENT EXPENSES**

You might have read articles suggesting you should plan to replace 70 percent of your working-years' income in retirement. That is a reasonable suggestion for long-range planning, but it is only a starting point— *your needs may be very different, and you must examine your current spending and project your retirement expenses to develop a reliable forecast.*

Figure 18.1 provides a modified version of the expense worksheets from Chapter 1. Use it as a template for projecting your retirement expenses. The example assumes that the couple will retire in one year.

After projecting expenses for your first year in retirement, you need to consider *inflation.* Although some of your expenses will remain constant, many others will increase over time. Figure 18.2 lists the figures from Figure 18.1, adjusted upward in following years for an average 4 percent inflation rate. Note the additional $25,000 expense in year 2 under "Variable Expenses—Other." The couple in this example plan to buy a car that year and estimate it will cost $25,000.

FIGURE 18.1 PROJECTED RETIREMENT EXPENSES.

	Current	Retirement: Year 1
Fixed expenses		
Mortgage loan payments	$ 7,200	$ 0
Utilities	3,600	3,600
Property insurance	400	400
Property taxes	3,000	3,000
Medical insurance	2,000	4,000
Long-term care insurance	—	—
Other expenses	—	—
Total fixed expenses	$16,200	$11,000
Variable expenses		
Charitable contributions	$ 1,000	$ 500
Clothing	1,500	500
Education	500	1,000
Food	5,000	5,000
Gifts	2,000	2,000
Travel/vacation	2,500	4,800
Other		
Total variable expenses	$12,500	$13,800
Total expenses	$28,700	$24,800

Projecting expenses in this fashion offers an excellent opportunity to review *why* you spend your money, not just *how*. As you think about your current expenses, rank each item's importance to your lifestyle. If you need to cut back on expenses, the rankings will help you identify the least painful reductions.

PROJECTING RETIREMENT INCOME

Projecting expenses shows you how much you will need each year; your next step is to identify the sources of the income to pay those expenses. There are two generic categories: pension income and asset-based income. Figure 18.3 lists the most common sources of pension income, using the hypothetical couple's pretax figures. Social Security payments increase by 3 percent each year.

FIGURE 18.2 MULTIYEAR EXPENSE PROJECTIONS.

	Year 1	Year 2	Year 3	Year 4	Year 5
Fixed expenses					
Mortgage loan payments	—	—	—	—	—
Utilities	$ 3,600	$ 3,744	$ 3,894	$ 4,050	$ 4,211
Property insurance	400	416	433	450	468
Property taxes	3,000	3,120	3,245	3,375	3,510
Medical insurance	4,000	4,160	4,326	4,499	4,679
Long-term care insurance	—	—	—	—	—
Other expenses	—	—	—	—	—
Total fixed expenses	$11,000	$11,440	$11,898	$12,374	$12,868
Variable expenses					
Charitable contributions	$ 500	$ 520	$ 541	$ 562	$ 585
Clothing	500	520	541	562	585
Education	1,000	1,040	1,082	1,125	1,170
Food	5,000	5,200	5,408	5,624	5,849
Gifts	2,000	2,080	2,163	2,250	2,340
Travel/vacation	4,800	4,992	5,192	5,399	5,615
Other		25,000			
Total variable expenses	$13,800	$39,352	$14,926	$15,522	$16,144
Total expenses	$24,800	$50,792	$26,824	$27,896	$29,012

When you estimate your pension benefits, ask your personnel department if the plan is integrated with Social Security retirement benefits. Many firms reduce an employee's monthly pension benefit by part of the Social Security benefit the employee receives. If your plan is integrated, you should ask about your expected net (after-integration) benefit.

FIGURE 18.3 PROJECTED PENSION INCOME.

	Year 1	Year 2	Year 3	Year 4	Year 5
Social Security (H)	$10,000	$10,300	$10,609	$10,927	$11,255
Social Security (W)	10,000	10,300	10,609	10,927	11,255
Pension (H)	6,000	6,000	6,000	6,000	6,000
Pension (W)	0	0	0	0	0
Total pension income	$26,000	$26,600	$27,218	$27,854	$28,510

Compare the projected expenses in year 4 with the projected pension income and you will note that expenses exceed pretax pension income. This is not unusual for retirees, and it demonstrates the need for an additional source of income: *investment assets.* This is a broad category that includes personal retirement plans such as 401(k) accounts and IRAs, dividends, interest, and rents from assets held outside retirement plans. Incorporating these assets requires two steps. First, you project the value of the assets at reasonable rates of return. You then project the income and withdrawals of principal needed from these assets to cover any expected cash flow deficits. Figure 18.4 shows the projected values of the couple's investment assets, using the following assumptions:

- Savings account and mutual fund pay annual 3 percent income distributions.

- Mutual fund has 5 percent annual capital growth.

- $25,000 withdrawal from mutual fund to pay for new car.

- 401(k) and IRA average 8 percent annual growth.

Figure 18.5 summarizes the couple's cash flow projections for years 1 through 5.

Note that the couple's projected cash flow surplus is dwindling each year; eventually they will be forced to take additional distributions from their mutual fund and start distributions from their retirement plans.

FIGURE 18.4 PROJECTED VALUE OF INVESTMENT ASSETS.

	Year 1	Year 2	Year 3	Year 4	Year 5
Savings	$ 12,000	$ 12,000	$ 12,000	$ 12,000	$ 12,000
Mutual funds	50,000	27,500	28,875	30,319	31,835
401(k) (H)	110,000	118,800	128,304	138,568	149,654
IRA (W)	60,000	64,800	69,984	75,583	81,629
Total value	$232,000	$223,100	$239,163	$256,470	$275,118
Investment Assets:					
Income					
Savings	$ 360	$ 360	$ 360	$ 360	$ 360
Mutual funds	1,500	825	866	910	955
401(k) (H)	0	0	0	0	0
IRA (W)	0	0	0	0	0
Total income	$ 1,860	$ 1,185	$ 1,226	$ 1,270	$ 1,315

FIGURE 18.5 CASH FLOW SUMMARY.

	Year 1	Year 2	Year 3	Year 4	Year 5
Pension income	$26,000	$26,600	$27,218	$27,855	$28,510
Asset income	1,860	1,185	1,226	1,270	1,315
Asset withdrawals		25,000			
Less income taxes	0	0	0	0	0
Net income	27,860	52,785	28,444	29,125	29,825
Less projected expenses	−24,800	−50,792	−26,824	−27,897	−29,012
Net cash flow	$ 3,060	$ 1,993	$ 1,620	$ 1,228	$ 813

FUNDING TARGETS

KEY CONCEPT

As your income increases, you will find that Social Security and other pension sources replace a smaller percentage of your desired retirement income. This means you will need to fund more of your retirement income from personal investment.

The following examples illustrate one method for estimating the amount you should start saving each month to accumulate sufficient retirement funds. The key factors here are as follows:

- Retirement date: 10 years from now.
- Projected final working year's combined pretax income: $100,000.
- Retirement pretax income needed (year 1): $50,000 (50 percent).
- Current retirement savings: $100,000.
- Assumed annual rates of return: working years, 12 percent; retirement years, 8 percent.
- Assumed annual inflation rate: 4 percent (working and retirement years).
- Assumed life expectancy: 90 years (25 years in retirement).

Step 1. Estimate annual (pretax) retirement income needed.
After estimating the amount of Social Security, pensions, and employment income they will receive, combined with their reduced expenses, the couple estimate they will need to generate 50 percent of their preretirement income from their investment assets.

Line no.

1	Final annual income	$100,000
2	Replacement target	50%
3	Replacement amount	$50,000

Step 2. Estimate total funding needed.

The couple's goal is to have 50 percent of their annual preretirement income, or $50,000, available in the first year of retirement. Assuming 4 percent inflation, they will need $52,000 in year 2, $54,080 in year 3, and so on. To estimate the present value of their estimated retirement income, the couple finds the factor for 4 percent inflation and 8 percent return in Figure 18.6 (50 percent replacement income). In other words, if the couple has $412,000 available at retirement, and that money earns an annual 8 percent with inflation at 4 percent, they can withdraw the income needed each year and the fund will last until they reach age 90.

Line no.

4 *After retirement:*

5 Expected annual inflation   4%

6 Expected annual return   8%

7 Percentage factor (from Figure 18.6)   824%

8 Target amount (line 3 × line 7) $412,000

If the couple's goal were to replace 75 percent of their income, they would use the values listed in Figure 18.7.

FIGURE 18.6 AMOUNT REQUIRED TO REPLACE 50 PERCENT OF CURRENT INCOME.

Annual Inflation	Annual Return		
	6%	8%	10%
3%	905%	750%	634%
4%	1,004	824	691
5%	1,118	910	756

FIGURE 18.7 AMOUNT REQUIRED TO REPLACE 75 PERCENT OF CURRENT INCOME.

Annual Inflation	Annual Return		
	6%	8%	10%
3%	1,357%	1,125%	951%
4%	1,506	1,237	1,037
5%	1,677	1,365	1,134

Step 3. Estimate future value of existing savings.
The couple has $100,000 in retirement savings. If this amount earns an annual 12 percent return over the next 10 years, it will be worth roughly $311,000 when they retire.

Line no.		
	Working years:	
9	Existing savings	$100,000
10	Years to retirement	10
11	Expected annual return	12%
12	Future value factor (from Figure 18.8):	3.11
13	Future value of savings	$311,000
13a	Net proceeds from sale of current residence	NA

Step 4. Estimate additional savings.
The couple needs to have $412,000 (line 8) saved by retirement. Their current savings of $100,000 are projected to grow to $311,000, leaving a net amount needed of $101,000. They use Figure 18.9 to find the appropriate future value factor of 232.3 (10 years, 12 percent). Dividing the net amount needed (line 14) by the factor (line 15) tells them how much they must save each month to reach the target of $101,000.

Line no.		
14	Net amount needed (line 8 – (line 13 + line 13a))	$101,000
15	Future value factor (from Figure 18.9)	232.3
16	Monthly savings needed to meet line 14 (line 14 ÷ line 15)	$435

Retirement Projections Worksheet: Summary

Line no.		
1	Final annual income	$100,000
2	Replacement target	50%
3	Replacement amount	$50,000
4	*After retirement:*	
5	Expected annual inflation	4%
6	Expected annual return	8%
7	Percentage factor (from Figure 18.6)	824%
8	Target amount	$412,000

FIGURE 18.8 FUTURE VALUE OF $1.

Annual Return

Years	6%	8%	10%	12%
1	1.06	1.08	1.10	1.12
2	1.12	1.17	1.21	1.25
3	1.19	1.26	1.33	1.40
4	1.26	1.36	1.46	1.57
5	1.34	1.47	1.61	1.76
6	1.42	1.59	1.77	1.97
7	1.50	1.71	1.95	2.21
8	1.59	1.85	2.14	2.48
9	1.69	2.00	2.36	2.77
10	1.79	2.16	2.59	3.11
11	1.90	2.33	2.85	3.48
12	2.01	2.52	3.14	3.90
13	2.13	2.72	3.45	4.36
14	2.26	2.94	3.80	4.89
15	2.40	3.17	4.18	5.47
16	2.54	3.43	4.59	6.13
17	2.69	3.70	5.05	6.87
18	2.85	4.00	5.56	7.69
19	3.03	4.32	6.12	8.61
20	3.21	4.66	6.73	9.65
21	3.40	5.03	7.40	10.80
22	3.60	5.44	8.14	12.10
23	3.82	5.87	8.95	13.55
24	4.05	6.34	9.85	15.18
25	4.29	6.85	10.83	17.00
26	4.55	7.40	11.92	19.04
27	4.82	7.99	13.11	21.32
28	5.11	8.63	14.42	23.88
29	5.42	9.32	15.86	26.75
30	5.74	10.06	17.45	29.96

Working years:

9	Existing savings	$100,000
10	Years to retirement	10
11	Expected annual return	12%
12	Future value factor (from Figure 18.8):	3.11
13	Future value of savings	$311,000
13a	Net proceeds from sale of current residence	NA
14	Net amount needed (line 8 – (line 13 + line 13a))	$101,000

FIGURE 18.9 FUTURE VALUE OF $1 MONTHLY SAVINGS.

Annual Return

Years	6%	8%	10%	12%
1	$ 12.4	$ 12.5	$ 12.7	$ 12.8
2	25.6	26.1	26.7	27.2
3	39.5	40.8	42.1	43.5
4	54.4	56.7	59.2	61.8
5	70.1	74.0	78.1	82.5
6	86.8	92.6	98.9	105.8
7	104.6	112.9	122.0	132.0
8	123.4	134.8	147.4	161.5
9	143.5	158.5	175.5	194.8
10	164.7	184.2	206.6	232.3
11	187.3	212.0	240.9	274.6
12	211.2	242.1	278.7	322.3
13	236.6	274.7	320.6	375.9
14	263.6	310.1	366.8	436.4
15	292.3	348.3	417.9	504.6
16	322.7	389.8	474.4	581.4
17	355.0	434.7	536.7	667.9
18	389.3	483.3	605.6	765.4
19	425.7	535.9	681.6	875.3
20	464.4	592.9	765.7	999.1
21	505.4	654.7	858.5	1,138.7
22	549.0	721.6	961.1	1,295.9
23	595.2	794.0	1,074.4	1,473.1
24	644.3	872.4	1,199.6	1,672.7
25	696.5	957.4	1,337.9	1,897.6
26	751.8	1,049.4	1,490.7	2,151.1
27	810.6	1,149.0	1,659.4	2,436.7
28	873.0	1,256.9	1,845.8	2,758.6
29	939.2	1,373.7	2,051.8	3,121.3
30	1,009.5	1,500.3	2,279.3	3,529.9

15	Future value factor (from Figure 18.9)	232.3
16	Monthly savings needed to meet line 14	$435

As the example demonstrates, assumptions such as inflation rates and investment returns play an important role in retirement planning. Because these assumptions may be erroneous, you need to recalculate your projections periodically in case adjustments are needed. Review your retirement plan

annually so you have sufficient time to make any
needed corrections.

Long-term retirement projections are subject to error
because you cannot predict the key variables with
certainty. Build some flexibility into your plans by
setting acceptable target ranges for retirement income
and asset values.

ALTERNATIVE CALCULATIONS

If you prefer to avoid the previous funding
calculations, you can use Figures 18.10 and 18.11 to
make rough estimates for retirement planning. Figure
18.10 lists the amount of savings (as a percent of current annual income) needed to replace 75 percent of
your current income after you retire, based on the
number of years until you retire and your investment

FIGURE 18.10 ARE YOU SAVING ENOUGH?

Strategy	Years to Retirement							
	0	5	10	15	20	25	30	35
Aggressive	957%	675%	463%	307%	193%	109%	48%	3%
Moderate	1,046	773	558	393	268	172	98	42
Conservative	1,148	890	676	505	369	261	174	105

Source: T. Rowe Price Associates, reported in "Retirement Honing: How Much Should You Have Saved for
a Comfortable Life?" by Jonathan Clements, Wall Street Journal, January 28, 1997, p. C1. Reprinted by
permission of the Wall Street Journal, copyright © 1997 by Dow Jones & Company, Inc. All rights reserved worldwide.

FIGURE 18.11 HOW LONG WILL YOUR RETIREMENT ASSETS LAST?

Withdraw	Average Annual Rate of Return									
	1%	2%	3%	4%	5%	6%	7%	8%	9%	10%
15%	6	7	7	7	8	8	9	9	10	11
14%	7	7	8	8	9	9	10	11	11	13
13%	8	8	8	9	9	10	11	12	13	15
12%	8	9	9	10	11	11	12	14	16	18
11%	9	10	10	11	12	13	14	16	19	25
10%	10	11	12	13	14	15	17	20	26	
9%	11	12	13	14	16	18	22	28		
8%	13	14	15	17	20	23	30			
7%	15	16	18	21	25	33				
6%	18	20	23	28	36					
5%	22	25	30	41						

Source: The Vanguard Group, Investing During Retirement (New York: McGraw Hill, 1998).

strategy. Figure 18.11 shows how many years your retirement savings will last, based upon your withdrawal
rate and rate of return.

The following assumptions apply to Figure 18.10:

Investors save 8 percent of their gross salary; and
inflation averages 4 percent annually.

Aggressive strategy.   80 percent stocks, 20 percent
bonds before retirement; 65 percent stocks, 35 percent bonds after retirement.

Moderate strategy.   65 percent stocks, 35 percent
bonds before retirement; 50 percent stocks, 50 percent bonds after retirement.

Conservative strategy.   50 percent stocks, 50 percent bonds before retirement; 35 percent stocks, 65
percent bonds after retirement.

END POINT

Planning for retirement poses a unique challenge, because you will not know how much wealth you need
until you reach retirement. If you wait too long to start
planning and saving, however, it becomes almost impossible to accumulate sufficient funds. One solution is
to maintain flexibility in your plans. Set a range for
your desired income and then aim for the high end of
that range. Even if your efforts are less than 100 percent successful, this approach will help you achieve an
acceptable level of retirement income.

CHAPTER

Retirement Planning

SAVINGS STRATEGIES

CONCEPT The amounts required to fund a comfortable retirement may seem large, but the government provides tax incentives to encourage retirement savings. You should consider these incentives as you select among the retirement plan alternatives.

First Choice: Deductible and Deferred Accounts

This group includes 401(k)s, 403(b)s, and the qualified plans available to self-employeds and small businesses. These plans offer the double benefit of reducing current taxable income and growing tax deferred. If you have access to one of these plans, contribute the maximum allowed, assuming the after-tax cost will not strain your budget excessively.

Two pointers with 401(k) plans: (1) The IRS now allows employers to credit the value of unused vacation time to employee accounts. If you anticipate that you will have unused days, ask your personnel department if they will consider crediting them to your accounts. (2) Check the method your company uses for crediting the employer's matching contribution. If the company spreads out its contribution evenly over the year and you reach the maximum allowable contribution limit before year-end, you might lose out on part of the maximum employer match.

 Do not overlook the basic investment rule of diversification in your 401(k) plan. A 1996 study by the Institute of Management and Administration found that employees at 246 of the nation's largest companies kept 42 percent of their retirement plan assets in their employer's stock. A more conservative approach would be to diversify among a range of stocks and fixed-income accounts. Monitor your plan's investments and rebalance periodically as needed within the context of your overall portfolio.

Second Choice: Deductible IRAs and Roth IRAs

In 1997 Congress passed legislation introducing the Roth IRA. You can make nondeductible contributions up to $2,000 each year, and withdrawals after five years and age 59½ are tax-exempt. Congress also increased the income limits for deducting IRA contributions, making those contributions deductible for more taxpayers.

The Roth IRA will be an attractive alternative for many taxpayers, but the decision of which IRA is the better choice depends on several factors. These factors include your current and anticipated retirement tax bracket, the number of years that your funds will remain in an IRA, and your anticipated rates of return. Figure 19.1 shows a comparison of total benefits from the Roth IRA, a deductible IRA, a nondeductible IRA, and a regular taxable account. The key assumptions behind the figures in Figure 19.1 are as follows:

- Annual individual contribution until age 65: $4,000 per couple.

- Withdrawals over 20-year period in retirement.

- An 8 percent annual return before retirement; 7 percent after retirement.

- A 28 percent federal tax bracket, 5 percent state rate (before and after retirement).

- Roth IRA distributions exempt from federal and state income taxes.

- Taxpayer reinvests annual tax savings from deductible IRA contribution into a taxable account earning these same rates.

T. Rowe Price Associates has produced an outstanding set of worksheets and low-cost PC software for analyzing the various IRA options. You can order the software by calling 800-332-6407.

 **CONVERTING REGULAR IRAs TO ROTH IRAs**

Besides creating the Roth IRA, the 1997 Tax Act allows taxpayers whose adjusted gross income is less than $100,000 to transfer their existing IRA account balances to a Roth IRA. The advantage to the transfer is

FIGURE 19.1 IRA COMPARISONS.

	30-Year-Old Couple		40-Year-Old Couple		55-Year-Old Couple	
	Pretax value at Retirement	Total After-Tax Withdrawals in Retirement	Pretax value at Retirement	Total After-Tax Withdrawals in Retirement	Pretax value at Retirement	Total After-Tax Withdrawals in Retirement
Roth IRA	$744,409	$1,313,400	$315,818	$557,214	$62,582	$110,417
Deductible IRA	877,277	1,098,214	383,747	483,308	79,724	101,309
Nondeductible IRA	744,409	942,606	315,818	412,734	62,582	88,165
Regular taxable account	420,469	632,432	214,966	323,334	54,248	81,596

Source: Special Report: The New Tax Legislation, T. Rowe Price Associates Inc., 1997.

that withdrawals of funds from the Roth IRA in retirement (after age 59½) will be tax-free; the disadvantage is that you must pay income taxes on the taxable part of the funds transferred to the Roth IRA. (The usual 10 percent penalty for early IRA withdrawals is waived for these transfers.) Also, if you transfer the funds before the end of 1998, you can spread the taxable amount of the IRA distribution over four years.

You must calculate the costs and benefits based on your situation to determine if the conversion makes sense. As general guidelines, the benefits of converting increase if (1) you plan to pay the income taxes from sources other than the IRA, (2) you have a longer investment period, and (3) you expect to earn higher rates of return. Figures 19.2 and 19.3 illustrate the conversion calculations for two taxpayers based on the following assumptions:

- No additional IRA contributions after conversion.
- The investor retires at age 65 and withdraws the money over a 20-year period in retirement.
- An 8 percent annual return before retirement; 7 percent after retirement.
- A 28 percent federal tax bracket, 5 percent state rate (before and after retirement).
- The tax savings account assumes that the taxes that would have been paid on conversion are invested in a taxable account growing at the same rate.
- Taxes due upon conversion are paid from other assets so the full IRA balance is transferred.

 RETIREMENT PLAN
CONCEPT DISTRIBUTIONS

At some point you will be ready (or required) to take distributions from your retirement plans. You will face

FIGURE 19.2 IRA CONVERSION: AGE 45 WITH $25,000 TRANSFER. FEDERAL AND STATE INCOME TAXES DUE: $7,900.

	Pretax Value at Retirement		Total After-Tax Withdrawals in Retirement		Net Gain for Roth IRA
	Current IRA	Roth IRA	Current IRA	Roth IRA	
	$116,524	$116,524	$140,623	$205,589	
Tax savings account	$ 21,205	N/A	$ 31,894	N/A	
Total value	$137,729	$116,524	$172,518	$205,589	$33,071

Source: Special Report: The New Tax Legislation, T. Rowe Price Associates Inc., 1997.

FIGURE 19.3 IRA CONVERSION: AGE 55 WITH $50,000 TRANSFER. FEDERAL AND STATE INCOME TAXES DUE: $15,800.

	Pretax Value at Retirement		Total After-Tax Withdrawals in Retirement		Net Gain for Roth IRA
	Current IRA $107,946	Roth IRA $107,946	Current IRA $130,271	Roth IRA $190,455	
Tax savings account	$ 24,894	N/A	$ 37,443	N/A	
Total value	**$132,840**	**$107,946**	**$167,715**	**$190,455**	**$22,740**

Source: Special Report: The New Tax Legislation, *T. Rowe Price Associates Inc., 1997.*

several critical decisions, and advance planning can re-duce the stress that dealing with potentially large sums can produce. Before making these decisions, you should consider several factors: income taxes, retire-ment income needs, your (and your spouse's) invest-ment management skills, and your estate plan. Use the following material for assistance as you discuss your options with your advisors.

Defined Benefit Plan Participants

The classic defined benefit plans pay the retiree a monthly retirement income that is typically based on his or her salary and years spent with the company. At retirement, you must tell your employer how you wish to receive the pension. Figure 19.4 lists the usual op-tions, with dollar amounts given as examples.

For married employees, some form of the joint and survivor annuity is automatic, and the nonretiree spouse must voluntarily waive his or her rights to that pension. Single taxpayers are usually offered a single life annuity. Roughly 40 percent of companies with defined benefit plans offer employees the additional option of taking their pension as a *lump-sum payout.*

Joint and survivor annuities make sense in the following cases:

- Your spouse is likely to outlive you and your pension will be an important source of retirement income for him or her.
- Your employers provide some form of medical bene-fits to retirees and spouses who are receiving pen-sion payments.
- You are single and your plan allows you to name a nonspousal beneficiary. For instance, if you help

FIGURE 19.4 TYPICAL PENSION OPTIONS.

Method	Amount
Single life annuity	$1,820 per month for pensioner's (retiree's) life. Payment stops at retiree's death.
Single life with guaranty	Payments made for retiree's life with a guaranteed minimum period. 10-year guaranty: $1,710 per month. 20-year guaranty: $1,560 per month.
Joint and survivor annuity	Payments made for both retiree's and beneficiary's lives. 50% survivor benefit: $1,700 for retiree's life; $850 to survivor for life if retiree dies first. 100% survivor benefit: $1,500 per month for life for retiree and beneficiary.

Source: The Vanguard Group, Investing During Retirement (New York: McGraw Hill, 1998).

support a parent, naming that person as beneficiary would help replace your financial contribution in case you died.

Defined Contribution Plan Participants

Defined contribution plans include 401(k), 403(b), and other qualified retirement plans. These plans usually give employees several choices for withdrawing their account balance:

- *Lump-sum distribution.* Employer distributes full balance, net of any outstanding loans, to employee.
- *Partial distributions.* Employee can withdraw part of his or her funds from the plan as desired.
- *Annuity.* The employer purchases an annuity for the employee.

KEY CONCEPT Lump-Sum Distributions

The lump-sum distribution is the most common option, and it deserves special consideration. Its advantages include increased control and withdrawal flexibility, potentially higher retirement income with positive investment results, and no drop in income at the retiree's death (as there is with several annuity options). But there are also risks to taking a lump-sum distribution. The primary risk is that you mismanage the distribution by squandering, overspending, or investing the funds poorly. Another factor to consider is your beneficiary's ability to manage the funds if you become incompetent or die.

If you decide to take the lump sum, you face several other decisions. Figure 19.5 lists the pros and cons of the options.

In general, rolling over a lump-sum distribution to an IRA is the best option for preserving your retirement plan funds, although you should consider the special averaging treatment, if it is available. If the distribution includes your employer's stock, however, a rollover might *increase* your taxes. By transferring the shares to a regular (non-IRA) brokerage account, you will incur taxes and any early distribution penalty on the *cost* of the transferred shares, not the shares' appreciation over your cost basis. If you have a gain on the shares (technically known as *net unrealized appreciation*), that gain is not taxed until you sell the shares, and then it is taxed as a long-term capital gain.

Required Distributions

To prevent tax deferral for an indefinite period, the IRS requires you to take minimum distributions from your retirement plans after reaching age 70½. The rules are complicated, and if you withdraw too little, the IRS has the right to charge you a 50 percent insufficient withdrawal penalty. Here is a summary of the required distribution rules.

FIGURE 19.5 LUMP-SUM DECISIONS.

Option	Implications
Keep the distribution.	Distribution typically taxed as ordinary income; 10% penalty if you are under age 59½ in many cases.
Roll over distribution to IRA.	Avoids current taxation and extends deferral.
Income averaging.	One-time special income tax calculation for those over age 59½ that treats distribution as if it were received over a 5- or 10-year period. After 1999, 5-year averaging will be repealed; 10-year averaging available only to those born before 1936; participant must have been in plan for 5 years.

Starting date. You must begin withdrawals by April 1 of the year after the year in which you reach age 70½. If you continue working, you have until April 1 of the year following the year in which you retire. (Employees who own more than 5 percent of the business must start distributions in the year after reaching 70½.) But if you take no distributions during the year you reach 70½, you must take two distributions the following year: the first by April 1 and the second by December 31.

Calculate the tax impact of receiving your first two distributions in the same year. It might be less expensive to take the first distribution in your age 70½ year.

Required withdrawals. The required payout amount will depend on the calculation method you choose and your beneficiary's age. The following example demonstrates the required calculation.

John reached age 70½ in 1997, so he must take his first distribution by April 1, 1998. His IRA account had a balance of $30,000 on December 31, 1996, and his wife, who is age 65, is his beneficiary.

Step 1: Determine account balance as
of previous December 31 (1996). $30,000

Step 2: Determine joint life expectancy
from IRS tables in Publication 939.   22.8 years

Step 3: Divide $30,000 by 23.1 to get
first distribution amount. $1,316

To figure his second distribution, John will need his account balance as of December 31, 1997, reduced by his $1,316 distribution. Assuming that his account was worth $32,000, the base figure for the next distribution will be $28,684 ($30,000 – $1,316). (*Note:* John must take the second withdrawal by December 31, 1998.)

Step 4: Determine account balance as
of previous December 31 (1997). $28,684

Step 5: Determine joint life expectancy
from IRS tables in Publication 939.
John's age is 72 and his wife's is
now 66.   21.9 years

Step 6: Divide $28,684 by 21.9 to get
second distribution amount. $1,310

As an alternative to recalculating their joint life expectancies each year, John could use the *term-certain* method. With this method, he would simply reduce the joint life expectancy each year by one year: 21.8 in year 2, 20.8 in year 3, and so on. If your beneficiary is not your spouse, the rules are more complicated. You cannot use the actual joint life expectancy figure if your nonspousal beneficiary is more than 10 years younger than you. The maximum allowable age difference is 10 years, so you must treat your beneficiary as if he or she is age 61 if you are taking your first distribution in the year after you turn 70½.

The rules for minimum IRA distributions are complex, especially with nonspousal beneficiaries. Many plan sponsors, such as banks and mutual funds, will provide guidance in calculating the required distributions. A tax advisor could also assist you with the IRS paperwork.

CONVERTING HOME EQUITY

For many retirees, home equity is a substantial financial asset, but it is an illiquid asset that produces no cash flow to supplement other retirement incomes. As a result, it is not unusual for retirees to be *house poor,* a condition in which a person or couple has substantial home equity but few other assets. If you (or your parents) encounter this problem, consider the following possible remedies to improve retirement cash flow.

1. *Sell the existing home and buy a less expensive replacement.* This solution has the advantage of freeing up equity while still retaining the advantages of home ownership. The primary disadvantage is the stress of selling the existing home, finding a suitable replacement, and moving.

2. *Consider a reverse mortgage.* The availability of reverse mortgage programs continues to improve. The U.S. Department of Housing and Urban Development and private lenders offer reverse mortgages, and the development of the Federal National Mortgage Association's (FNMA, also known as Fannie Mae) Home Keeper(sm) program has led to increased interest in these loans. The Home Keeper program gives borrowers several options for withdrawing equity from the home:

   - *Tenure option.* Equal monthly payments for as long as you occupy the home as your principal residence.
   - *Line of credit option.* You decide the timing and amount of withdrawals.
   - *Modified tenure option.* A mix of loan payments and available line of credit.

   The amount available for borrowing under the Home Keeper program depends on the age of the borrower(s) and the property's value. Figure 19.6, which is from FNMA's *Home Keeper* booklet, shows the amounts available under the line of credit option.

FIGURE 19.6 MAXIMUM LINE OF CREDIT AVAILABLE.

Single Borrower   **Property Value**

Age	$100,000	$150,000	$200,000
70	26,514	42,369	58,223
80	42,668	66,435	90,201
90	58,285	89,429	120,573

Two Borrowers   **Property Value**

Age	$100,000	$150,000	$200,000
70	9,461	16,789	24,117
80	31,211	49,249	67,287
90	48,907	75,362	101,817

Source: Fannie Mae, Home Keeper, 1995.

In addition to the traditional reverse mortgage, FNMA recently introduced its Home Keeper for Home Purchase loan. This program is designed for retirees (age 62+) who wish to sell their existing home and buy a new one without having to make mortgage payments on the new home. For example, assume that a 76-year-old woman sells her home for $75,000 and wants to buy a new one that costs $115,000. She applies to FNMA for a reverse mortgage for $60,000 and buys the new home, keeping the additional $20,000 for expenses and income. When she moves or dies, the house is sold and FNMA receives its payment (including interest).

The American Association of Retired Persons (AARP) offers a variety of informational brochures about home equity conversion programs. You can request these brochures by calling 202-434-6042. For information about FNMA's Home Keeper program, call the agency at 800-732-6643. The National Center for Home Equity Conversion also offers materials at 800-247-6553.

END POINT

Effective retirement planning involves several issues, ranging from savings strategies to pension plan distributions. The goal is to accumulate sufficient assets and income to meet your retirement needs. Reaching that requires you to maximize the available opportunities.

Estate Planning Fundamentals

You cannot escape the problems caused by aging and mortality. As you get older, the *risk of physical and mental impairment* increases. If an impairment becomes severe enough, your ability to manage your affairs might diminish significantly. That condition could lead to the appointment of a guardian to handle your finances, and the court might appoint a person whom you would not have selected if you were competent.

The *risk of premature death* raises different problems: Who should settle your affairs? If you have minor children, who should raise them after you are gone? How should your assets be distributed? If you die without a will, the laws of your state of residence determine how the property owned in your name gets distributed to your heirs. Depending on the circumstances, the state might also be required to choose guardians for your minor children after your death. To prevent these problems, you need to plan your estate.

 ESTIMATING THE VALUE OF YOUR ESTATE

The first step in estate planning is to estimate the value of your gross estate, which includes assets that you own (or control) in your name and your share of anything you own jointly with others. Chapter 1 introduced the personal balance sheet that listed your assets and liabilities. As Figure 20.1 shows, you can use much of the information from your personal balance sheet in

FIGURE 20.1 GROSS ESTATE VALUATION.

Property	Value of Property Owned in Your Name	Value of Your Share of Property Owned with Others	Total
Items from personal balance sheet			
Cash and bank accounts	_____	_____	_____
Investments	_____	_____	_____
Retirement plans	_____	_____	_____
Personal property	_____	_____	_____
Autos	_____	_____	_____
Residence(s)	_____	_____	_____
Business interests	_____	_____	_____
Other	_____	_____	_____
Additional assets to include			
Life insurance policies you own or that are payable to your estate (include value of death benefit)	_____	_____	_____
Value of Uniform Transfer to Minors Accounts (UTMA) or Uniform Gifts to Minors Accounts (UGMA) for which you are custodian (if you created the accounts)	_____	_____	_____
Present value of annuities and other incomes being paid to you or that are owed to you	_____	_____	_____
Other	_____	_____	_____
Total	_____	_____	_____

calculating your gross estate, but there are additional items to include. Figure 20.2 explains some of the terminology used in valuing estates.

DANGER! Most assets are fairly easy to value, but others, such as real estate and privately owned businesses, frequently require expert valuation. It is acceptable to use your own estimates to start the estate planning process, but you need expert, impartial valuations before finalizing your plans.

FIGURE 20.2 ESTIMATING ESTATE VALUES.

Asset	Explanation
Ownership category	
Individual	Owned solely in your name; current value of asset included in your estate.
Assets owned jointly with right of survivorship (JWROS)	If you own the asset with your spouse, include 50 percent of its current value in your estate. If the co-owner is not your spouse, estimate your share of the contribution to buy the asset. That percentage of the asset's current value is included in your estate. (Technically, 100 percent of the asset's value is included in the estate of the joint owner who dies first. In that case, your executor must prove that the other owner contributed to the asset's purchase.)
Tenancy by the entirety	Exists only between husband and wife; 50 percent of the asset's value included in your estate
Tenancy in common	Estimate your share of the contribution to buy the asset. That percentage of the asset's current value is included in your estate.
Asset category	
Life insurance policies you own or that are payable to your estate (include value of death benefit)	If you own or control a life insurance policy, the value of the death benefit will be included in your estate, even if you are not the beneficiary. Also, if a policy names your estate or executor as beneficiary, the value of the death benefit will be included in your estate, even if you have no ownership or of control over the policy.
Uniform Transfer to Minors Accounts (UTMA) or Uniform Gifts to Minors Accounts (UGMA) for which you are custodian (if you created the accounts)	Establishing UTMAs and UGMAs is a popular method for transferring assets to children. If you establish an account for your child and name yourself custodian, you have retained control over the account and it will be included in your estate.
Present value of annuities and other incomes paid or owed to you.	If the income stops at your death, it has no value in your estate. If a beneficiary receives payments after your death, the present value of the expected future income is considered an asset of your estate.

KEY CONCEPT · EFFECTIVE ESTATE PLANNING

Effective estate planning focuses on several primary goals: (1) *providing backup financial management* if you are incapacitated, (2) *distributing your assets efficiently* according to your wishes after your death, and (3) *appointing guardians* for minor children and dependents, if necessary. To achieve these goals, you must coordinate the use of several estate planning techniques and documents. These instruments are the basic tools of estate planning:

- Powers of attorney and living wills.
- Trusts.
- Forms of property ownership (individual, joint).
- Beneficiary designations (insurance policies, retirement plans).
- Wills.
- Letters of instruction.

In a well-designed estate plan, there are no conflicts among these instruments. Although each serves a different purpose, their actions are coordinated. In contrast, a poorly designed estate plan often lacks this coordination, and there may be direct conflicts among the various instruments.

There are two widely held misconceptions about estate planning that you should avoid. The first is that joint ownership of all property solves every estate planning problem. It does not, and joint ownership actually can introduce unexpected complications and costs. The second misconception is that a will is the only estate planning document you need. It is true that you need a will, but a will becomes effective *only after death.* You also need the documents that provide backup management while you are alive.

LIFETIME PLANNING TOOLS

Lifetime planning tools provide continuity in managing your affairs if you suffer an impairment that affects your physical or mental abilities. By implementing these techniques while you are competent, you ensure that your wishes will be followed if you become impaired, and you can choose the people who will follow your instructions. The most important techniques to consider using are these:

- Durable power of attorney (legal and medical).
- Living will.
- Revocable living trust.

Durable Power of Attorney: Legal

With a *durable power of attorney* for legal matters, you name another person to act as your attorney-in-fact, or agent. As your agent, this person can sign checks and contracts, buy and sell assets, and make any other financial decision in your place. A durable power of attorney takes effect when you sign it. The power remains in effect even if you become incompetent, although you can revoke it or change your agent at any time. In contrast, a *springing power of attorney* becomes valid only after you become incompetent. Because of the difficulty in judging incompetence, many advisors recommend against using the springing power version.

Durable Power of Attorney: Medical

A *durable power of attorney for medical care,* also known as a *health care proxy,* allows you to name another person who can act as your attorney-in-fact, or agent, for medical decisions if you are incapacitated. As your agent, this person can make health care decisions for you. The document also allows you to express your wishes about accepting or refusing medical treatments. Because you are authorizing your agent to make critical decisions *about your life,* you obviously need to select that agent very carefully.

Living Will

With a living will, you can express your wishes about receiving life-sustaining medical treatments if you become terminally ill or lapse into a coma. If you have strong feelings about receiving or refusing the care you might receive under these circumstances, write a living will to record your feelings. There is no guarantee that health care providers will follow your wishes, but if you don't express them in writing, you might be unable to communicate them later.

 You should get legal advice in preparing a durable power of attorney for legal and financial management, but you don't necessarily need a lawyer for a health care power of attorney or living will. If your state government has an agency that specializes in servicing the elderly, that department might be able to send you the necessary forms for little or no cost. You can also write to Choice in Dying (200 Varick Street, New York, NY 10014) for a kit that includes instructions on drafting a living will and durable power of attorney for health care.

Revocable Living Trust (RLT)

As its name implies, you create an RLT while you are living, and you can change or revoke it at any time. In a typical arrangement, you (as creator of the trust, or *grantor*) would name yourself *trustee* (the person responsible for managing the trust) and *beneficiary* (the person who receives the trust's income and distri-butions). You would also name a *successor trustee,* who would take over the trust's management if you (as grantor/trustee) become incapacitated or die. As trustee, the grantor retains control of any assets placed in the trust. During your lifetime, you as the grantor can contribute assets to the trust, and if you name yourself as beneficiary, you will continue to receive any income generated by the trust's assets. If the grantor/trustee becomes incapacitated or dies, the successor trustee takes over and follows the instructions contained in the trust document. (Not all states allow the grantor to be the sole trustee, so check your local laws.)

The RLT has several valuable features. It avoids probate court, possibly saving considerable cost and delay in distributing assets after the grantor's death. The successor trustee also provides backup financial management in case the grantor becomes unable to manage his or her affairs. By combining the RLT with a properly structured durable power of attorney, you as the grantor can ensure continuity in the handling of your finances if you become impaired. During the grantor's lifetime, trust administration is simple and you do not have to complete any special tax returns for the trust.

There are drawbacks to the RLT, though. Depending on the complexity of the grantor's finances, you might incur substantial setup fees for legal work and asset transfers. Also, the RLT is not suited for everyone. A person with a modest estate whose finances are not complicated probably can accomplish the same results that an RLT produces with other estate planning techniques while avoiding the expense of setting up the trust.

Many estate planners are promoting revocable living trusts as the cure-all for every estate planning problem. You might be able to achieve the benefits of the RLT without the setup costs by carefully coordinating your will with property ownership, beneficiary designations, and a durable power of attorney. Investigate whether these techniques will work for you before creating an RLT.

Because possession of a durable power of attorney gives your agent permission to act in your name, you should choose that person carefully. As an additional safeguard, consider leaving the original power of attorney document with the attorney who drafts it for you. Give your agent instructions on how to contact the attorney to get the documents if you become incompetent or incapacitated. Then you don't have to worry about the agent using the power of attorney before you intended.

PROBATE COURT

Each state has its own probate court system for overseeing the distribution of estates. After someone dies, the executor named in the will presents that will to the probate court for verification. The executor then assumes responsibility for collecting and protecting the estate's assets, paying the decedent's bills, and distributing the estate's remaining assets to heirs according to the will's instructions. Not all assets go through the probate court, though. Assets that name beneficiaries (life insurance and retirement plans), jointly owned property, and property held in trust are not part of the probate estate. These assets are distributed directly to the beneficiary or co-owner, or they remain held in trust.

Avoiding probate is a common estate planning goal. There are several good reasons to keep assets out of probate court. The first is the potential delay in distributing the assets. Although most estates distribute assets within nine months, some probate proceedings can last much longer, especially those for complex estates. The second reason to avoid probate is to reduce estate administration fees. An executor must pay probate court fees and legal fees (if he or she hires an attorney). While court fees are generally low, a lawyer's fees can add up quickly. By keeping assets out of probate court, you can reduce both distribution delays and estate administration fees.

Some lawyers bill for estate administration based on a percentage of the amount of assets in the estate. As an alternative, consider asking the lawyer to bill by the hour, and request an initial estimate and a final accounting of the time he spends on the estate. The lawyer might not like the arrangement, but it can help control the legal fees.

DISTRIBUTING YOUR ASSETS

At some point, life ends and an estate enters the distribution stage. To plan for this stage you need to answer three questions:

- Who should receive my property?
- When should these heirs receive the property I am leaving to them?
- In what form will I leave the property: outright or in trust?

Your personal circumstances and goals will determine your answer to these questions. For example, married spouses often leave everything outright to each other. In marriages where one or both spouses had children from previous marriages, a typical goal is to divide assets so that both the spouse and the children receive some benefit. This type of arrangement frequently involves the use of trusts. Other individuals may leave all assets to a charity or an alma mater. The point is, *you need to think about how you want your assets distributed after your death.* This is a critical step, because your decisions will influence your choice of estate planning techniques and the actions needed to coordinate your efforts.

Many people assume that their will controls the distribution of all their assets. That is a mistake, because other instruments take priority over the will. These higher-ranked instruments include jointly owned property, beneficiary designations on life insurance and retirement plans, and bequest instructions for assets held in trusts. Because these instruments take precedence over your will's instructions, you need to coordinate the distribution instructions of all the estate planning instruments you use.

To avoid distribution conflicts in your asset distribution plan, you must review any existing beneficiary arrangements you have in place already. (Figure 20.3 can help you get started.) This is particularly important

FIGURE 20.3 BENEFICIARY REVIEW.

Asset	Desired Beneficiary	Current Beneficiary (current co-owner for jointly owned assets)	Date Corrected
Jointly owned assets			
Life insurance policies			
Retirement plans			
Trusts			

if you are divorced, because it is not unusual for individuals to leave a former spouse unintentionally listed as the beneficiary on retirement plans and insurance policies.

 Some personal property (e.g., cars and furnishings) is owned individually, and you cannot designate a contractual beneficiary for that property. While you could list your distribution instructions for these assets in your will, it is easier and more convenient to list personal property bequests in your *letter of instructions,* which will be discussed shortly.

After you decide who will receive which assets, you must address the issues of the *timing* and *form* of the distributions. The simplest approach is to distribute the assets immediately and directly to the recipients (i.e., with no strings attached). That might be the easiest solution, but it could lead to disaster. The traditional alternative to outright distributions is to leave the assets in trust for the beneficiaries for a specified period of time. You can create the trust while you are alive or you can create it in your will and have your estate fund it. As grantor of the trust, you give the trustee instructions for distributing the assets. Your instructions can be very specific, or you can give the trustee greater latitude.

Before making your final distribution decisions, try to evaluate each of your proposed heirs objectively. Do they seem to manage their finances well? Do they have experience with investments? Are their personal lives stable? These questions may seem intrusive, but countless inheritances have been squandered because the heirs were not prepared to manage the money they received. If you do not want that to happen, consider using a trust as an alternative to outright bequests.

 If you create a trust to hold assets after your death, choose your trustees carefully. The ideal trustee will be an expert in estate planning, taxation, administration, and investments. Trustees also need a background in psychology to handle the inevitable problems that develop with heirs. Because most people lack this unique combination of skills, you might want to consider using a *corporate trustee* such as a bank or trust company. These institutions specialize in estate and trust administration, and most of them provide competent service. One possible solution is to appoint a cotrustee, such as a trusted friend or relative, who would work with the institution and share decision making authority. Also consider giving your beneficiaries the right to replace trustees, in case your original choices do not perform as expected.

Several states (Arizona, California, Idaho, Louisiana, New Mexico, Texas, and Washington) have *community property* laws. (Wisconsin is considered a quasi–community property state.) In these states, property acquired during marriage is treated as if each spouse owned half, no matter how much each spouse contributed to the property's acquisition. When one spouse dies, one-half the community property passes to the surviving spouse, with the remaining half going to other heirs. Under certain conditions, these states also recognize *separable property,* which is wholly owned by one spouse. Generally, this is property that one spouse brought into the marriage or received as a gift or inheritance after marriage. Because of the added complexity of asset distribution laws in these states, residents should seek professional estate planning advice.

 There are potential drawbacks to holding property jointly. Joint ownership can sometimes increase estate taxes for married couples. In another common scenario, a widow or widower names an adult child who lives locally as joint owner on bank and brokerage accounts. The goal is convenience: The adult child who lives nearby can access the account easily if the parent cannot. The are two risks with this type of joint ownership. If the adult child is sued for divorce or liability, the accounts may be considered part of his assets. The second risk occurs when the parent dies and the local child becomes sole owner of the account. If the parent's wish was to have the account distributed equally among all surviving children, there could be a problem if the child who was listed as co-owner decides not to split the funds with siblings.

WRITING AN EFFECTIVE WILL

Your will is the cornerstone of your estate plan. Surprisingly, though, almost two-thirds of adult Americans die *intestate,* that is, without a valid will. In those cases, the *intestacy laws* of the decedent's state of residence dictate how the estate will be distributed. In a sense, the state provides a will for those who fail to write their own. (This doesn't affect assets that are passed by joint ownership, trust, or beneficiary designation. As stated earlier, those transfer methods take precedence over a will or a state's intestacy laws.)

Dying without a will creates numerous problems. It delays distribution of the estate's assets because the estate must go through probate court. It also creates additional hardship for heirs and beneficiaries who lack the decedent's instructions on handling the estate. Given the relatively low cost of having a lawyer draft a will (usually less than $200 for the average estate), there is no excuse for not having a current, valid will.

If you must make changes to your will, you do not have to rewrite the entire document. Instead, you can make changes by adding a *codicil,* which is a legal amendment to the will that changes an existing provision. To ensure the codicil takes effect, have it drawn up by a lawyer, witnessed, and signed.

Provisions of a Will

- Identification of the person writing the will and his or her places of residence.
- Clauses to prove the validity of the will and to revoke any prior wills.
- Instructions for payment of funeral and burial costs, estate debts, taxes, and administrative costs.
- Instructions for specific bequests to individuals and charities.
- Instructions for distributing remainder of estate after bequests and expenses.
- Survivorship clause (how to distribute assets if both spouses die simultaneously).
- Instructions for creating trusts (if any).
- Appointment of minor children's guardians.
- Clause allowing executor and guardians to serve without requiring them to post bond.

Letter of Instructions

It is generally not a good idea to list funeral and burial instructions and detailed bequests for specific items of personal property in your will. You might change your burial plans or dispose of those assets before your death, and you do not want to revise your will too frequently—it can get expensive. A more convenient method is to write a *letter of instructions* in which you list your instructions for funeral, burial, and specific bequests. Because this is an informal, personal document, you can change it as frequently as needed without incurring legal fees.

END POINT

There is a widely held misconception that estate planning is only for wealthy retirees. In reality, every adult who owns property needs to plan for the possibility of impairment and premature death. Effective estate planning requires coordination of lifetime planning tools such as powers of attorney and living trusts with post-mortem (after-death) tools such as wills and beneficiary designations.

Reducing Estate Taxes

Estate taxes can significantly reduce the net amount of assets that you can leave to heirs. Under current (1997) tax law, marginal tax rates on estates valued at over $600,000 start at *37 percent* and climb to *over 50 percent* on larger estates. While the $600,000 threshold is scheduled to gradually increase, the potential impact of estate taxes on wealth transfers is still enormous. This chapter discusses methods for reducing estate taxes.

ESTATE TAX CALCULATIONS

Figure 21.1 illustrates how estate taxes are calculated for an unmarried decedent's estate using the $600,000 exemption allowed in 1997. This simplified example follows the flow of IRS Form 706, "United States Estate (and Generation-Skipping Transfer) Tax Return" (revised April 1997).

From a tax planning perspective, the focus is on minimizing the amount reported under "Taxable Estate." This means reducing the gross estate, increasing the estate's deductions, or both. Before examining methods for achieving these goals, you should understand how the unified credit works.

TAX-EXEMPT ESTATES AND THE UNIFIED CREDIT

Only taxable estates valued at more than $600,000 pay estate taxes. In 1995, 31,564 decedents paid estate taxes, generating roughly $15.1 billion in tax revenues

FIGURE 21.1 FEDERAL ESTATE TAX CALCULATION (UNMARRIED DECEDENT).

Item	Amount ($)
Total gross estate	$1,000,000
Less allowable deductions	−40,000
Taxable estate	$ 960,000
Gross estate tax	$ 330,200
Less allowable unified credit	−192,800
Less credit for state death taxes	−30,000
Net estate tax	$ 162,800

for the government. Unfortunately for taxpayers, that number is projected to grow to 73,000 estates by 2007.[1] The 1997 Tax Act included legislation to gradually increase the $600,000 taxable estate threshold to $1 million by the year 2006, as shown in Figure 21.2.

The planned increase in the exempted amount has important implications for many U.S. citizens. More taxpayers will avoid estate taxes completely, and married taxpayers will be able to leave combined estates up to $2 million after 2006 by using some basic planning techniques.

It is important to understand that the exemption is actually an equivalent amount that is derived from the *unified credit,* which has a maximum of $192,800. In other words, a $600,000 estate would generate a $192,800 tax liability based on 1997 tax rates. Giving each estate a $192,800 tax credit has the same impact as a giving an exemption of $600,000. Also, the unified credit is a *lifetime limit*—you can use it up while you are living or allow your estate administrator to use it after your death. The section on gift-giving techniques

FIGURE 21.2 EXEMPTED AMOUNTS.

Year	Exempted Amount
1998	$ 625,000
1999	650,000
2000	675,000
2001	675,000
2002	700,000
2003	700,000
2004	850,000
2005	950,000
2006	1,000,000

explains how and why you would use part of that unified credit while still living.

REDUCING THE GROSS ESTATE

The determining factors for including an asset in your estate are *ownership* and *control.* If you own an asset individually or with others, your share of the asset's value is included in your estate. Also, *if you effectively control an asset,* such as a trust, that asset's value will be included in your estate. As with all tax issues, the question of estate inclusion can be extremely complex.

If you have a sizable or complicated estate, you must hire competent legal and tax advisors to help you plan. Because estate tax rates are prohibitively high, do-it-yourself estate planning errors can be extremely expensive. Also, review the amount of assets in your gross estate (and your spouse's, if married) periodically. Your estate plan should recognize the growth in your assets' value and the impact that growth has on potential taxes.

The simplest way to avoid taxation on an asset is to remove it from your estate by giving it away. This technique, frequently referred to as *gifting,* is easy to implement. You give the asset to a recipient, and assuming the gift was legitimate (i.e., you received nothing in return), the asset is removed from your gross estate, thus reducing estate taxes.

The IRS imposes an annual limit of $10,000 that you can give to a noncharitable recipient (also referred to as *beneficiary* or *donee*) without incurring gift taxes. (The $10,000 limit will be indexed for inflation starting in 1999.) For example, if you give three people $10,000 each (in a year), you are within the limits. But if you give them $20,000 each, you have made a *taxable gift* of $30,000 and you must report the transaction to the IRS. If you are married, you and your spouse can combine gifts to give up to $20,000 annually to each recipient.

Several points are worth noting. First, you are *not* required to give gifts of cash—you can give other assets. While cash may be the recipient's preferred gift, it might not be the most convenient asset for you to give away, particularly if you are retired and need the funds. Second, you are not required to pay the gift tax in cash—you can use part of your $192,800 unified credit, which reduces the amount that will be available to your estate. Third, you can give gifts in trust, or if the donee is a minor, you can use the Uniform Transfers (or Gifts) to Minors Act, which provides a convenient method for giving to children.

Outright gifts are the simplest to make. You simply write a check or transfer an asset's title to a recipient.

Making outright gifts is not always the best transfer method, however. For instance, if you wish to give $10,000 annually to each of your three children, that equals $30,000 each year, or a total of $300,000 over 10 years. If you counted on those funds as a supplemental retirement income source, you risk depleting your assets prematurely and accepting a lower standard of living.

Another issue with gifts of cash or marketable securities (stocks, bonds, etc.) is the recipient's ability to handle the funds wisely. Many recipients come to expect their annual gifts, and they factor those amounts into their short-term spending plans rather than investing the funds for longer-term goals. If you lack confidence in a recipient's financial management skills, you should avoid giving them cash or an asset that is easily converted to cash.

Retaining control over the assets you give away requires careful planning. If the IRS determines that you attached too many strings to the transfer, then it will not be considered a gift, and the asset's value will remain in your estate. There are several techniques for making qualifying gifts while subsequently retaining some control over the asset's disposition. The following sections review these techniques.

FAMILY LIMITED PARTNERSHIPS (FLPs)

An FLP has one or more *general partners* and one or more *limited partners*. The general partners manage the partnership and assume the financial and legal liability associated with its operation. Limited partners have no control over the partnership, and their liability is limited to the amount of their investment.

The following FLP is a typical example. The family's parents own real estate and a successful small business worth $2 million, both of which continue to increase in value. The parents want to make annual gifts to their two adult children, but they do not want to give them cash and they want to retain control of the assets. They create an FLP and name themselves as both general and limited partners. They transfer the business and real estate into the FLP and divide the partnership units as 2 percent general partner (1 percent each) and 98 percent limited partners (49 percent each). At this point *nothing has changed except titles—the FLP now owns the assets.* Each parent owns a 1 percent general partner's interest and a 49 percent limited partner's interest in an FLP that holds $2 million in assets. The parents now begin to make annual gifts of limited-partner interests to their two children. If the FLP is worth $2 million, then 1 percent of the FLP is worth

$20,000. By agreeing to make joint gifts, the parents can give each child a 1 percent limited-partner interest in the FLP without incurring gift taxes. (If the FLP's assets increase in value, the parents will need to adjust the percentages they give away each year to stay under $20,000.) Because the parents own the general-partner interests, they retain control of the partnership. The FLP also facilitates the annual gifts—it is simpler to give partnership interests than it is to change fractional ownership of the business and real estate each year.

The FLP offers another planning opportunity that makes it even more attractive. A limited partner's interest is illiquid and offers no control over the FLP's operation. Realistically, it would be very difficult, perhaps impossible, to find an investor outside the family who would want to buy an FLP interest. In cases like this where the asset being transferred is illiquid and lacks control, the IRS allows the donor to apply a *discount* to the asset's value. In this example, the parents probably could apply up to a 40 percent discount to the value of each transferred interest. This discount allows the parents to transfer roughly $33,000 of limited partnership interest each year ($33,000 × .6 = $19,800). Instead of transferring $40,000 from their estates each year, the parents can shift $66,000, a 65 percent increase.

FLPs are being touted as a panacea for a wide variety of estate planning and asset-protection problems. While they are an excellent solution for many situations, they can be expensive due to fees for the initial setup and ongoing accounting and legal services. Also, if you discount the transferred assets too aggressively, the IRS may challenge the valuation.

Valuation discounts can be used conveniently with other entities besides FLPs. If the parents own a Subchapter S corporation, they can create non-voting shares and give shares to their children each year, taking a discount on the shares' value for the lack of voting control.

 IRREVOCABLE LIFE INSURANCE TRUSTS (ILITs)

As the name implies, an ILIT is an irrevocable trust that holds life insurance. When designed properly, these trusts remove life insurance proceeds from an estate, and the premiums used to pay for the trust's policy qualify for the annual gift exclusion. The donor, also known as the *grantor* (usually a parent), creates an irrevocable trust that will own a life insurance policy. The donor can give the trust an existing policy, or, in a typical arrangement, the trust can apply for a new policy on the donor's life.

Each year, the parent/donor makes a cash gift to the trust, which uses the cash to pay the policy's premium. At the donor's death, the trust's assets (i.e., the life insurance proceeds) are not included in the donor's estate, so the assets avoid estate taxes. If the estate needs cash, the trust is usually authorized to buy assets from the estate, thus providing the liquidity needed for debts and taxes.

There is a potential weakness with the ILIT arrangement. In order for the donor's cash gifts to qualify for the annual $10,000 exclusion, the trust's beneficiaries must be given the right to withdraw the funds for a reasonable period, such as 30 days, after they are deposited in the trust. This is known as a *Crummey* power, and the ILIT must include it. Although it may serve the beneficiary's best long-term interest to leave the funds in the trust to pay the policy's premiums, he or she can demand a distribution.

Establishing an ILIT requires you to follow the trust's legal formalities. First, gifts to the trust must be genuinely irrevocable. Second, you must adhere to the beneficiary notification requirements and give the beneficiaries adequate notice and opportunity to exercise their right of withdrawal. Failure to meet the IRS's requirements could disqualify the trust.

Financial advisors are beginning to consider FLPs as an alternative to ILITs, because the FLP offers more control and avoids the Crummey power issue. If you are considering an ILIT, ask your advisor to discuss the pros and cons of using an FLP instead.

PRESENT AND FUTURE INTERESTS

There is a range of estate planning techniques (including several methods for making charitable contributions) that allow you to split an asset into two components: current income and remaining principal (also known as the *remainder*). While this might seem like an artificial separation, the following example shows that the concept reflects economic reality. Suppose that a person has $1 million of fixed-income assets producing a 6 percent annual yield. He needs the assets' income for the next 10 years, after which he plans to give the assets to his children. If he gave them the assets outright today, he would lose the income, use up his unified credit, and incur a substantial gift tax. Instead, he creates an irrevocable trust and funds it with the assets. The trust pays him an annual income (fixed income or percentage of the trust's value) for 10 years or until his death, whichever occurs first. The trust then terminates and distributes its assets to the donor's children.

From the recipients' perspective, the promise to receive $1 million in 10 years is not the same as receiving that amount outright today—it is worth considerably less than $1 million. The IRS recognizes that money has a time value, and it allows donors to divide gifts into current interest and remainder interest. The division between the income and remainder interests depends on the prevailing IRS discount rate and the term and type of the income interest. For example, with a discount rate of 7 percent and a 10-year trust period, the income interest is worth roughly 49 percent of the trust contribution, and the remainder interest is worth 51 percent. If you lengthen the income period from 10 to 15 years, the income interest is worth 64 percent, and the remainder's value drops to 34 percent.[2]

Some of these splitting techniques involve uncertainty, which you should recognize before creating the trust. Specifically, if you die before the trust terminates, the remainder is pulled back into your estate. But if you do nothing and retain ownership of the asset, its value will be included in your estate anyway, so you really have little to lose from transferring it to the trust. If you survive the trust's term, the asset's remainder value, *including its appreciation,* will not be included in your estate.

Splitting a transfer into present and future interests increases flexibility in removing assets from the gross estate. Figure 21.3 lists several frequently used estate planning techniques that provide opportunities for using the income interest versus remainder interest approach.

Among these techniques, the qualified personal residence trust has been attracting significant publicity lately. Figure 21.4 provides an example to demonstrate a QPRT's potential tax savings. Assume that a couple wish to leave their home to their children, but they want the right to live in the home for the next 20 years. The home is worth $600,000, and its value is increasing by 5 percent annually.

As the example in Figure 21.4 demonstrates, the home is projected to increase in value by roughly $1 million over the next 20 years. If the parents transfer the home to the QPRT and live longer than 20 years, that appreciation will not be included in their estates, thus saving several hundred thousand dollars in taxes.

Removing assets from your estate can reduce your potential estate taxes significantly, but achieving those savings can restrict your financial flexibility. Be sure you integrate your estate plans with the other aspects of your financial plan, particularly the need for sufficient income-producing assets to fund your retirement.

FIGURE 21.3 TECHNIQUES FOR DIVIDING INCOME AND REMAINDER.

Method	Description
Grantor retained income trust (GRIT) Qualified personal residence trust (QPRT)	These trusts are used to place a personal residence in trust, with the grantor retaining the right to use the residence for a specified period.
Grantor retained annuity trust (GRAT)	Grantor receives a specified dollar distribution for the trust's term.
Grantor retained unitrust (GRUT)	Grantor receives a specified percentage of the trust's value as his or her distribution for the trust's term.
Charitable lead trust (CLT)	Charity receives income annuity for trust's term. At trust termination, principal reverts to trust beneficiaries. Contribution to trust also generates current income tax deduction.
Charitable remainder trusts (CRT)	Trust beneficiaries receive income annuity for trust's term. At trust termination, principal reverts to charity. Contribution to trust also generates current income tax deduction.

FIGURE 21.4 QUALIFIED PERSONAL RESIDENCE TRUST.

Current value of residence	$ 600,000
Less value of retained interest	−466,000
Value of remainder (taxable gift)	134,000
Unified credit used	34,000
Projected future value of home (excluded from parents' estates)	$1,592,000

THE UNLIMITED MARITAL DEDUCTION

The IRS allows a variety of deductions to reduce the gross estate. Categories include funeral and administrative expenses, mortgages and debts, charitable bequests, and bequests to a surviving spouse. Using these deductions properly, particularly the charitable and marital bequests, can reduce and possibly eliminate your estate taxes.

 If you plan to have your estate make charitable bequests, consider making them while you are living by using some form of a charitable trust. Lifetime charitable contributions have the added benefits of reducing current income taxes and removing the contributed assets from your estate. Most charitable organizations are eager to discuss and facilitate charitable trusts, even if the amount is relatively small.

Estate tax law allows spouses to give (while alive) or bequest (via estate) unlimited amounts to each other without taxation. This provision ensures that a surviving spouse will not face the hardship imposed by taxes when a spouse dies, but it does create a potential tax trap for the surviving spouse's beneficiaries. The following example demonstrates this problem using 1997 tax rates (ignoring state taxes). The example in Figures 21.5 and 21.6 assumes that the couple own most of their property together in some form of joint ownership and that they name each other as beneficiaries on individually owned property.

The surviving wife dies in 1997. Her estate includes her assets, her share of the previously owned joint property, and the $400,000 in assets she inherited from her husband.

The wife's estate taxes are $59,400, reducing her estate by roughly 7.4 percent. Unfortunately for her heirs, the entire federal estate tax *could have been avoided* with some basic planning. The problem stemmed from her husband's estate claiming a full marital deduction and failing to use his unified credit. The bequest from her husband caused the wife's estate to exceed the $600,000 threshold and incur federal taxes.

FIGURE 21.5 HUSBAND'S ESTATE CALCULATIONS: 100% MARITAL DEDUCTION.

Item	Amount
Husband's gross estate (died in 1996)	$400,000
Less marital deduction for bequest to spouse	−400,000
Taxable estate	0
Less allowable unified credit	0
Total federal estate tax	$ 0*

*Ignores state taxes.

FIGURE 21.6 WIFE'S ESTATE TAX CALCULATIONS.

Item	Amount
Total gross estate	$800,000
Less allowable deductions	−40,000
Taxable estate	$760,000
Gross estate tax	$252,200
Less allowable unified credit	−192,800
Total federal estate tax	$ 59,400*

*Ignores state taxes.

If you are married and your combined assets exceed the current exemption amount, consider creating *marital bypass* or *credit shelter* trusts. By using these trusts, your combined estates can pass up to two times the current exemption amount without federal estate taxes: $1.2 million in 1997, gradually increasing to $2 million by 2006. If the couple in this example had bypass trusts, both estates would remain under the exemption limit, as the revised figures in Figures 21.7 and 21.8 show.

FIGURE 21.7 HUSBAND'S ESTATE CALCULATIONS: MARITAL BYPASS TRUST.

Item	Amount
Husband's gross estate (died in 1996)	$400,000
Less marital deduction (all assets to bypass trust)	0
Taxable estate	$400,000
Gross estate tax	$121,800
Less allowable unified credit	−121,800
Total federal estate tax	$ 0*

*Ignores state taxes.

FIGURE 21.8 WIFE'S ESTATE TAX CALCULATIONS, REVISED.

Item	Amount
Total gross estate	$400,000
Taxable estate	400,000
Gross estate tax	$121,800
Less allowable unified credit	−121,800
Total federal estate tax	$ 0*

*Ignores state taxes.

Under the revised scenario, the husband's assets pass to a trust that is established for the benefit of his wife instead of a direct bequest to her. She would have a corresponding arrangement in place in case she died first. The trust can distribute its income to the surviving spouse, who may also be given a limited, noncumulative right to withdraw part of the trust's assets, perhaps up to 5 percent each year. At the surviving spouse's death, the trust's assets are not included in her estate and are distributed according to the trust's terms.

 There are several types of trusts that can be used in conjunction with the marital deduction. These trusts can be very useful in extended family situations, where each spouse wants to ensure that children from previous marriages eventually receive assets. An experienced estate planner can illustrate the pros and cons of the different trust arrangements.

 If you create a marital bypass trust, you must structure your property ownership properly to use the trust or you could thwart the arrangement. This may require you to transfer property from joint to single ownership and change beneficiary designations, so make your estate advisors aware of how you hold title to your property.

 ## TAX RELIEF FOR FAMILY-OWNED BUSINESSES

The 1997 Tax Act included an estate exclusion for qualified family businesses that are left to family members after December 31, 1997. The amount that can be excluded is the difference between $1.3 million and the amount exempted under the unified credit for the year. There are restrictions on claiming the exclusion, including the following[3]:

- Decedent must be a U.S. citizen or resident at the time of death.

- The principal place of business must be in the United States.

- The business must comprise more than half the estate.

- The business must be *family-owned* (that is, a single family owns at least 50 percent, two families own at least 70 percent, or three families own more than 90 percent).

- To qualify, an heir must have been actively employed by the trade or business for at least 10 years before the decedent's death.

END POINT

The 1997 Tax Act will allow an increased number of estates to avoid estate taxation in the coming years. If you believe that your estate could be taxable, however, you should consider techniques to reduce or eliminate that taxation or to provide the liquidity your estate will need to pay its obligations.

PART 5

Other Issues

Other Issues

Paying for College

Tuition shock is a common experience for many parents. Although the overall inflation rate has remained low for much of the 1990s, college costs continue to soar. The average tuition expense has more than doubled since 1976, *even after factoring in inflation.* For academic year 1997–1998, the College Board estimates that tuition and fees at four-year private institutions rose 5 percent, from an average $12,994 to $13,664. With room and board added in, the average total cost at a private university is over $21,400. At four-year public schools, tuition and fees also increased by 5 percent, to over $3,000, with total costs approaching $7,500 per year.[1]

The ideal solution to paying for children's college costs is to start saving when the children are very young. By investing regularly, you can accumulate a portion of the funds needed before they enroll. Unfortunately, many parents do not (or cannot) start saving until the children are in high school (if they save for college at all). A late start is better than no start, but most families must rely on some form of financial aid to help cover college costs. Even if the student receives aid, putting a child through college is one of life's major expenses. This chapter discusses college savings strategies and the financial aid process.

PROJECTING COLLEGE COSTS

KEY CONCEPT If your child has already selected a college and will start within the next year, you can estimate the expense fairly accurately by increasing the current cost by an inflation rate for each subsequent year. For example, if the current cost is $15,000 and you assume 6 percent annual inflation, Figure 22.1 illustrates the estimated costs.

Longer-term projections follow the same approach, although the projection becomes less certain as the time span increases. Figure 22.1 is an example of a future value calculation, which was discussed extensively in Chapter 4. Follow these steps to project future costs, using the future value factors from Figure 22.2:

Step 1:

Current annual cost	$15,000
Years until child enrolls	7
Assumed inflation rate	5%

Step 2: Look up the future value factors from Figure 22.2 for periods 7 through 10 (college years 1 to 4) and a 5 percent inflation rate. (If you need numbers below 5 percent or above 10 percent, or for more than 18 periods, see Figure A.1 in the appendix.)

Year	Future value factor
1	1.407
2	1.477
3	1.551
4	1.629

Step 3: Project the future costs.

Current cost	$15,000
Year 1	$15,000 × 1.407 = $21,105
Year 2	$15,000 × 1.477 = $22,155
Year 3	$15,000 × 1.551 = $23,265
Year 4	$15,000 × 1.629 = $24,435
Total	$90,960

If the projected cost seems like an unattainable amount, don't be discouraged. These numbers are projections of *total* costs and do not include any financial aid for which your child might qualify. Also,

FIGURE 22.1 SHORT-TERM COST PROJECTIONS.

Current cost	$15,000
Year 1	$15,000 × 1.06 = $15,900
Year 2	$15,900 × 1.06 = $16,854
Year 3	$16,854 × 1.06 = $17,865
Year 4	$17,865 × 1.06 = $18,937

FIGURE 22.2 FUTURE VALUE OF $1 (SINGLE CASH FLOW).

Period	5%	6%	7%	8%	9%	10%
1	1.050	1.060	1.070	1.080	1.090	1.100
2	1.103	1.124	1.145	1.166	1.188	1.210
3	1.158	1.191	1.225	1.260	1.295	1.331
4	1.216	1.262	1.311	1.360	1.412	1.464
5	1.276	1.338	1.403	1.469	1.539	1.611
6	1.340	1.419	1.501	1.587	1.677	1.772
7	1.407	1.504	1.606	1.714	1.828	1.949
8	1.477	1.594	1.718	1.851	1.993	2.144
9	1.551	1.689	1.838	1.999	2.172	2.358
10	1.629	1.791	1.967	2.159	2.367	2.594
11	1.710	1.898	2.105	2.332	2.580	2.853
12	1.796	2.012	2.252	2.518	2.813	3.138
13	1.886	2.133	2.410	2.720	3.066	3.452
14	1.980	2.261	2.579	2.937	3.342	3.797
15	2.079	2.397	2.759	3.172	3.642	4.177
16	2.183	2.540	2.952	3.426	3.970	4.595
17	2.292	2.693	3.159	3.700	4.328	5.054
18	2.407	2.854	3.380	3.996	4.717	5.560

realize that these are estimates, and the actual costs may be higher or lower.

KEY CONCEPT — SAVINGS STRATEGIES

There are varying philosophies about saving for college expenses. At one extreme is the position that it is a waste of time to plan and save because any amount you accumulate will reduce your child's chances for financial aid. At the other extreme are those parents who attempt to save enough to cover the entire cost, regardless of the impact their savings have on the school's financial aid decisions.

Assuming you have the funds available, it is better to save too much for your children's college costs for several reasons. First, schools expect some contribution from you, but they do not expect you to spend all of your income and assets on your children's education. Second, assuming that financial aid will cover any shortfall is a risky strategy. The final and most important reason is the financial flexibility that the savings can give you. If your child decides to enroll in an inexpensive school or does not attend college, you can use the excess college savings for other financial goals.

After projecting the total cost, you need to estimate the amount you should save each month. Figure 22.3

FIGURE 22.3 GROWTH OF $100 MONTHLY INVESTMENT.

Years	Rate				
	4%	6%	8%	10%	12%
1	$ 1,222	$ 1,234	$ 1,245	$ 1,257	$ 1,268
2	2,494	2,543	2,593	2,645	2,697
3	3,818	3,934	4,054	4,178	4,308
4	5,196	5,410	5,635	5,872	6,122
5	6,630	6,977	7,348	7,744	8,167
6	8,122	8,641	9,203	9,811	10,471
7	9,675	10,407	11,211	12,095	13,067
8	11,292	12,283	13,387	14,618	15,993
9	12,974	14,274	15,743	17,405	19,289
10	14,725	16,388	18,295	20,484	23,004
11	16,547	18,632	21,058	23,886	27,190
12	18,444	21,015	24,051	27,644	31,906
13	20,417	23,545	27,292	31,795	37,221
14	22,471	26,230	30,802	36,381	43,210
15	24,609	29,082	34,604	41,447	49,958
16	26,834	32,109	38,721	47,044	57,562
17	29,149	35,323	43,180	53,226	66,131
18	31,559	38,735	48,009	60,056	75,786
19	34,067	42,358	53,238	67,602	86,666
20	36,677	46,204	58,902	75,937	98,926

shows the growth of a $100 monthly investment for rates of return ranging from 4 percent to 12 percent.

Figure 22.3 shows how an early start and a higher return have a dramatic impact on the amount you can accumulate. To use the table with monthly amounts other than $100, multiply the table's figures by the amount you can save. For example, if you save $250, multiply the table's values by 2.5.

Continuing with the previous example, assume that the parents want to accumulate 75 percent of the projected total cost, or $68,000 ($90,960 × .75 = $68,220) by their daughter's freshman year. They project a 10 percent return on their funds, so they need to save roughly $560 per month. Here is the calculation: $68,000 ÷ $12,095 (from the 7 years, 10 percent box) = 5.62. Multiply 5.62 times 100. The total projected cost is $90,960, so they will need to keep saving throughout their daughter's enrollment, not just up to the start of her freshman year.

If you have access to a PC-based spreadsheet or a financial planning program, you can generate fairly accurate answers to the question, "How much should I save each month?" But remember, although the answer may be mathematically accurate, you are working with estimates based on *assumptions* you make about college cost, inflation, and investment rates of return. Hopefully, your projection will be reasonably accurate, but it is still an estimate.

DANGER! Planning for children's education can be extremely discouraging because you cannot imagine how you will find the necessary savings. Do not let this reaction prevent you from starting a savings program. Financial aid is designed to fill the gap between the cost of a higher education and a family's resources, but it is not meant to replace the family's contribution. Save whatever you can, even if that amount is less than your ideal target.

DANGER! It is common for parents of college-bound students to find their financial resources stretched to the limit. Between saving for children's college costs, planning for their own retirement, and attempting to assist their own parents financially if needed, these parents have few if any discretionary funds. If you are in this situation, consider the option of *helping* your children finance their education but not bearing the entire cost. Although you may wish to pay for their education, you must recognize the trade-off you are making with your own financial security. If necessary, consider alternative funding techniques. For example, you can co-sign student loans or lend your children funds with favorable postgraduation repayment terms. You can ask them to compromise on their choice of schools to reduce the expense. You are *not* required to pay 100 percent of your children's college costs, especially if the expense will reduce your financial security.

KEY CONCEPT ### FINANCIAL AID

If you dislike completing federal income tax forms, you will find the financial aid application forms even more intrusive. Unfortunately, there is no easy way to avoid completing the forms unless you plan to pay all of your child's college expenses with your own funds. There are two commonly used aid applications: the Free Application for Federal Student Aid (FAFSA) and the Financial Aid Profile. The FAFSA form is required, but not all schools use the Profile. Some schools may also request additional information on proprietary forms.

The forms ask for information about your assets and income and the student's assets and income. This information is used to develop an *expected family contribution* (EFC), which is the amount of your assets and

income (and your child's) that you can afford to contribute toward college expenses. Subtract your EFC
from the annual cost of attending a school and you will
know how much aid your child is eligible to receive.

You can get copies of the financial aid application
forms from your child's guidance department, college
financial aid offices, or by calling 1-800-4FED-AID. You
generally submit the completed forms between January
1 and May 31, although some state aid agencies have
March 1 submission deadlines. When you submit the
forms for the first time, you will complete them during
your child's senior year in high school.

Your goal in the aid process is to minimize your EFC so
you can maximize your child's aid package. This
requires advance planning, because the aid
applications you complete for the first time when your
child is a high school senior reflect your family finances
for the *previous year.* (Financial aid advisors call this
period the *first base year.*) Assuming it is not too late,
you should focus on making your numbers look as good
as possible (from an aid standpoint) for that period.

The key to maximizing aid is to minimize your EFC,
and that requires an understanding of which asset and
income categories are included and which are excluded.
The incomes that are considered available for the EFC
include those used for tax purposes, such as wages and
salaries, interest and dividends, and business income.
The EFC also includes several categories that are not
taxable: child support, tax-free interest, and deferred
compensation. Most assets are included in the EFC
computations: cash, savings and checking accounts,
investments and real estate (not including your home),
businesses, and nonresidential farm interests.

Financial aid computations consider a much higher
percentage of a student's income and assets as eligible
than parents' income and assets. A college will assess
parents' income up to 47 percent and assets up to 5.65
percent. But students can be assessed up to 50 percent
on their income and 35 percent on their assets.[2] If you
want to maximize your financial aid eligibility, do not
accumulate assets in your children's names.

Placing assets in your children's name has another
drawback in addition to its impact on financial aid.
Your child can take control of assets held in his or
her name at age 18 or 21, depending on your state's
law. You lose control of the funds at that time and cannot prevent your child from spending it. Keeping college funds in your name may increase your taxes, but it
also ensures that *you* will decide how to spend the
money.

Your income and asset information is adjusted for allowances and certain debts. For instance, you cannot deduct the value of personal or consumer loans, student loans, or any loans not related to an included asset. You can exclude the value of retirement plans, annuities, and the cash value of life insurance policies.

The *included* and *excluded* categories create planning opportunities. If you can shift assets from an included status to excluded, you decrease your EFC and increase your eligibility. To accomplish this reduction of EFC, consider the following strategies as you plan for the first base year[3]:

- Keep assets in parents' names.
- Increase the number of family members simultaneously enrolled in college.
- Spend student's assets and income first.
- Make any major purchases now to reduce cash holdings.
- Minimize capital gains.
- Maximize contributions to retirement plans and other excluded assets.
- Reduce any outstanding educational debt.
- Prepay your mortgage (some private schools include home equity).

Use a worksheet to determine the impact of different aid strategies on your EFC. You can find these worksheets on-line or in books such as *Paying for College Without Going Broke, 1998 Edition* (Random House/Princeton Review), by Kalman Chany.

Figure 22.4 lists the estimated percentages of public and private college costs paid for by financial aid in the academic year 1997–1998 for a family of four, with no other family members attending college (from

FIGURE 22.4 FINANCIAL AID COVERAGE.

Pretax Income

Assets[1]	$30,000 Public	$30,000 Private	$50,000 Public	$50,000 Private	$70,000 Public	$70,000 Private	$90,000 Public	$90,000 Private
$ 20,000	80%	91%	53%	78%	0%	47%	0%	20%
40,000	80	91	53	78	0	47	0	20
60,000	75	88	33	69	0	40	0	15
80,000	70	86	24	64	0	37	0	9
100,000	69	85	12	58	0	31	0	4

[1] *Does not include equity in home.*

Source: Paying for College, *T. Rowe Price;* Peterson's Guide to Four Year Colleges 1997.

Peterson's Guide to Four Year Colleges 1997; the percentages were calculated using The College Board's average, comprehensive public college cost of $10,069 and private college cost of $21,424 for 1997–1998). Cross-reference your family's pretax income and total assets (not including home equity) to get an idea of how much aid you can expect.

 If you don't like certain aspects of a school's financial aid offer, try negotiating a better deal. There is no guarantee you will convince the school's financial aid office to modify its offer, but it is worth the effort if you can build a strong case.

 ALTERNATIVE STRATEGIES

Besides maximizing financial aid, you can take other steps to reduce the cost of educating your children:

- Student completes degree in three years instead of four.
- Co-op (combined work and study) programs.
- Student spends two years at a less expensive public school, then transfers to four-year college.
- Student attends a Canadian college.
- Student qualifies for independent student status (if eligible).
- Student enrolls in ROTC or service academy.
- Prepaid tuition plans. Seventeen states currently offer prepaid tuition plans, and roughly 30 more states are considering them. Examine these factors before you deposit funds with a plan:
  Fees.
  Limitations on selection of schools.
  Anticipated investment return on your funds.
  Refund policy.

RECENT TAX LAW CHANGES

The 1997 Tax Act includes several measures that affect families who are planning for children's college expenses:

- *HOPE credit.* Starting in 1998, parents can claim a tax credit for the first $1,000 of their children's first two years' college tuition and fees and 50 percent of the next $1,000. This credit phases out for taxpayers filing joint with modified adjusted gross incomes between $80,000 and $100,000, or $40,000 to $50,000 for single filers.

- *Lifetime learning credit.* For expenses paid after June 30, 1998, any taxpayer can claim a credit of up to 20 percent of the first $5,000 in tuition and fees. The credit gradually increases to 20 percent of the first $10,000 by the year 2003. This credit is subject to the same income phaseout as the HOPE credit.

- *Student loan interest deduction.* Payments of student loan interest made after December 31, 1997, may be deductible, even for taxpayers who do not itemize. The deductions will be allowed for interest paid during the first 60 months in which payments are required. The annual deduction limits are $1,000 in 1998, $1,500 in 1999, $2,000 in 2000, $2,500 in 2001 and thereafter. Taxpayers claimed as dependents on another taxpayer's return cannot take the deduction, and it is phased out for taxpayers with modified AGI of $40,000 to $55,000 for single and $60,000 to $75,000 for joint returns.

- *Education IRAs.* Beginning in 1998, you can make up to a $500 nondeductible annual contribution for each child under age 18. Funds can be withdrawn tax-free for education expenses. A phaseout starts for single taxpayers with incomes over $95,000 and married filing jointly with incomes over $150,000.

- *Penalty-free IRA withdrawals.* The 10 percent penalty on IRA distributions taken after December 31, 1997, for taxpayers under age 59½ is waived for distributions used to pay college expenses. The distribution is taxed as ordinary income, however.

END POINT

Paying for children's college expenses has become one of the largest expenditures most parents incur. The ideal solution is to establish a long-term, growth-oriented investment plan while the children are very young. If that strategy is not feasible, combine a short-term savings strategy with an effort to maximize financial aid.

Time Value of Money Tables

FIGURE A.1 FUTURE VALUE OF $1 (SINGLE CASH FLOW).

Period	1%	2%	3%	4%	5%	6%	7%	8%	9%	10%
1	1.010	1.020	1.030	1.040	1.050	1.060	1.070	1.080	1.090	1.100
2	1.020	1.040	1.061	1.082	1.103	1.124	1.145	1.166	1.188	1.210
3	1.030	1.061	1.093	1.125	1.158	1.191	1.225	1.260	1.295	1.331
4	1.041	1.082	1.126	1.170	1.216	1.262	1.311	1.360	1.412	1.464
5	1.051	1.104	1.159	1.217	1.276	1.338	1.403	1.469	1.539	1.611
6	1.062	1.126	1.194	1.265	1.340	1.419	1.501	1.587	1.677	1.772
7	1.072	1.149	1.230	1.316	1.407	1.504	1.606	1.714	1.828	1.949
8	1.083	1.172	1.267	1.369	1.477	1.594	1.718	1.851	1.993	2.144
9	1.094	1.195	1.305	1.423	1.551	1.689	1.838	1.999	2.172	2.358
10	1.105	1.219	1.344	1.480	1.629	1.791	1.967	2.159	2.367	2.594
11	1.116	1.243	1.384	1.539	1.710	1.898	2.105	2.332	2.580	2.853
12	1.127	1.268	1.426	1.601	1.796	2.012	2.252	2.518	2.813	3.138
13	1.138	1.294	1.469	1.665	1.886	2.133	2.410	2.720	3.066	3.452
14	1.149	1.319	1.513	1.732	1.980	2.261	2.579	2.937	3.342	3.797
15	1.161	1.346	1.558	1.801	2.079	2.397	2.759	3.172	3.642	4.177
16	1.173	1.373	1.605	1.873	2.183	2.540	2.952	3.426	3.970	4.595
17	1.184	1.400	1.653	1.948	2.292	2.693	3.159	3.700	4.328	5.054

Period	11%	12%	13%	14%	15%	16%	17%	18%	19%	20%
18	1.196	1.428	1.702	2.026	2.407	2.854	3.380	3.996	4.717	5.560
19	1.208	1.457	1.754	2.107	2.527	3.026	3.617	4.316	5.142	6.116
20	1.220	1.486	1.806	2.191	2.653	3.207	3.870	4.661	5.604	6.727
25	1.282	1.641	2.094	2.666	3.386	4.292	5.427	6.848	8.623	10.835
30	1.348	1.811	2.427	3.243	4.322	5.743	7.612	10.063	13.268	17.449
35	1.417	2.000	2.814	3.946	5.516	7.686	10.677	14.785	20.414	28.102
40	1.489	2.208	3.262	4.801	7.040	10.286	14.974	21.725	31.409	45.259
45	1.565	2.438	3.782	5.841	8.985	13.765	21.002	31.920	48.327	72.890
50	1.645	2.692	4.384	7.107	11.467	18.420	29.457	46.902	74.358	117.391
1	1.110	1.120	1.130	1.140	1.150	1.160	1.170	1.180	1.190	1.200
2	1.232	1.254	1.277	1.300	1.323	1.346	1.369	1.392	1.416	1.440
3	1.368	1.405	1.443	1.482	1.521	1.561	1.602	1.643	1.685	1.728
4	1.518	1.574	1.630	1.689	1.749	1.811	1.874	1.939	2.005	2.074
5	1.685	1.762	1.842	1.925	2.011	2.100	2.192	2.288	2.386	2.488
6	1.870	1.974	2.082	2.195	2.313	2.436	2.565	2.700	2.840	2.986
7	2.076	2.211	2.353	2.502	2.660	2.826	3.001	3.185	3.379	3.583
8	2.305	2.476	2.658	2.853	3.059	3.278	3.511	3.759	4.021	4.300

FIGURE A.1 FUTURE VALUE OF $1 (SINGLE CASH FLOW). (Continued)

Period	11%	12%	13%	14%	15%	16%	17%	18%	19%	20%
9	2.558	2.773	3.004	3.252	3.518	3.803	4.108	4.435	4.785	5.160
10	2.839	3.106	3.395	3.707	4.046	4.411	4.807	5.234	5.695	6.192
11	3.152	3.479	3.836	4.226	4.652	5.117	5.624	6.176	6.777	7.430
12	3.498	3.896	4.335	4.818	5.350	5.936	6.580	7.288	8.064	8.916
13	3.883	4.363	4.898	5.492	6.153	6.886	7.699	8.599	9.596	10.699
14	4.310	4.887	5.535	6.261	7.076	7.988	9.007	10.147	11.420	12.839
15	4.785	5.474	6.254	7.138	8.137	9.266	10.539	11.974	13.590	15.407
16	5.311	6.130	7.067	8.137	9.358	10.748	12.330	14.129	16.172	18.488
17	5.895	6.866	7.986	9.276	10.761	12.468	14.426	16.672	19.244	22.186
18	6.544	7.690	9.024	10.575	12.375	14.463	16.879	19.673	22.901	26.623
19	7.263	8.613	10.197	12.056	14.232	16.777	19.748	23.214	27.252	31.948
20	8.062	9.646	11.523	13.743	16.367	19.461	23.106	27.393	32.429	38.338
25	13.585	17.000	21.231	26.462	32.919	40.874	50.658	62.669	77.388	95.396
30	22.892	29.960	39.116	50.950	66.212	85.850	111.065	143.371	184.675	237.376
35	38.575	52.800	72.069	98.100	133.176	180.314	243.503	327.997	440.701	590.668
40	65.001	93.051	132.782	188.884	267.864	378.721	533.869	750.378	1,051.668	1,469.772
45	109.530	163.988	244.641	363.679	538.769	795.444	1,170.479	1,716.684	2,509.651	3,657.262
50	184.565	289.002	450.736	700.233	1,083.657	1,670.704	2,566.215	3,927.357	5,988.914	9,100.438

FIGURE A.2 FUTURE VALUE OF $1 (MULTIPLE CASH FLOWS).

Period	1%	2%	3%	4%	5%	6%	7%	8%	9%	10%
1	1.000	1.000	1.000	1.000	1.000	1.000	1.000	1.000	1.000	1.000
2	2.010	2.020	2.030	2.040	2.050	2.060	2.070	2.080	2.090	2.100
3	3.030	3.060	3.091	3.122	3.153	3.184	3.215	3.246	3.278	3.310
4	4.060	4.122	4.184	4.246	4.310	4.375	4.440	4.506	4.573	4.641
5	5.101	5.204	5.309	5.416	5.526	5.637	5.751	5.867	5.985	6.105
6	6.152	6.308	6.468	6.633	6.802	6.975	7.153	7.336	7.523	7.716
7	7.214	7.434	7.662	7.898	8.142	8.394	8.654	8.923	9.200	9.487
8	8.286	8.583	8.892	9.214	9.549	9.897	10.260	10.637	11.028	11.436
9	9.369	9.755	10.159	10.583	11.027	11.491	11.978	12.488	13.021	13.579
10	10.462	10.950	11.464	12.006	12.578	13.181	13.816	14.487	15.193	15.937
11	11.567	12.169	12.808	13.486	14.207	14.972	15.784	16.645	17.560	18.531
12	12.683	13.412	14.192	15.026	15.917	16.870	17.888	18.977	20.141	21.384
13	13.809	14.680	15.618	16.627	17.713	18.882	20.141	21.495	22.953	24.523
14	14.947	15.974	17.086	18.292	19.599	21.015	22.550	24.215	26.019	27.975
15	16.097	17.293	18.599	20.024	21.579	23.276	25.129	27.152	29.361	31.772
16	17.258	18.639	20.157	21.825	23.657	25.673	27.888	30.324	33.003	35.950
17	18.430	20.012	21.762	23.698	25.840	28.213	30.840	33.750	36.974	40.545

FIGURE A.2 FUTURE VALUE OF $1 (MULTIPLE CASH FLOWS). (Continued)

Period	1%	2%	3%	4%	5%	6%	7%	8%	9%	10%
18	19.615	21.412	23.414	25.645	28.132	30.906	33.999	37.450	41.301	45.599
19	20.811	22.841	25.117	27.671	30.539	33.760	37.379	41.446	46.018	51.159
20	22.019	24.297	26.870	29.778	33.066	36.786	40.995	45.762	51.160	57.275
25	28.243	32.030	36.459	41.646	47.727	54.865	63.249	73.106	84.701	98.347
30	34.785	40.568	47.575	56.085	66.439	79.058	94.461	113.283	136.308	164.494
35	41.660	49.994	60.462	73.652	90.320	111.435	138.237	172.317	215.711	271.024
40	48.886	60.402	75.401	95.026	120.800	154.762	199.635	259.057	337.882	442.593
45	56.481	71.893	92.720	121.029	159.700	212.744	285.749	386.506	525.859	718.905
50	64.463	84.579	112.797	152.667	209.348	290.336	406.529	573.770	815.084	1,163.909

Period	11%	12%	13%	14%	15%	16%	17%	18%	19%	20%
1	1.000	1.000	1.000	1.000	1.000	1.000	1.000	1.000	1.000	1.000
2	2.110	2.120	2.130	2.140	2.150	2.160	2.170	2.180	2.190	2.200
3	3.342	3.374	3.407	3.440	3.473	3.506	3.539	3.572	3.606	3.640
4	4.710	4.779	4.850	4.921	4.993	5.066	5.141	5.215	5.291	5.368
5	6.228	6.353	6.480	6.610	6.742	6.877	7.014	7.154	7.297	7.442
6	7.913	8.115	8.323	8.536	8.754	8.977	9.207	9.442	9.683	9.930

7	9.783	10.089	10.405	10.730	11.067	11.414	11.772	12.142	12.523	12.916
8	11.859	12.300	12.757	13.233	13.727	14.240	14.773	15.327	15.902	16.499
9	14.164	14.776	15.416	16.085	16.786	17.519	18.285	19.086	19.923	20.799
10	16.722	17.549	18.420	19.337	20.304	21.321	22.393	23.521	24.709	25.959
11	19.561	20.655	21.814	23.045	24.349	25.733	27.200	28.755	30.404	32.150
12	22.713	24.133	25.650	27.271	29.002	30.850	32.824	34.931	37.180	39.581
13	26.212	28.029	29.985	32.089	34.352	36.786	39.404	42.219	45.244	48.497
14	30.095	32.393	34.883	37.581	40.505	43.672	47.103	50.818	54.841	59.196
15	34.405	37.280	40.417	43.842	47.580	51.660	56.110	60.965	66.261	72.035
16	39.190	42.753	46.672	50.980	55.717	60.925	66.649	72.939	79.850	87.442
17	44.501	48.884	53.739	59.118	65.075	71.673	78.979	87.068	96.022	105.931
18	50.396	55.750	61.725	68.394	75.836	84.141	93.406	103.740	115.266	128.117
19	56.939	63.440	70.749	78.969	88.212	98.603	110.285	123.414	138.166	154.740
20	64.203	72.052	80.947	91.025	102.444	115.380	130.033	146.628	165.418	186.688
25	114.413	133.334	155.620	181.871	212.793	249.214	292.105	342.603	402.042	471.981
30	199.021	241.333	293.199	356.787	434.745	530.312	647.439	790.948	966.712	1,181.882
35	341.590	431.663	546.681	693.573	881.170	1,120.713	1,426.491	1,816.652	2,314.214	2,948.341
40	581.826	767.091	1,013.704	1,342.025	1,779.090	2,360.757	3,134.522	4,163.213	5,529.829	7,343.858
45	986.639	1,358.230	1,874.165	2,590.565	3,585.128	4,965.274	6,879.291	9,531.577	13,203.424	18,281.310
50	1,668.771	2,400.018	3,459.507	4,994.521	7,217.716	10,435.649	15,089.502	21,813.094	31,515.336	45,497.191

FIGURE A.3 PRESENT VALUE OF $1 (SINGLE CASH FLOW).

Period	1%	2%	3%	4%	5%	6%	7%	8%	9%	10%
1	0.990	0.980	0.971	0.962	0.952	0.943	0.935	0.926	0.917	0.909
2	0.980	0.961	0.943	0.925	0.907	0.890	0.873	0.857	0.842	0.826
3	0.971	0.942	0.915	0.889	0.864	0.840	0.816	0.794	0.772	0.751
4	0.961	0.924	0.888	0.855	0.823	0.792	0.763	0.735	0.708	0.683
5	0.951	0.906	0.863	0.822	0.784	0.747	0.713	0.681	0.650	0.621
6	0.942	0.888	0.837	0.790	0.746	0.705	0.666	0.630	0.596	0.564
7	0.933	0.871	0.813	0.760	0.711	0.665	0.623	0.583	0.547	0.513
8	0.923	0.853	0.789	0.731	0.677	0.627	0.582	0.540	0.502	0.467
9	0.914	0.837	0.766	0.703	0.645	0.592	0.544	0.500	0.460	0.424
10	0.905	0.820	0.744	0.676	0.614	0.558	0.508	0.463	0.422	0.386
11	0.896	0.804	0.722	0.650	0.585	0.527	0.475	0.429	0.388	0.350
12	0.887	0.788	0.701	0.625	0.557	0.497	0.444	0.397	0.356	0.319
13	0.879	0.773	0.681	0.601	0.530	0.469	0.415	0.368	0.326	0.290
14	0.870	0.758	0.661	0.577	0.505	0.442	0.388	0.340	0.299	0.263
15	0.861	0.743	0.642	0.555	0.481	0.417	0.362	0.315	0.275	0.239
16	0.853	0.728	0.623	0.534	0.458	0.394	0.339	0.292	0.252	0.218

Period	11%	12%	13%	14%	15%	16%	17%	18%	19%	20%
1	0.901	0.893	0.885	0.877	0.870	0.862	0.855	0.847	0.840	0.833
2	0.812	0.797	0.783	0.769	0.756	0.743	0.731	0.718	0.706	0.694
3	0.731	0.712	0.693	0.675	0.658	0.641	0.624	0.609	0.593	0.579
4	0.659	0.636	0.613	0.592	0.572	0.552	0.534	0.516	0.499	0.482
5	0.593	0.567	0.543	0.519	0.497	0.476	0.456	0.437	0.419	0.402
6	0.535	0.507	0.480	0.456	0.432	0.410	0.390	0.370	0.352	0.335
7	0.482	0.452	0.425	0.400	0.376	0.354	0.333	0.314	0.296	0.279
8	0.434	0.404	0.376	0.351	0.327	0.305	0.285	0.266	0.249	0.233
17	0.844	0.714	0.605	0.513	0.436	0.371	0.317	0.270	0.231	0.198
18	0.836	0.700	0.587	0.494	0.416	0.350	0.296	0.250	0.212	0.180
19	0.828	0.686	0.570	0.475	0.396	0.331	0.277	0.232	0.194	0.164
20	0.820	0.673	0.554	0.456	0.377	0.312	0.258	0.215	0.178	0.149
25	0.780	0.610	0.478	0.375	0.295	0.233	0.184	0.146	0.116	0.092
30	0.742	0.552	0.412	0.308	0.231	0.174	0.131	0.099	0.075	0.057
35	0.706	0.500	0.355	0.253	0.181	0.130	0.094	0.068	0.049	0.036
40	0.672	0.453	0.307	0.208	0.142	0.097	0.067	0.046	0.032	0.022
45	0.639	0.410	0.264	0.171	0.111	0.073	0.048	0.031	0.021	0.014
50	0.608	0.372	0.228	0.141	0.087	0.054	0.034	0.021	0.013	0.009

FIGURE A.3 PRESENT VALUE OF $1 (SINGLE CASH FLOW). (Continued)

Period	11%	12%	13%	14%	15%	16%	17%	18%	19%	20%
9	0.391	0.361	0.333	0.308	0.284	0.263	0.243	0.225	0.209	0.194
10	0.352	0.322	0.295	0.270	0.247	0.227	0.208	0.191	0.176	0.162
11	0.317	0.287	0.261	0.237	0.215	0.195	0.178	0.162	0.148	0.135
12	0.286	0.257	0.231	0.208	0.187	0.168	0.152	0.137	0.124	0.112
13	0.258	0.229	0.204	0.182	0.163	0.145	0.130	0.116	0.104	0.093
14	0.232	0.205	0.181	0.160	0.141	0.125	0.111	0.099	0.088	0.078
15	0.209	0.183	0.160	0.140	0.123	0.108	0.095	0.084	0.074	0.065
16	0.188	0.163	0.141	0.123	0.107	0.093	0.081	0.071	0.062	0.054
17	0.170	0.146	0.125	0.108	0.093	0.080	0.069	0.060	0.052	0.045
18	0.153	0.130	0.111	0.095	0.081	0.069	0.059	0.051	0.044	0.038
19	0.138	0.116	0.098	0.083	0.070	0.060	0.051	0.043	0.037	0.031
20	0.124	0.104	0.087	0.073	0.061	0.051	0.043	0.037	0.031	0.026
25	0.074	0.059	0.047	0.038	0.030	0.024	0.020	0.016	0.013	0.010
30	0.044	0.033	0.026	0.020	0.015	0.012	0.009	0.007	0.005	0.004
35	0.026	0.019	0.014	0.010	0.008	0.006	0.004	0.003	0.002	0.002
40	0.015	0.011	0.008	0.005	0.004	0.003	0.002	0.001	0.001	0.001
45	0.009	0.006	0.004	0.003	0.002	0.001	0.001	0.001	0.000	0.000
50	0.005	0.003	0.002	0.001	0.001	0.001	0.000	0.000	0.000	0.000

FIGURE A.4 PRESENT VALUE OF $1 (MULTIPLE CASH FLOWS).

Period	1%	2%	3%	4%	5%	6%	7%	8%	9%	10%
1	0.990	0.980	0.971	0.962	0.952	0.943	0.935	0.926	0.917	0.909
2	1.970	1.942	1.913	1.886	1.859	1.833	1.808	1.783	1.759	1.736
3	2.941	2.884	2.829	2.775	2.723	2.673	2.624	2.577	2.531	2.487
4	3.902	3.808	3.717	3.630	3.546	3.465	3.387	3.312	3.240	3.170
5	4.853	4.713	4.580	4.452	4.329	4.212	4.100	3.993	3.890	3.791
6	5.795	5.601	5.417	5.242	5.076	4.917	4.767	4.623	4.486	4.355
7	6.728	6.472	6.230	6.002	5.786	5.582	5.389	5.206	5.033	4.868
8	7.652	7.325	7.020	6.733	6.463	6.210	5.971	5.747	5.535	5.335
9	8.566	8.162	7.786	7.435	7.108	6.802	6.515	6.247	5.995	5.759
10	9.471	8.983	8.530	8.111	7.722	7.360	7.024	6.710	6.418	6.145
11	10.368	9.787	9.253	8.760	8.306	7.887	7.499	7.139	6.805	6.495
12	11.255	10.575	9.954	9.385	8.863	8.384	7.943	7.536	7.161	6.814
13	12.134	11.348	10.635	9.986	9.394	8.853	8.358	7.904	7.487	7.103
14	13.004	12.106	11.296	10.563	9.899	9.295	8.745	8.244	7.786	7.367
15	13.865	12.849	11.938	11.118	10.380	9.712	9.108	8.559	8.061	7.606
16	14.718	13.578	12.561	11.652	10.838	10.106	9.447	8.851	8.313	7.824
17	15.562	14.292	13.166	12.166	11.274	10.477	9.763	9.122	8.544	8.022
18	16.398	14.992	13.754	12.659	11.690	10.828	10.059	9.372	8.756	8.201

FIGURE A.4 PRESENT VALUE OF $1 (MULTIPLE CASH FLOWS). (Continued)

Period	1%	2%	3%	4%	5%	6%	7%	8%	9%	10%
19	17.226	15.678	14.324	13.134	12.085	11.158	10.336	9.604	8.950	8.365
20	18.046	16.351	14.877	13.590	12.462	11.470	10.594	9.818	9.129	8.514
25	22.023	19.523	17.413	15.622	14.094	12.783	11.654	10.675	9.823	9.077
30	25.808	22.396	19.600	17.292	15.372	13.765	12.409	11.258	10.274	9.427
35	29.409	24.999	21.487	18.665	16.374	14.498	12.948	11.655	10.567	9.644
40	32.835	27.355	23.115	19.793	17.159	15.046	13.332	11.925	10.757	9.779
45	36.095	29.490	24.519	20.720	17.774	15.456	13.606	12.108	10.881	9.863
50	39.196	31.424	25.730	21.482	18.256	15.762	13.801	12.233	10.962	9.915

Period	11%	12%	13%	14%	15%	16%	17%	18%	19%	20%
1	0.901	0.893	0.885	0.877	0.870	0.862	0.855	0.847	0.840	0.833
2	1.713	1.690	1.668	1.647	1.626	1.605	1.585	1.566	1.547	1.528
3	2.444	2.402	2.361	2.322	2.283	2.246	2.210	2.174	2.140	2.106
4	3.102	3.037	2.974	2.914	2.855	2.798	2.743	2.690	2.639	2.589
5	3.696	3.605	3.517	3.433	3.352	3.274	3.199	3.127	3.058	2.991
6	4.231	4.111	3.998	3.889	3.784	3.685	3.589	3.498	3.410	3.326
7	4.712	4.564	4.423	4.288	4.160	4.039	3.922	3.812	3.706	3.605

8	5.146	4.968	4.799	4.639	4.487	4.344	4.207	4.078	3.954	3.837
9	5.537	5.328	5.132	4.946	4.772	4.607	4.451	4.303	4.163	4.031
10	5.889	5.650	5.426	5.216	5.019	4.833	4.659	4.494	4.339	4.192
11	6.207	5.938	5.687	5.453	5.234	5.029	4.836	4.656	4.486	4.327
12	6.492	6.194	5.918	5.660	5.421	5.197	4.988	4.793	4.611	4.439
13	6.750	6.424	6.122	5.842	5.583	5.342	5.118	4.910	4.715	4.533
14	6.982	6.628	6.302	6.002	5.724	5.468	5.229	5.008	4.802	4.611
15	7.191	6.811	6.462	6.142	5.847	5.575	5.324	5.092	4.876	4.675
16	7.379	6.974	6.604	6.265	5.954	5.668	5.405	5.162	4.938	4.730
17	7.549	7.120	6.729	6.373	6.047	5.749	5.475	5.222	4.990	4.775
18	7.702	7.250	6.840	6.467	6.128	5.818	5.534	5.273	5.033	4.812
19	7.839	7.366	6.938	6.550	6.198	5.877	5.584	5.316	5.070	4.843
20	7.963	7.469	7.025	6.623	6.259	5.929	5.628	5.353	5.101	4.870
25	8.422	7.843	7.330	6.873	6.464	6.097	5.766	5.467	5.195	4.948
30	8.694	8.055	7.496	7.003	6.566	6.177	5.829	5.517	5.235	4.979
35	8.855	8.176	7.586	7.070	6.617	6.215	5.858	5.539	5.251	4.992
40	8.951	8.244	7.634	7.105	6.642	6.233	5.871	5.548	5.258	4.997
45	9.008	8.283	7.661	7.123	6.654	6.242	5.877	5.552	5.261	4.999
50	9.042	8.304	7.675	7.133	6.661	6.246	5.880	5.554	5.262	4.999

CHAPTER 3

1. Brooke Stephens, *Talking Dollars and Making Sense: A Wealth Building Guide for African-Americans* (New York: McGraw-Hill, 1997), pp. 20–23.

2. Olivia Mellan, *Money Harmony: Resolving Money Conflicts in Your Life and Relationships* (New York: Walker and Company, 1994), p. 30.

3. Elizabeth Razzi, "How Smart Couples Manage Their Money," *Kiplinger's Personal Finance Magazine* (June 1996), pp. 49–53; *Wise Financial Moves for Couples, Newlyweds and Young Families* (Bryn Mawr: American Society of CLU & ChFC, 1996).

CHAPTER 6

1. "Survey: Doing Business at Big Banks Costs More," *CNN Interactive,* 31 July 1997 (CNN: CNN Interactive, 1997).

2. Ibid.

3. Ellen Stark, "Lift Your Returns with 15 Top Money Funds," *Money* (March 1997), p. 41.

4. Ibid.

5. Christopher Oster, "Banking on the Stock Market," *SmartMoney* (September 1997), p. 44.

6. Federal Deposit Insurance Corporation, *Your Insured Deposit* (Washington, DC: Federal Deposit Insurance Corporation, 1997), Question 17.

7. Bureau of the Public Debt, *A Great Way to Save: U.S. Savings Bonds Investor Information* (Washington, DC: Department of the Treasury, 1996), p. 3.

8. "Lipper Indexes," *Wall Street Journal* (29 August 1997), p. C23.

9. Lisa Reilly Cullen, "Finally, You Could Profit by Banking Online," *Money* (September 1997), p. 31.

10. "MasterCard Lowers Debit Card Liability to $50," MasterCard International Inc. press release (30 July 1997).

11. "VISA Caps Debit Card Liability," *CNNfn,* 13 August 1997, (CNN: CNNfn, 1997).

12. Jean Sherman Chatzky, "An AMA Switch: In Your Best Interest?" *SmartMoney* (August 1996), p. 91.

CHAPTER 7

1. "Credit Fuels Bankruptcies," *CNNfn,* 9 June 1997 (CNN: CNNfn, 1997).

2. "Seven Signals of Credit Over-Extension," National Credit Counseling Services Web site (National Credit Counseling Services, 1997).

3. "Consumer Debt Facts," National Credit Counseling Services Web site (National Credit Counseling Services, 1997).

4. "Credit Fuels Bankruptcies," *CNNfn.*

5. Richard Eisenberg, *The Money Book of Personal Finance* (New York: Warner Books, 1996), p. 172.

6. Adapted from E. Thomas Garman and Raymond E. Forgue, *Personal Finance,* 4th ed. (New York: Houghton Mifflin, 1994), p. 181.

CHAPTER 8

1. "Chart 2: Average Number of Days Worked to Pay Taxes by Type of Tax and Level of Government, 1997," Tax Foundation Web site (Tax Foundation, 1997).

2. "Taxes as Percentage of Income for the Median One- and Two-Income Families, 1955–1996," Tax Foundation Web site (Tax Foundation, 1997).

3. Kalman A. Chaney with Geoff Martz, *Paying for College: 1997 Edition* (New York: Random House, Inc., 1996), pp. 22–23.

CHAPTER 9

1. "National Appreciation Rate Returns to 4 Percent," *Secondary Mortgage Markets* (April 1997), p. 7.

2. Carlos Tejada, "In Mortgage Hunt, Home Buyers Hold the Hammer," *Wall Street Journal* (3 October 1997), p. C1.

3. Ken Harney, "Lenders Offer 10% down, No PMI," *Providence Journal Bulletin* (28 September 1997), p. G1.

4. Ken Harney, "Reform Bill Offers Relief from Insurance Premiums," *Providence Journal Bulletin* (12 October 1997), p. G1.

CHAPTER 10

1. Source: 1985 Commissioners Disability Table, reported in "You Could Lose Your Income, Your Home, Your Savings," from the UNUM Life Insurance Company of America.

2. Ibid.

3. Source: HIAA Sourcebook of Health Insurance Data, 1994, reported in "You Could Lose Your Income, Your Home, Your Savings," from the UNUM Life Insurance Company of America.

4. William W. Thomas III, ed., *Social Security Manual,* 1997 ed. (Cincinnati: The National Underwriter Company, 1997), p. 335; and "Monthly Information Package, August 1997," Social Security Web site (Social Security Administration, 1997).

5. William W. Thomas III, ed., *Social Security Manual,* 1997 ed., pp. 82–83.

6. Janet Bamford, "Are You Protected?" *Bloomberg Personal* (November/December 1996), pp. 119–130.

7. Employee Benefit Research Institute, *Fundamentals of Employee Benefit Programs,* 5th ed. (Washington, DC: Employee Benefit Research Institute, 1997), pp. 289–297.

8. Accident Facts, 1994, National Safety Council, reported in "Long Term Disability: Risks and Realities," from the UNUM Life Insurance Company of America.

9. *Fundamentals of Employee Benefit Programs,* 5th ed., pp. 293–294.

10. Janet Bamford, pp. 119–130.

11. Marlene Y. Satter and Liana Camporeale, "Disability Insurance 1997," *Dow Jones Investment Advisor* (December 1997), pp. 80–89.

12. "LTC Insurance in 1995: Premiums Down 5 Percent, Sales Reach All-Time High," Health Insurance Association of America press release, 17 May 1997.

13. Jacquelyn S. Coy and Paul J. Winn, "Long-Term Care— A Vital Product in an Evolving Environment," *Journal of the American Society of CLU & ChFC* (September 1997), pp. 68–75.

14. National Association of Insurance Commissioners, *A Shopper's Guide to Long-Term Care Insurance* (Kansas City, MO: National Association of Insurance Commissioners, 1996), p. 5.

15. William W. Thomas III, ed., *All About Medicare,* 1997 ed. (Cincinnati: The National Underwriter Company, 1997), pp. 123–125.

16. Coy and Winn, p. 70.

17. Health Insurance Association of America press release, 17 May 1997.

18. Jeff Sadler, *The Long Term Care Handbook* (Cincinnati: The National Underwriter Company, 1996), p. 193.

19. National Association of Insurance Commissioners, 1997 insert, p. 1.

CHAPTER 11

1. Adapted from Stephan R. Leimberg and Robert J. Doyle, Jr., *The Tools and Techniques of Life Insurance Planning* (Cincinnati: The National Underwriter Co., 1993), pp. 12–13.

2. Adapted from Stephan R. Leimberg et al., *The Tools and Techniques of Financial Planning,* 4th ed. (Cincinnati: The National Underwriter Co., 1993), pp. 336–337.

3. Ibid.

4. James A. Hunt, *Analysis of Cash Value Life Insurance Policies: A Report on CFA's Rate of Return Service* (Washington, DC: Consumer Federation of America, July 1997), p. 5.

5. Stephan R. Leimberg and Robert J. Doyle, Jr., p. 69.

6. Hunt, p. 5.

7. Consumer Federation of America and U.S. Public Interest Research Group, *Most Credit Life Insurance Still a Rip-Off* (Washington, DC: Consumer Federation of America and U.S. Public Interest Research Group, 1997).

8. Thomas W. Johnson, "Life Insurance As a Liquid Asset," *Financial Planning* (December 1996), pp. 102–105.

CHAPTER 12

1. Employee Benefit Research Institute, *EBRI Databook on Employee Benefits,* 4th ed. (Washington, DC: Employee Benefit Research Institute, 1997), Table 27.1.

2. Nancy Ann Jeffrey, "Say Aah," *Wall Street Journal* (1 December 1997), p. R10.

3. *EBRI Databook on Employee Benefits,* 4th ed., Chart 29.3.

4. Nancy Ann Jeffrey, "Healthy Switch: New Law Eases Job-Hops, Sometimes," *Wall Street Journal* (30 August 1996), p. C1.

5. Jane Bennett Clark, "Me and My Health Insurance," *Kiplinger's Personal Finance Magazine* (October 1997), pp. 67–75.

6. Health Care Financing Administration, *1996 Guide to Health Insurance for People with Medicare* (Baltimore: Health Care Financing Administration, 1996), p. 14.

7. Robert A. Gilmour, *How to Cover the Gaps in Medicare* (Great Barrington: American Institute for Economic Research, 1997), p. 48.

8. Ibid.

9. Galina Espinoza, "What You Need to Know About Medicare HMOs," *Money* (March 1997), pp. 120–128.

CHAPTER 13

1. Amanda Walmac, "The Best Way to Protect Yourself and Your Assets Against a Lawsuit," *Money* (August 1996), p. 29.

2. Leslie Scism, "Not All Umbrella Policyholders Can Expect Presidential Service," *Wall Street Journal* (13 February 1996), p. C1.

3. Richard W. Duff, "Asset Protection Strategies Du Jour: An Interview with Barry Engel," *Journal of Financial Planning* (December 1996), pp. 32–35.

4. Adapted from James A. Keller et al., *Guide to Asset Protection Planning* (Fort Worth: Practitioners Publishing Company, 1997).

5. Barbara Monaco, "Offshore Trusts Come to the Mainland," *MSNBC,* 17 September 1997 (MSNBC, 1997).

6. Duff, pp. 32–35.

7. Nick Ravo, "The Offshore Trusts: A Shield Against Certain Swords," *New York Times,* 24 July 1997 (America Online: New York Times, 1997).

8. Keller et al., *Guide to Asset Protection Planning,* pp. 12–23.

9. Ibid.

CHAPTER 14

1. "Plan Participants More Comfortable with Equities, But Don't Understand Fixed Income Risks," *PRNewswire,* 14 April 1997 (AOL: PRNewswire, 1997).

CHAPTER 15

1. Charles Molineaux, "Stocks Win in Long Run," *CNNfn,* 3 September 1997 (CNN: CNNfn, 1997).

CHAPTER 16

1. "Big Year for Variables," *Financial Planning* (March 1997), p. 121.

2. Harold R. Evensky, *Wealth Management* (Irwin/ McGraw-Hill, 1997), pp. 68–70.

3. Rich Fortin and Stuart Michelson, "What Mutual Funds Really Return After Taxes," *Journal of Financial Planning* (April 1996), pp. 60–65.

4. Steven T. Goldberg, "Funds for Tax-Shy Investors," *Kiplinger's Personal Finance Magazine* (November 1997), pp. 119–124.

5. NAREIT Online, Web site.

6. Barry Vinocur, "Real Estate Funds, Judging More Than Performance," *Property 97* (1997), pp. 24–27.

7. Suzanne McGee, "Smart Plays or Hype? Unit Investment Trusts Are Hot," *Wall Street Journal* (10 October 1997), p. C1.

8. Margie C. Welder, "Why and How to Use Convertible Securities in Client Portfolios," *Journal of Financial Planning* (August 1997), pp. 78–86.

CHAPTER 17

1. "Trends in Mutual Fund Investing: June 1997," press release from the Investment Company Institute, 30 July 1997.

2. "Mutual Funds Quarterly Review," *Wall Street Journal* (3 October 1997), p. D1.

3. Edward Wyatt, "Market Place: Investor Exuberance Borders on Irrational, Survey Finds," *The New York Times* on the Web, 10 October 1997 (New York Times, 1997).

4. The Vanguard Group, *Index Investing* (Valley Forge: Vanguard Marketing Corporation, 1996), p. 4.

5. Source: The Vanguard Group Web site.

6. Michael R. Sesit, "Stock Pickers Beat Indexers in Other Lands," *Wall Street Journal* (6 March 1997), p. C1; Karen Damato, "Funds Haven't Done Well by Indexing Small Stocks," *Wall Street Journal* (28 January 1997), p. C1.

7. Karen Damato, "Many Funds' 10-Year Figures to Get a Lift," *Wall Street Journal* (7 July 1997), p. C1.

8. Gary Gentile, "Open the Door to Closed-End Funds," *Financial Planning* (June 1997), pp. 140–146.

9. Jeffrey M. Laderman, "Your Guide to Closed-End Funds," *Business Week* (17 February 1997), pp. 86–92.

CHAPTER 18

1. "Survey: 30% of Pre-Retirees Have Saved Less Than $10,000," *CNN Interactive,* 27 May 1997 (CNN: CNN Interactive, 1997).

2. "Older Baby Boomers Starting to Save More, Merrill Lynch Baby Boom Retirement Index[(sm)] Finds," Merrill Lynch, Pierce, Fenner & Smith Inc. Web site (Washington, DC: Merrill Lynch, Pierce, Fenner & Smith Inc., 1997).

3. Internal Revenue Service Publication 939.

CHAPTER 21

1. Tom Herman, "Tax Report," *Wall Street Journal* (12 February 1997), p. 1.

2. Adapted from Stephan R. Leimberg et al., *The Tools and Techniques of Financial Planning,* 4th ed. (Cincinnati: The National Underwriter Co., 1993), Appendix D, Table B.

3. Deloitte & Touche LLP, *Promises Kept: The 1997 Tax Act* (Washington, DC: Deloitte & Touche LLP, 1997), p. 21.

CHAPTER 22

1. "College Costs at a Glance," Associated Press (24 September 1997), as reported on *CNN Interactive.*

2. Kalman A. Chaney with Geoff Martz, *The Princeton Review Student Advantage Guide to Paying for College, 1997 Edition* (New York: Random House, 1996), pp. 23–24.

3. Adapted from "Strategies for Maximizing Aid Eligibility," FinAid Page, Inc., Web site (FinAid Page, Inc., 1997).